Fragments

10. Fertile Soil
WATER CYCLE
NURTURING LANDSCAPE

Resource Spaces
UNDERGROUND SPACES
BROWNFIELD SITES
CONTINUOUS ARCHITECTURE

Time as Resource

92. Projected Territories
SUPPORT FOR DECISION-MAKING
TAKING CARE OF OUR TERRITORIES

Invited Research
INHABITANT CO-DESIGN
EXPLORATORY PROCESS

New Models
METROPOLITAN LABORATORY
AUGMENTED PROGRAMMING

Shared Narratives

158. Low Carbon
RESTRAINT
BIO-BASED
CIRCULARITY

Resilience
CAPABILITY
AGILITY
ANTICIPATION

Welcoming the living

Compasses

228. A Heuristic Approach
Grégory Quenet

Designing Differently
RE.SITUATING THROUGH THE PROJECT
RE.DEFINING THE COMMONS
NEW PARADIGMS
MEASURING WITH TIME

Orienting Oneself
RESOURCES
GOVERNANCE
BLUE ECONOMY

Tracé Bleu

Que faire en ce lieu,
à moins que l'on y songe ?

Architecturestudio, March 2023.

René-Henri ARNAUD, Roueïda AYACHE, Grégory AZAR, Dohhoon BAEK, Yuxin BAI, Alexandre BARON, Aymeric BARTHEL, Constantin BATACH, Yasmine BEN AMEUR, Emna BEN HAMIDA, Imène BERCHE, Nicolas BIEN, Chen BINGHUA, Amandine BLONDELET, Jacky BOISTEAU, Jean-François BONNE, Raphael BORG, Valeriya BORISOVA, Guillaume BOUBET, Romain BOURSIER, Maïlyss BRENNER, Alain BRETAGNOLLE, Carsten BROGE, Justyna BUCZKOWSKA, Lucie CALZADA, Bertrand CAU, Moez CHATMEN, Eve Lena CHAUDEL, Cédric CHAUSSE, Badr CHAWKI, Philippe CHEHAB, Yara CHEHADE, Alain CHIFFOLEAU, Lucas CLEMENT, Didier COLIN, Laura COLIN, Roberto D'ALU, Shen DAN, Nicolas DE FRANCONY, Tiphaine DE VEAUX DE SANCY, Carole DEAU, Laurent DEGREMONT, Donovan DELAUNAY, Loic DEVAY, Maxence DUBOIS, Christophe DUCHESNE, Claire DUCLOS PREVET, Mariano EFRON, Sana EL ABDALLAH, Imane EL HABAZI, Jurgen FALLERT, Lin FANGRONG, Antoine FERRIEN, Laurent-Marc FISCHER, Luka FORRESTER, Widson Magno FORTES MONTEIRO, Aziza FOURATTI, Adélaïde FOURCADE, Zoé FROMMER, Marta GALLO, Ons GHARSALLI, Raissa GOHI, Honglei GU, Luce GUIGNARD, Isabelle GUNASENA, Teresa HADDAD, Vincent HANNOTIN, Po-Hsien HOU, Alexander JACOBI, Halim JAMEI, Gaspard JOLY, Hyunah KANG, Yacine KHARCHI, Young-Baek KIM, Céleste KOTTMAN, Wilfried KOUADIO, Thomas KRAHENBHUL, Chanyoung KWAK, Justine LAM, Emmanuelle LEFORT LAMOURETTE, Marc LEHMANN, Franck LEON, Oscar LERCH, Caroline LEVEQUE, Yongkang LI, Flore LUPOLI, Mohamed MARCHOUD, Thomas MARCONI, Sophie MATHURIN, Yassin MATNI, Farida MEFTAH, Li MEI, Alessandra MERLI, Zhi MO, Walter MONLOUBOU, Marion MOUSTEY, Jaeyoung MUN, Dimitru Alexandru MUSTEATA, Yara NEHME, Diana NORIEGA, Raffaele PAPADIA, Nikola PAROL BAILLIF, Julien PASTEAU, Annonciade PERRON, Céline PIETTE, Nathanael PINARD, Marie-Caroline PIOT, Ananie POIRIER, Alexis POTIER, Kolja PREUSS, Selma RAIS, Matheus RENNO SARTORI, Carole RICHARD, Paul RINGUEZ, Taehoon RO, Martin ROBAIN, Philippe RODRIGUES, Ismail SAHNOUN, Rodolphe SCHVARTZ, Junhao SHI, Xiaoqing TAN, Romain TER HOFSTEEDE, Gwenn TEXIER, Rodo TISNADO, Sofia Naida TOUJDINE, Marie-Christine TRAN, Daliana VASILACHE, Rexa VIDAL ALLEN, Manh Thang VU, Se-Jun WHANG, Xiaoyu XU, Wanli XU, Laura YAKAN, Hwasuck YEOM, Liu YUNXUAN, Andrea ZAMORA, Juan Francisco ZEGARRA, Ye ZHANG, Dejun ZHANG, Jin Bao ZHANG, Zhao ZHENDYANG, Kuo ZHENG, Danny ZHOU, Mohand Said ZIRI

Preface

2073

The climate has changed drastically, the global population is only seven billion, our ways of life have become more sustainable, and nature has resumed the course of its evolution. Thanks to political and ecological action by citizens of the world, we have entered the era of the Anthrobiocene... and Architecturestudio is one hundred years old.

2023

Architecturestudio is fifty years old and rather than looking backwards, the firm is projecting itself over the fifty years to come. The results of this endeavour are presented in this book.

Tracé Bleu is a holistic approach to the new paradigms now imposed by the climate crisis to everyone, and particularly to architects. This uncertain exploration, we wanted to share it with philosophers, researchers, geographers, environmentalists, artists and art directors, politicians, and environmental historians. We would like to thank them for the richness of their contributions.

It is true that we have been already receptive to the concern of the century. The book *The Ecological City*, published in 2009 by Ante Prima Editions, witnessed that sensibility, as do all the fragments featured within the present book, partial elements of a “blue” strategy in the making. However, we go further here.

Tracé Bleu is also a methodology, equally original and contributive, systemic and inclusive of new skills that should enable us to better apprehend architectural projects and preserve inhabited environments with all their specificities and their complexities. This method is a continuation of our work, it coincides with the collective design approach which has been the signature of Architecturestudio since the beginning, while adding new dimensions and enriching it with a new relationship with time, that of the cycles of the “Blue Economy”.

Tracé Bleu, is also, for the studio, the transition from a quote by Kierkegaard often used to illustrate our philosophy—"Leave open the wounds of possibilities"—to the magnificent phrase suggested by Jose-Manuel Gonçalvès and borrowed from Jean de la Fontaine : *Que faire en ce lieu, à moins que l'on y songe?* A transition from the static to the dynamic through a new ethic of action. In the last sentence in French, all the meaning stems from the polysemy of the "y" vowel, both adverb and pronoun: pondering, imagining, dreaming in this place, our planet, and at the same time reflecting on the place itself.

For what is at stake today is also, and above all, a battle of ideals for a new society, capable of living in harmony with all living beings and passing on to future generations their share of dreams.

Introduction

The history of architecture accelerated in the last century, following the rhythm of western technological development. Our discipline is now associated with the degradation of inhabited environments. Modernity, however, was merely a parenthesis. Other notions of architecture co-existed; new ones are both possible and necessary to face the challenges of our time. We are living in a new climatic regime that calls for a different architecture. The twenty-first century must build its counterproposal to technological modernity. *Tracé Bleu* is our working hypothesis. Defining both a methodological framework and a philosophical grounding, it aims to reorient our practice as architects, with regard to the concerns of our time. It doesn't relay its conclusions here but rather opens up new lines of questioning. We have grouped these into four themes: "Re.source," "Re.act," "Re.generate," and "Inhabiting the world differently."

As Explore

These four themes were developed starting from distinct textual registers. As reflection begins through discussion, and change is built through listening, the first register is the transcription of a series of debates which took place within the office over several months, debates between personalities from different backgrounds and disciplinary fields: researchers, practitioners, politicians, and cultural actors. With the title As Explore, these public events are part of the firm's culture and its inclination for intellectual debate and collective work. Our idea of ecology centers on a science of complexity, and invites the agents transforming environments to engage in systemic practice.

The truth, if there is truth, can only be plural, and to approach this truth today means multiplying points of view, opening up inter- and trans-disciplinary debates, and accepting the contradictions and paradoxes that define our time.
Discussions thus focused on four questions:

→ How can we envision territories to guarantee housing for all?
→ What set of actors can define the commons?
→ What are the regenerative economies for our territories?
→ Which representations can support our relations with living beings and with processes of care for inhabited Environments?

Fragments

The second register of texts is titled Fragments. An anthology of experiences of AS that testify to our search for an ecological future, dozens of projects are presented and highlight the diversity of programs and key ideas of our practice today, and even more for tomorrow: caring for ecosystems, recomposing brownfield sites and interstitial zones, programming the capacity for evolution into spaces, integrating uncertainty, investing in the commons, governing with the living, building with restraint, evaluating occupation and the long-term... these fragments, put forward by the world in its entirety, are associated with a diagrammatic or synthetic iconography which illustrates the firm's toolbox. They testify to our concern for the environment, all while acknowledging an approach to the issue that is still too fragmented.

Compasses

To guide our questions and reflections, the texts on fragments are supplemented by compasses. The compasses, addressed in Chapter 4, are presented as new methodological tools that integrate temporal dimensions and constitute a heuristic approach to the project, allowing us to resituate ourselves. The "Resource" compass raises the question of a cyclical relationship to our resources in a long-term perspective; the "Governance" compass considers the inclusion of ecological and climatic agents in the design process, either existing or those still to come; and finally the "Blue Economy" compass makes possible the decompartmentalization of the sustainable aims of projects, whether they relate to low-carbon economies, knowledge, resilience or regeneration, or the benefit of a symbiotic approach.

Tracé Bleu

The third register, finally, is that of the essay. Entitled *Tracé Bleu*, this text sets out the theoretical and philosophical questions relevant to us today. These start from our experience of the field and the richness of the transcribed debates, organized along the four main themes mentioned above. This text, written with the architect and researcher Marc-Antoine Durand, acts as the book's connecting thread.

Re.source

Throughout history, the transition from one time to another has always been accompanied by a shift in our perception of the world, and the emergence of new representations. The Anthropocene is no exception to this rule. The impact of our activities is now visible in the very materiality of the planet. This new frame of reference is unyielding: we are faced with the evidence of the finiteness and fragility of our world.

This observation directly concerns architecture and the fields of construction or planning, situating the exploitation and sharing of resources as central issues of the twenty-first century. At the scale of our profession, two avenues are addressed here. First: our space is no longer extendable, rendering preservation and the regeneration of land priorities within projects. Second is the assertion of resource-time as the material of projects, and the consideration of its implementation in cycles. The proposed hypothesis is that sustainable architecture—meaning architecture that lasts—is inherently an architecture connected to its natural system, and capable of regenerating itself.

Re.act

The difficulty of implementing an efficient response to this statement relates to both the complexity and the urgency of the issues at hand. If the environmental crisis has significantly changed citizens' expectations, the coordination of actions and the sharing of decisions calls for questioning our systems of governance. The opening up of who is involved is a first response to the complexity of emerging environmental topics.

Our future is uncertain, and the environmental crisis is perceived as a threat to humanity. This new awareness confronts us with new ethical questions: how can we decide, today, the future of those that can't express themselves, either as they haven't been born—the case of future generations—or in the case of non-human agents, as they aren't represented? Despite the harshness of this observation, the Anthropocene also reveals, in a way without precedent, a planetary community united in its fragility. Architecture is invited to contribute to an ecology of action concerned with all living beings, and to defend that which we share.

Re.generate

How can we make our notions of a market economy compatible with this new roadmap? In order to facilitate an evolution of the world and of the design project, we must rediscover the value of exchange. The blue economy, as defined by Gunter Pauli, is a consideration of the value of exchange as qualitative rather than quantitative. This is a model of restraint and of justified need which we can rely on to support our ways of life, both individual and collective.

By prioritizing systemic cooperation and striving for balance and sharing, rather than interest and profit, it is a model that makes it possible to reform the practice of architecture or planning starting from a logic of support and the regeneration of inhabited environments. The very notion of design projects is enhanced by taking into consideration the long time frame of transformation, and of synchronization—in action—of human and natural cycles.

Inhabiting the world differently

Within the uncertainty that characterizes our time, *Tracé Bleu* is a hypothesis. A direction for our research. A tool to approach projects differently. A strategy to re-source architecture.

Re-sourcing architecture means considering another modernity, one simultaneously globalized, concerned with inhabited environments, and attentive to climatic inequalities. Re-sourcing architecture also means working for goodwill and for community, whether human or non-human, and designing with awareness of these new agents. Re-sourcing architecture means, finally, a different mode of inhabiting time, resynchronizing human cycles with those of all other beings and rediscovering a cosmology in which nature has its place.

Building the memory of humans and responding to their needs, with the same gesture. Taking care of what we inherit to imagine how we might intervene in that same building, in the future. The future emerging through architecture is not a mirage. It is always a choice, an engagement. The battle of imaginaries will be difficult, and architects will have their role. The future is an eminently political question. It is up to us to respond and to build the world differently, for a desirable future!

Re. source

How can we envision territories to guarantee housing for all?

François Gemenne Researcher, GIEC Member, and Specialist in Environmental Geopolitics

Luc Gwiazdzinski Geographer and Professor at the École National Supérieure d'Architecture of Toulouse

Grégory Quenet Environmental Historian, University Professor

AS Explore, moderated by Alain Bretagnolle and Romain Boursier, Partner Architects/Urban Planners, Architecturestudio

Faced with the ecological turmoil that threatens the inhabitability of our planet, Architecturestudio interrogates our ability to define a new relationship to resources through ways of living in step with the conditions of life on Earth. Resource scarcity is the result of continuous anthropogenic pressure on a planet that inherently seeks equilibrium. It manifests in numerous ways: the degradation of air quality and the water cycle, and a reduction in biodiversity, soils, and subsoils. Can we change our relationship to natural resources by considering the impacts on all living things? Are we capable of contributing to the necessary regeneration of biodiversity? Is it not, in the end, simply about a return to roots? Access to resources creates new inequalities and causes environmental and climatic migrations. How can we connect chains of actors and of values that respond to ecological issues? At what scales? Are there, under our own eyes, available yet unexpected deposits of new resources?

17. **Fertile soil**

WATER CYCLE
- Living in flood-prone areas | Montpellier, France
- Teaching around a lake | Hanoi, Vietnam
- Redeveloping in the presence of water | Abidjan, Ivory Coast
- Socially enhancing an ecosystem | Lomé, Togo
- Conserving a wadi | Lusail, Qatar

NURTURING LANDSCAPE
- Urban micro-forest | Bussy-Saint-Georges, France
- An agri-neighborhood | Lucé, France
- "Positive Food" Neighborhood | Herblay, France
- Productive edges | Réau, France

47. **Resource spaces**

UNDERGROUND SPACES
- City infrastructure | Nanterre, France
- Inverted skyscraper | Jinan, China

BROWNFIELD SITES
- From a city entrance to a new metropolitan element | Nice, France
- From a motorway junction to a mixed connected neighborhood | Créteil, France
- An eco-neighborhood in a military fort | Issy-les-Moulineaux, France
- From a linear plot to an inhabited promenade | Buenos Aires, Argentina

CONTINUOUS ARCHITECTURE
- Intensifying a school complex | Saint-Étienne, France
- Densifying and inhabiting the "concrete slab" | Paris, France
- Reinvesting roofs and courtyards | Paris, France
- Amplifying modern heritage | Paris, France
- Augmenting architecture | Douala, Cameroon
- Transforming a UNESCO heritage site into a post-carbon model | Pingyao, China

87. **Time as Resource**

- A shared campus | Dijon, France
- A Cité des Arts open to all commons | Montpellier, France

Anthropocene

The Anthropocene refers to a new geological era whose beginning corresponds to the Industrial Revolution of the nineteenth century and inscribes, physically, the impact of the acceleration of human-technical activities in the surface strata of our planet. Theorized by the Dutchman Paul Josef Crutzen,[1] it is now commonly accepted. This awareness places the exploitation and the sharing of resources at the center of ecological debates unfolding in the twenty-first century.

1. Crutzen received the Nobel Prize in Chemistry in 1995. He took the term from the American biologist Eugene F. Stoermer, who used in the 1980s.

How can we envision territories to guarantee housing for all?

Romain Boursier
We would like to raise the question of the habitability of our territories with three professor-researchers—one being an environmental historian, the other a political climate scientist, and the third a geographer. Together we will start by questioning our over-consuming relationship with resources, before we consider the vulnerability of our territories and their capacity for resilience. In the third and final part, we will question our desire to work together towards renewing our collective imagination.

Alain Bretagnolle
Grégory Quenet, you are a holder of the Laudato Si' chair "For a new exploration of Earth" at the *Collège des Bernardins.*[1] Can you tell us about the starting point of this new exploration, and why you think it is necessary?

Grégory Quenet
The notion of exploration has been outdated since Lévi-Strauss' "*Tristes tropiques,*" which started with the sentence "I hate traveling and explorers." At the time, the context was one in which exploration was that of distant worlds, and seen from a colonial perspective that he wanted to criticize. The exploration that we are experiencing today is, on the contrary, in close proximity, which is very surprising. For what surrounds us is largely unknown to us. This notion of exploring what is closest to us applies to all disciplines, to all knowledge, including architecture. We can observe the ground, for example, and consider this thin film in which the conditions of the Earth's habitability are concentrated, to be a form of architecture: 300 meters above ground, and 300 meters into the ground. If an eighteenth century scientist had been asked to define the nature of a city, the first thing he would have said would have been: its subsoil. That is to say, caves, catacombs, abandoned quarries. Moreover, the notion of resource as it appeared in German cities in the sixteenth century refers to the subsoil. And towards the end of the 19th century, cities used subsoil areas to resolve conflicts between the different networks: waste water, information flows, and transport. They did this so well that it all became completely invisible, to the point that the cities we live in today no longer reveal what lies beneath them. The gigantic task of describing the world is the objective of this Chair: to cultivate a new way of looking around and investigating.

1 Training and research center in Paris.

From *Slow Violence*, Studio Joanie Lemercier

RWE's Bagger 290 excavator is the biggest man-made machine on earth. Just one of these machines can extract up to 240,000 tons of coal each day. If we count the emissions of the four power plants on location, each day 155,000 tons of CO_2 are emitted on this site, which in itself make it the biggest source of greenhouse gas emissions in Europe, the site is responsible for producing an emission of 480,000 tons of CO_2 total each day. If this extract from the audiovisual project *Slow Violence* demonstrates only destruction, the pathway is slow, contemplative, almost peaceful, a suspended moment in which one can easily imagine the irreversible and lasting asepcts of these events. Large-scale environmental annihilation occurs at another pace: it takes forty year for CO_2 emissions to have an impact on the planet's atmosphere, which makes climate change so difficult to understand at an individual level. This is what Rob Nixon, professor at Princeton University, calls "slow violence."

Kabul, Afghanistan.

The word *resource* reflects an interesting double semantics. It refers first of all to our means, material and intellectual, of existence. At the same time, it also describes what makes it possible to improve an unfortunate situation. By connecting what is vital to the human species to the improvement of its condition, this current definition of "resource" fits within a progressive and technological ideal, as evidenced by the overabundance of terminology linking technology to use of the word: we readily speak of resource deposits, of resource exploitation. This consumptive relationship to resources has fueled the use of technology in human development, fostering a dependence on growth and overconsumption. The Anthropocene, through the geological scale it invokes, now refers to both the excesses of this collective project and its questioning.

Alain Bretagnolle

Today, the notion of resources, whether energy, rare-earth elements or food, is at the heart of our concerns, both because we have become aware that they are finite, but also because this observation forces us to think differently about our relationship with the world, and particularly our relationship with non-human life, with biodiversity. Everyone agrees that anthropic pressure must be reduced, but how? Can we change our relationship with natural resources while considering the impacts on all living things? Are we capable of contributing to the regeneration of the environment and, in the end, does this not involve returning to our roots?

Grégory Quenet

First of all, I would say that one of the things that history teaches us is that nothing is inevitable, there is no linear time curve representing progress, nor is there a curve representing decline. Historical time is much more complex than that, and is made up of a certain number of potentialities, of bifurcations, and in this sense, everything is always possible.

Nevertheless, in order to understand this notion of resources, I would distinguish two levels of relationships with nature.

The first level is that of the possessiveness of the world: we describe it, exploit it, sell it, in other words, we have turned it into a commodity. A second level, which is just as important, is that of correspondence and meaning. If we focus on the sole level of possessiveness, we can naturally tell ourselves that we need to possess less, possess better, compensate for this possession, but are we not therefore limiting ourselves to this level? On the other hand, if we consider the second level, a different world opens up. We leave behind the extensiveness of a "more and more" approach, to move towards a more intensive relationship with things.

As for architecture, since we are in an architectural agency today, I think that one of the values of this discipline is that it acts on both levels, that of possessiveness and that of correspondence and meaning, and that it must deal with both at the same time. In this sense, new perspectives are opening up: other ways of living, of caring, of building connections.

Romain Boursier

How about the commons? They are collectively established, recognized, and defined as a collective possession, i.e. without exclusive property.

Grégory Quenet

Commons offer a way of living together as a society. They belong to the level of correspondences, and involve social relations, links between human beings. Resource is

Living in flood-prone areas

Montpellier, France

The Parc Marianne area is a sustainable neighborhood open onto a vast park for natural flood management. Bordered by two rivers that cross the site from north to south, the Lez and the Lironde, it is designed to be a continuation of its existing environment and creates visual access onto its natural and built environment. Strategically located between the historic center of Montpellier and the Mediterranean, and combining functional diversity with attractive public and landscaped areas, it aims above all to improve the quality of life of its inhabitants.

The orthogonal geometry of the vineyards of this former agricultural plain, and the undulation of the watercourses are the two movements that have influenced the urban composition of the neighborhood. The modified bed of the Lironde allows for precise flood management, floodwaters being captured by Georges Charpak Park in a seven-hectare retention area. The grassy area of the tramway line that runs down the center of Avenue Raymond Dugrand is also designed to receive and absorb run-off water from the roads. A vast reflective water feature in the square overlooking the park completes the design of the blue infrastructure.

The urban design of the neighborhood is thus based on the presence of water, with promenades along the Lironde and pedestrian footbridges crossing the planted bioswales of green corridors. Nature enters the city with endogenous plants and species adapted to the local climate to prolong the Mediterranean atmosphere of Montpellier's city center, with its shaded public spaces, tree-lined gardens in the heart of blocks, and tree-lined promenades.

The new neighborhood, which won the *EcoQuartier* 2011 award in the "overall ecological approach" category, is thus organized around blue-green infrastructure.

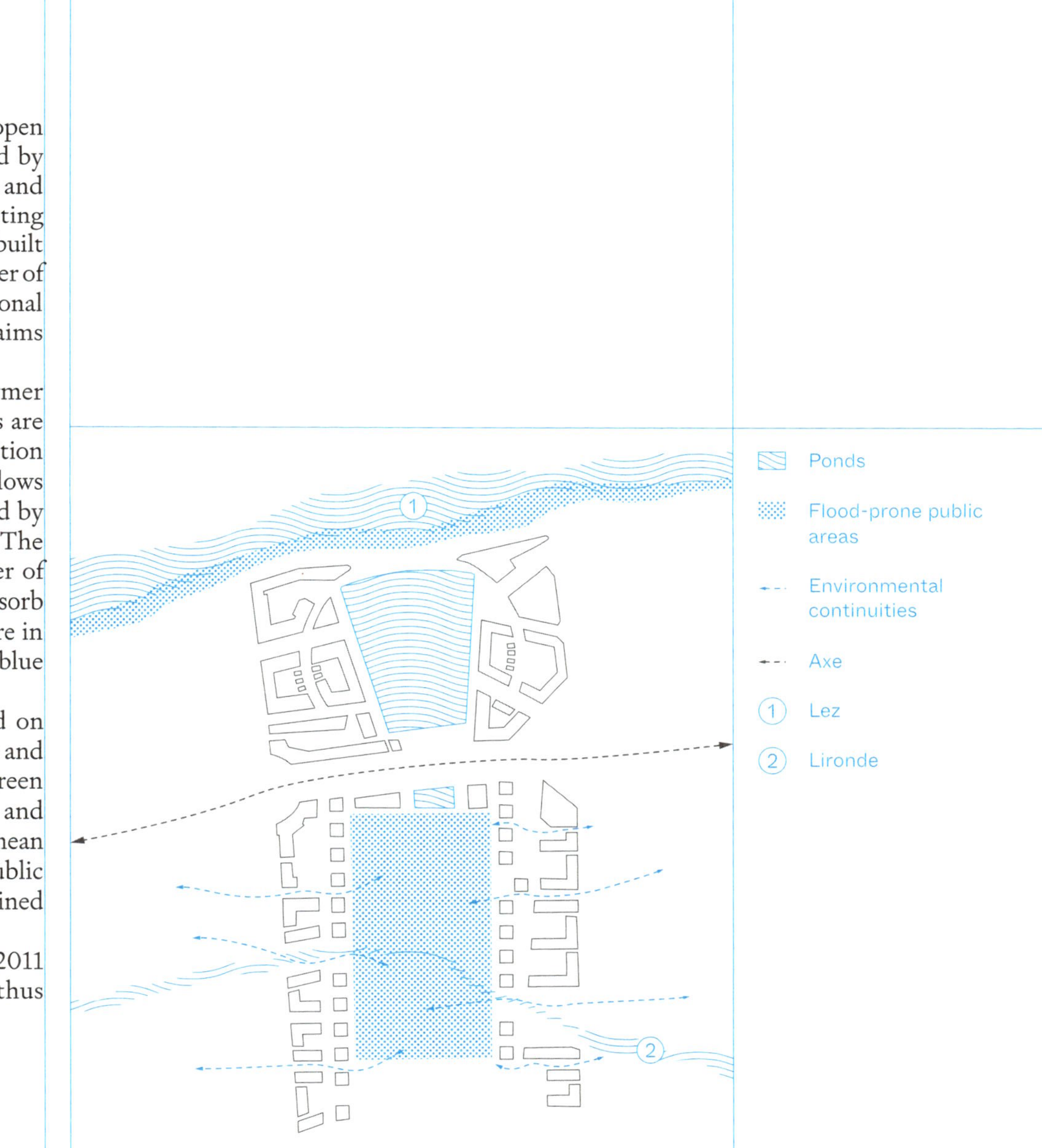

Port Marianne-Parc
Marianne Urban
Development Area,
Ville de Montpellier, SERM
Architecturestudio.

Montpellier, France, 2018.

actually a very interesting word. Its etymology does not reveal the meaning we have given it at all. A resource is that which resurfaces and is renewed. The great feat of neoclassical economics in the nineteenth century was to profoundly change this definition by associating resources with stocks. Hence the disastrous idea that nature is a kind of department store from which we can endlessly help ourselves. If we go back to its etymological meaning, that of resurgence, then it obviously involves something completely different: we have to take care of the way things resurface.

Romain Boursier
But can we add conditions to certain acts of possessing? Can we make people responsible or establish duties towards the regeneration of these resources?

Grégory Quenet
This is indeed tricky. Your agency is involved in both urban planning and architecture. We have to think beyond the limits of building to consider all these relationships. The problem is not that nature is changing—that is the typical argument of climate skeptics, to say that it is constantly changing—the problem is that today it is changing in the time-scale of a human life. That is the brand new issue at stake here. And I am quite struck by the fact that the sustainability of resources, which has been reflected on, conceptualized, for quite a long time, has only really become an issue and a practical problem very recently, notably in architecture.

François Gemenne
Basically, what makes it so difficult for us to phase out fossil fuels today is that we actually have these resources—which are literally fossil fuels, i.e. they are beneath our feet, and have been located—and that we exercise a form of sovereignty over them. Gas, petrol, coal, can be found in the subsoil of a specific country, and that country considers these resources as a kind of property that it is going to be able to use, or even use up completely. The great difficulty we are facing is to move from these resources that we possess to resources that will regenerate, i.e. renewable energy, resources that we will transform into energy thanks to technological infrastructures. It seems to me that our relationship with resources, with possessiveness and sovereignty, which has been completely neglected, is fundamentally shifting. We have a very technological perspective today, an engineer's perspective, on these questions of intermittency and capacity. But we lack a political perspective on our relationship with resources, which I think is necessary to move towards a post-fossil fuel world. One of the reasons why nuclear energy is so

The Anthropocene is also a rhetorical device with universalizing aims and a strong capacity to create narratives, thus requiring some intellectual precautions. Its political significance must first be put into perspective, as François Gemenne often points out. The concept gives the illusion that all humans are equally responsible for harm inflicted on the planet,[2] which is evidently not the case. The recent COP 27 is historic in this sense, as it recorded the North's environmental debt to the South. The Anthropocene is thus understood as critical, and so we speak of "Occidentalocene" or "Capitalocene."

2. François Gemenne, *Géopolitique du climat: Les relations internationales dans un monde en surchauffe*, Armand Colin, 2021.

Teaching around a lake

Hanoi, Vietnam

Hoa Lac is home to the new premises of the HUST (Hanoi University of Science and Technology), a Franco-Vietnamese university that develops scientific teaching cycles. Located about sixty kilometers from the center of Hanoi, the site chosen for the development of this City of Sciences, which will bring together the main units of excellence in Vietnamese research, is set in a vast landscape of lakes with winding contours.

We could have filled in the part of the lake that occupies the center of the site to allow the new constructions to take place on a virgin site detached from all contingencies. We chose to preserve and enhance it, in order to make this ecosystem the heart of the new university. The buildings thus form a framework with the lake as its motif, which students will be able to admire in every season.

Around the lake, the movement between the different entities of the campus follow a panoramic peripheral gallery, located on the first floor so as to cross the arms of the lake. At ground level, the shared spaces of the campus are designed to allow access to the banks, which are kept in their natural state, their profile changing with the water level according to the seasons. The riverbanks are landscaped and used for walks, as places of contemplation, and outdoor study rooms on the water's edge.

The mass of water contained in the lake, combined with the planting of tall trees, helps to regulate the temperature of the whole Campus and limits the heat island effects of the new buildings. The presence of the lake at the heart of this new living and working environment will allow scientific research to take place in symbiosis with the natural environment.

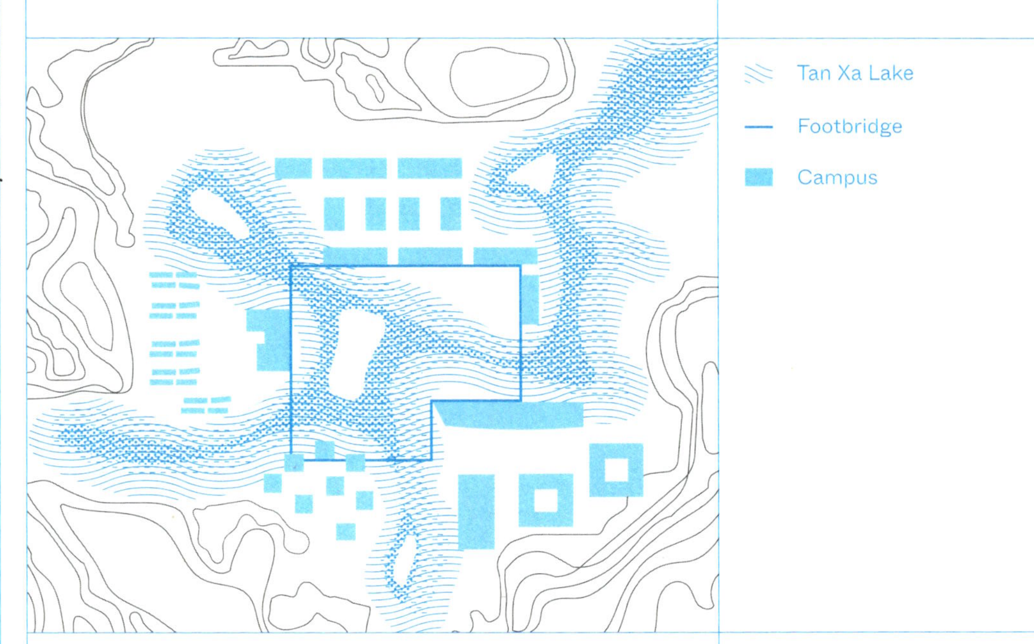

Tan Xa Lake
Footbridge
Campus

Kabul, Afghanistan.

The historian of science Jean-Baptiste Fressoz warns of the rhetorical risk.[3] In his book *The Shock of the Anthropocene*, Fressoz highlights the grandiosity of the phrase—a new era!—and explains how this rhetorical one-upmanship encourages us to create ruptures and to break with the history of ideas and knowledge of the past, placing us, paradoxically, in an analogous relationship with modern history. In the view of Fressoz, we either accept this rupture by considering that our knowledge of the environment has increased considerably, or we try to understand the continuities of an environmental history of our societies. This second hypothesis is the one that draws his attention, and to him is the only valid option for understanding the contemporary ecological crisis.

3. Christophe Bonneuil and Jean-Baptiste Fressoz, *The Shock of the Anthropocene: The Earth, History and Us*, Verso Books, 2017.

controversial today is not so much because of its costs, because of nuclear safety issues, or even—or perhaps marginally so—because of waste issues; it is because we are dealing with a form of energy that is neither one nor the other, which relies on a fossil fuel—in this case uranium—but which is then transformed into energy by sophisticated technological infrastructure.

Romain Boursier
What you are saying is similar to the question that arose at the beginning of the industrial era, particularly in England, as to whether industrialists should be satisfied with apparently free and abundant, but fickle energy sources—such as hydraulic energy, which involves the constraint of being located near rivers—or use other, more mobile, fluid and stable sources of energy.

Grégory Quenet
The difficulty with environmental issues is that they should not be thought of in terms of ecology. As soon as we use the word "ecology," we neglect the social dimension. It is a question of power, of a category that is used in different situations. In that sense, when you talk about the beginning of the industrial revolution, the debate concerned the type of energy that should be used, and what helped decide between coal and hydraulic energy, as Andreas Malm clearly identified for England, was the question of social rights. Renewable energy sources, such as hydro or wind power, are intermittent. This made it difficult to stabilize the workforce, which actually protested because it demanded stable working conditions, whereas the energy sources were not stable. Setting up wage labor and the operating forces that come with it required a source of energy that was not subject to variations. If English employers turned to fossil fuels, it was not because they were more efficient, nor because they produced better quality heat, but because they were stable and made it possible to impose a balance of power on wage-earners. Intermittent energy sources offered the latter much more effective forms of negotiation.

Romain Boursier
François Gemenne, I noted a very simple observation in your book *Géopolitique du climat* (The Geopolitics of Climate). You say that all the solutions imaginable exist in terms of reducing emissions and resource consumption, but that they are not being implemented.

François Gemenne
Yes, the mistake we often make is to believe that understanding is enough to trigger action. This is a very common mistake,

Redeveloping in the presence of water

Abidjan, Ivory Coast

The idea of rethinking the urban configuration of the neighborhoods of Anoumabo and Konan Raphaël in Abidjan followed the decision of the French State to fund a diagnostic study concerning the sanitation and waste management of the commune of Marcory, of which they are two emblematic neighborhoods. We pointed out that by implication, without a broader urban perspective, these technical elements would remain a dead letter, and therefore suggested a foresight exercise to the local authorities.

In addition to the technical diagnosis simultaneously carried out by Ginger, we conducted an in-depth survey of the local population, thus identifying urban areas and their respective histories, informal housing, the different uses of public space, and the governance systems in place. The development of the existing canal, which is both a dumping ground and a sewage system, into a landscaped area was one of the structural elements of the approach. Anoumabo is run according to customary law by a village chief, whereas Konan Raphaël bears the mark of 1980s social housing and of an expected urban transformation with the construction of the third bridge. Two distinct project approaches, conducted in consultation with the local population, led to the proposal of two eco-neighborhoods with very different characteristics and set-ups. They were presented by Ivory Coast at the COP 22 in Marrakech in 2016 as part of a sustainable city development program, Marcory 2030, with the aim of achieving an urban regeneration level characteristic of the African city of the future.

With nearly eight million inhabitants, the Ivorian capital, like all the major metropolises on the African continent, is experiencing very high demographic growth. The government has taken very clear positions regarding the end of urban sprawl in the Abidjan metropolis, and the need to rebuild the city on top of itself. These two urban renewal projects, which are still in progress, illustrate this approach in an emblematic way. They also bear witness to all sorts of difficulties—land availability, technical, operational and political—that are slowing down progress.

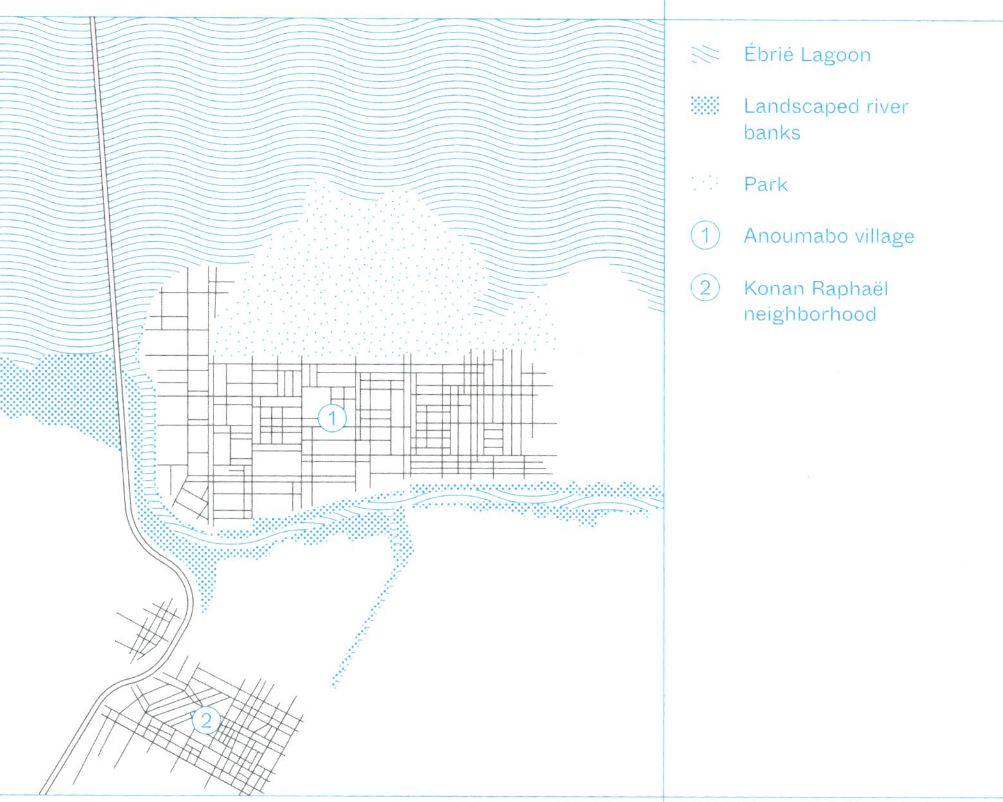

Ébrié Lagoon
Landscaped river banks
Park
(1) Anoumabo village
(2) Konan Raphaël neighborhood

Abidjan, Ivory Coast.

The finite nature of our world and the error of a project based on unlimited growth have long been recognized. The story was already unfolding, and it took almost a century to move from alarm to action. The work of Charbonneau and Ellul raised this point as early as the 1930s, when they questioned the technological society.[4] A century later it is clear that Western societies persist, in the name of "sustainable development," in attempting to reconcile the irreconcilable: technological progress and environmental conservation. How is it possible to explain this gap between conceptual understanding and sharing of findings on the one hand, and the implementation of concrete solutions to fix it on the other?

4. Bernard Charbonneau and Jacques Ellul are considered the forerunners of radical ecology.

particularly in environmentalist circles. But a fundamental question must initially be addressed, that of the organization of society. Insofar as our industrialized societies have largely developed based on the exploitation of fossil fuels, moving away from this, and on to a decarbonized world implies rethinking the organization of society itself, and our lifestyles as a whole. We often limit our questions to our production and consumption habits, whereas we obviously also need to rethink our housing habits, modes of transport, as well as concepts as fundamental as freedom, justice and sovereignty, and I think that we have so far been somewhat sparing with all this.
Where bike-sharing schemes are concerned, for example, we can see that the notion of mobility in cities has been transformed by what was initially a form of political experimentation (in La Rochelle in the 1970s). I am a great believer in the capacity of minorities to lead the way, precisely through experimentation, through the possibility of suggesting new pathways that the majority could then follow. I must admit that for a long time, I believed that it would be possible to raise awareness, to convince the majority of the population, and that all of a sudden there would be some kind of shift in society because most people would be convinced of the need to decarbonize the economy. I really believed in this, particularly at the time of the youth movements led by Greta Thunberg. However, I have to admit that this shift in society has not happened yet. Today I tend to believe much more in conscious and active minorities who will be able to carry out such experiments in architecture, urban planning, industrial processes and democratic innovation, who can pave the way and engage the rest of the population in their wake. I have more faith—but I could be wrong—in determined minorities than in a conscious majority.

Romain Boursier
In Paris, and elsewhere, we can see that public spaces are changing much more rapidly than buildings.

François Gemenne
Absolutely. It is even a challenge for buildings and architecture to keep up with urban planning.

Romain Boursier
Concerning the organization of urban and rural spaces, could we not start, for example, with the notion of resource pooling? Buildings thought of as reserves of uses and spaces?

François Gemenne
Urban areas are a breeding ground for experimentation, but also for the pooling of certain spaces, and perhaps for moving away

Socially enhancing an ecosystem

Lomé, Togo

Lomé's equalizing lagoon is a technical structure that occupies a central position between the recently developed residential areas in the north of the Togolese capital and the city center. It is also an essential element of the blue infrastructure, and is home to rich biodiversity. The project consists of opening it up to new uses, as part of a vast urban park which relies on hydraulic constraints and the existing ecosystem, in order to enhance its value.

The development of this twenty-hectare lagoon environment is based on the idea of an encounter between the natural and artificial elements of the site. The park is located on the northern edge of the equalization canal, between the eastern and western lakes of the lagoon system. A second canal, connected to the first, eliminates any risk of flooding. Between the two, the island area of the park creates a new landscape and initiates a rehabilitation process for the surrounding neighborhood for the benefit of the inhabitants of the metropolis.

Modular, thematic gardens whose design is open to modification contribute to the evolutionary construction of the site. They include architectural follies with different functions. The cultural garden includes a large landscaped esplanade, a scene for events of all types, an administrative building and a multi-purpose pavilion. The educational garden hosts a "green school" dedicated to educational and creative activities related to nature, local biodiversity, and the water cycle. The leisure garden includes kiosks, a restaurant and a fairground. The sports garden contains athletic tracks and fields adapted to different games and practices. Each garden is easily accessible and linked to the city by a full network of itineraries, with its footbridges and soft mobility ways.

By considering an existing ecosystem in a new light, which initially only had a technical function, the lagoon urban park project invents a new common area with a new status, that of an inhabited environment that welcomes all living beings.

Urban Park

Hydraulic continuity

1 Equalizing lagoon

2 Gulf of Guinea

↑ Hanoi, Vietnam.
→ Kabul, Afghanistan.

For Grégory Quenet it is the acceleration of the deterioration of our environment and our findings, at the scale of human life, on the decline of our resources, on air and water quality, on soil pollution, on the loss of biodiversity—that is, everything we could choose to not see is now visible and forces us, finally, to act.[5]

5. Grégory Quenet, *Qu'est-ce que l'histoire environnementale?* Champ Vallon, 2014.

from certain visions of ownership and appropriation that we have developed up to now. I sometimes get slightly annoyed with anti-capitalist positions that would like to make the fight against capitalism a sort of prerequisite for climate action, in which case I'm afraid that we would be chasing pipe dreams, and that we would have to wait a very long time before climate action were to be taken. But we need to be able to question some of the precepts of capitalism, particularly the way in which the exclusive appropriation of space and resources is envisaged. This is true for urban areas, but it can also be true for modes of transport, cars for instance. We are well aware today, even if there is a very strong increase in the use of electric cars, that if we replace the fleet of thermal cars with an equivalent fleet of electric cars, on the one hand this will raise a very important question about the resources to be used, particularly in terms of rare-earth elements, to operate and build batteries, and on the other hand it will also raise issues in terms of logic, travel, transport flows and quite simply traffic jams. Whereas today, we could rethink the way we use cars and move towards car-sharing.

Romain Boursier
And to think of mobility as a service.

François Gemenne
And to think of mobility as a service, absolutely.

Alain Bretagnolle
Luc Gwiazdzinski, you also use observation as an entry point to the project, but with a particular approach, that focuses on temporalities and is based on the notion of chronotopia.

Luc Gwiazdzinski
Yes, exactly. As a geographer, and also as an urban planner, I have tried, with others, to introduce the notion of time into my work. I consider it to be important where observation is concerned, but also later on, with action. When we ask someone to describe a part of a city, we ask them about the neighborhood involved, but we don't usually ask them about the time-scale. It is the same city, the materiality has changed very little, but a lot of things can change in a few hours. That was my initial question, the feeling that we tried to create a sort of average city for average people, with a continuous and constant way of functioning. Which is obviously not realistic.
Another surprising element is that we have always tried to develop space with a view to saving time—with the TGV[2] for instance—and maps have become distorted, we feel that distances have been shortened, and see how cities strive to

2 France's high-speed rail service.

Conserving a wadi

Lusail, Qatar

The new city of Lusail is being built on land reclaimed from the sea north of Doha, a blank page meeting the turquoise waters of the Gulf. Viable land for these urban developments in the desert climate of the Arabian Gulf lies either along the wadis (valleys), where the cultivated oases can traditionally be found, or along the coast, a case favored by modernity.

We initially imagined the architecture and public spaces of the commercial boulevard of Lusail—the main artery of this new city which grew out of the aridity of the desert all the way to the seaside—as well as the seafront promenade landmarks, the streets and squares, for which the challenge, innovative in this climate, was to create outdoor public space. We pursued this idea of creating the identity of the new city through its public spaces as part of the development of an ecological park occupying the site of a nearby wadi.

In this natural space shaped by age-old erosion, we have recreated and developed with Michel Desvigne Paysagistes, over two kilometers and in three sequences, the typical landscapes and environments of the wadis of Qatar: the aridity of the desert, the fertility of the oasis and the singularity of the mangrove where it meets the sea. These areas are dedicated to biodiversity. A wooden educational farm has been built in the oasis, with small pavilions, also made of wood, scattered along the way, to raise visitors' awareness of the ecosystem and associated agricultural practices.

The Eco-Wadi Park illustrates the evolution of pastoral, agricultural, nomadic, and sedentary activities in the area. By evoking, in particular, water catchment systems and the organization of nomadic pastoralism and of agriculture, in the context of human interaction with a desert environment, the trail illustrates the adaptability and ingenuity of local human communities in making the most of the scarce resources available to make their presence possible.

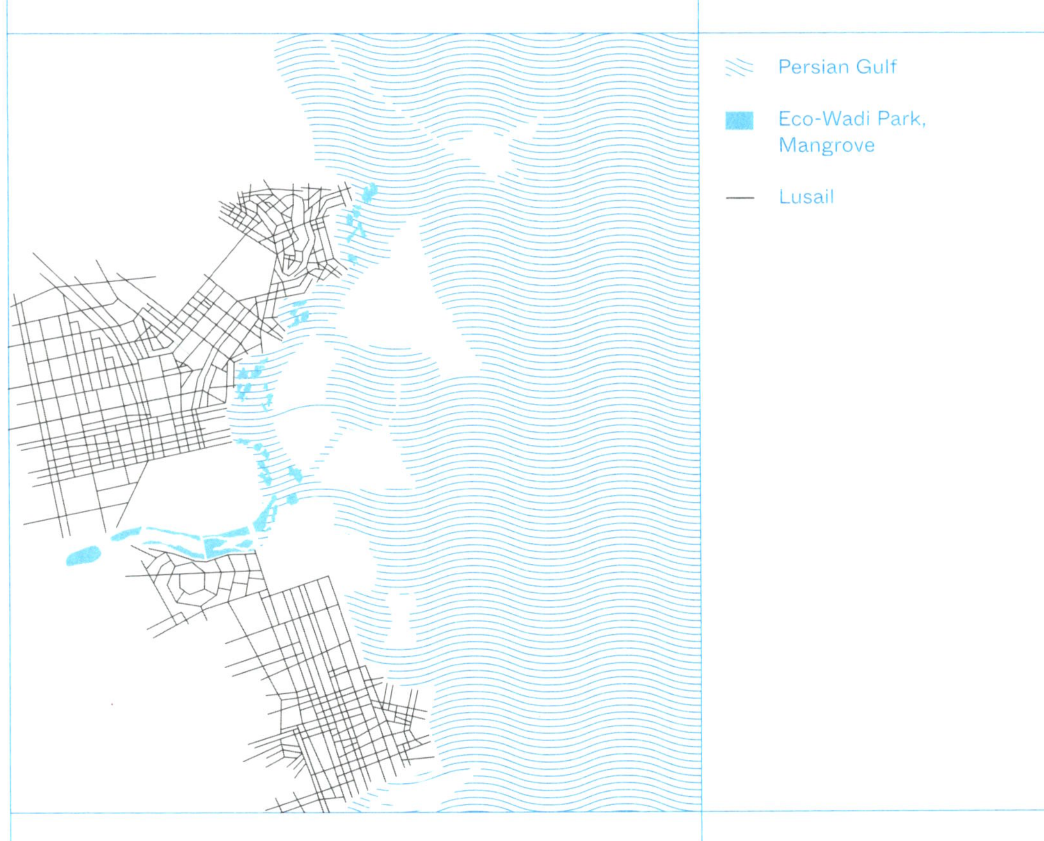

Persian Gulf

Eco-Wadi Park, Mangrove

Lusail

Urban and landscape development at Lusail, Qatari Diar, Architecturestudio, Michel Desvignes.

Lusail, Qatar, 2016.

One Earth, One World

Western modernity is built around a project of development without limits. This vision of the world helped initiate an expansive mode of development, one continuously seeking more material, energy, and human resources to accommodate its expansion. Yet the twentieth century ended with the acknowledgment of widespread depletion. First, with the oil crises of 1973 and 1980 our societies became aware of their dependence on fossil fuels. This was followed by the exhaustion, highlighted by scientists, of a world we had believed was unlimited, and the emergence of an international politics of ecology: "One Earth, one world," declared the United Nations' Brundtland report in 1987. For Bruno Latour we are living through a radical change, similar in importance to the Galilean revolution. We no longer inhabit the same planet.

be connected to these networks—whether motorways or long-distance rail services. On the other hand, the opposite has rarely been done, i.e. to manage time in order to save space. And the feeling I have is that in our disciplines, we are somewhat influenced by the metaphysics of stability, of permanence. Almost as if we were talking to an object that would forever be there. This is particularly true of architects. You mentioned chronotopia—I'm not going to try and define what it is, that would be too complex—but for me it is a form of articulation of time and space. Particularly in representations. To be able to work on the notion of time and space, and to be able to observe it, we must be able to define this spatio-temporal complexity. Chronotopia allows dynamic visions of a territorial or urban complexity.

Romain Boursier

It also allows us to understand time as a resource for architecture.

Luc Gwiazdzinski

Yes, this question can be approached from several angles. The first one is spatial, it concerns versatility. The versatility of spaces, hybridization. That is to say, how can we break the Athens Charter—I'm going to put it a little bluntly for the specialists here—how can we break zoning, and allow different populations, different activities, different uses and different temporalities to cohabit in the same space. Because a space which is dysfunctional is often a space which is mono-temporal, which has a single temporal color, a single type of use. So the first question concerns the versatility of spaces, and the city as a versatile space. Versatility does not fire our imagination, because it evokes the community centers of our childhood,[3] which were not the most hospitable or ergonomic of buildings. But this idea of versatility allows us to think about urban intensity, it forces us to think about the rules of conduct for those using these spaces. I'm only talking about human beings here, but we could also add non-humans to that. With plants, cohabitation is relatively smooth-running, with animals, it's a little more complex depending on the pace involved, but it bears thinking about.
This is the first notion: versatility. And we can see that the stakeholders involved, in order to improve or to become more competitive, or perhaps also for questions of equality between populations, are increasingly working towards hybridization. Today, a multitude of design processes are leading us to third places. It's interesting to note how institutions, whether universities, schools, or companies, exist beyond their walls.

3 Versatility is "*polyvalence*" in French, and "*salles polyvalentes*" are literally multi-purpose halls, i.e. community centers.

Urban micro-forest

Bussy-Saint-Georges, France

The town of Bussy-Saint-Georges is located on the northern edge of the Ferrière Regional Forest and the Domaine de Crécy Forest. Thanks to its exceptional location and its excellent access to the A4 motorway and the RER[1] A line, it has recently undergone urban development for the benefit of new inhabitants in the Val-de-Bussy sector of Marne-la-Vallée.

The study site extends along the motorway all the way to the RER train station. It is strategically located in terms of its future development and influence. More broadly, the site has a pivotal position between the natural environments of large forests to the south and the landscaped areas of the new city to the north.

How can we rethink a living entrance to the city? How can we recreate ecological continuity between the large forests and the green spaces of the different neighborhoods? A city entrance that enhances the ecological potential of the landscaped areas (whose vegetation was planted directly in the ground), that may support endogenous vegetation, and allow the surface management of rainwater? Which also develops the various benefits of nature in the city for its overall population?

The strategy of the project for a living entrance to the city consists of re-foresting interstitial spaces around facilities and public spaces in order to store carbon, to ensure ecological continuity for fauna and flora, and to reduce the impact of summer heat waves.

According to the method of micro-forests developed by the botanist and phyto-sociologist Arika Miyawaki, the project thus proposes the creation of an urban forest, by qualifying the surroundings of a future school and the development of a future bicycle highway. The ambition of the project is to extend this forest cordon along the other constructions, beyond our perimeter in coherence with neighboring projects, and up to the nearby forest and agricultural areas, thereby linking the territory's eco-systemic spaces.

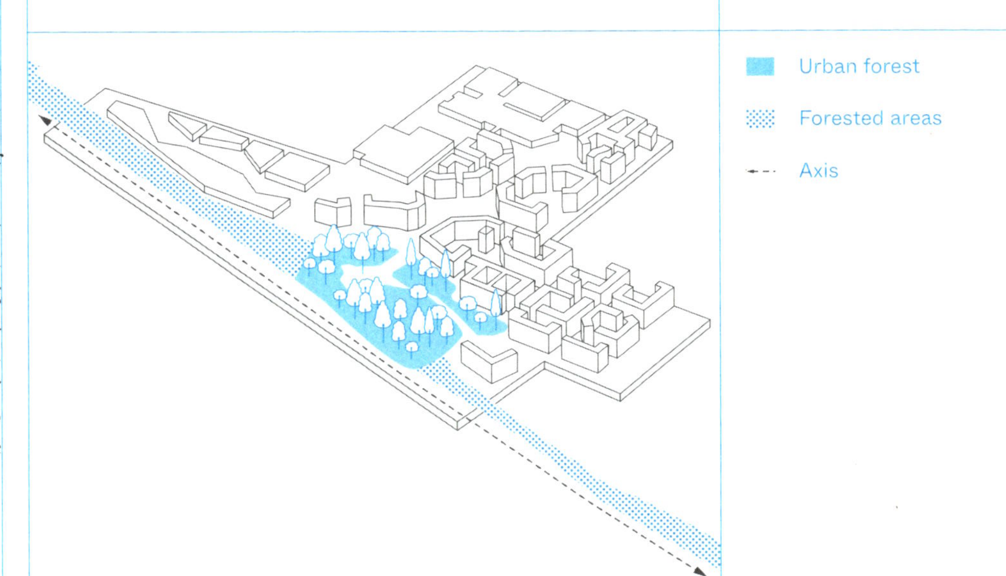

1. Suburban Express Railway in the Paris area

They exist beyond their core—I'm thinking spatially here—outside their walls, but also beyond time. Any activity that is developing today must have a nocturnal dimension, for example. The notion of nighttime is one of the tropisms in my research. If you want to exist, for example as a fairground, you need a night-time dimension. Theaters must put on events in the middle of the night. Today, I even found out about a "Night of the conservatories." We must leave the bunker we were in, to go out and meet others. This will actually create places for diversity, hybridization and interacting. This temporality, for example evenings, nighttime, has become a very important time for conviviality.
The second point concerns the rotation of activities over time. That is to say, the possibility of having several activities cohabit in the same space, so that they may take place one after another. And this raises a lot of questions. For example, a few years ago I lived in Strasbourg, not far from the European Parliament, which is used two days a month, whereas many institutions are looking for space. Another issue is that of housing for homeless people. I can't stand hearing anymore: "We can't take them in because we don't have the space." That is not true. All public buildings have space, and if we think in terms of chronotopia, as you suggest I do, then there is space available in the evenings. This element seems important to me: rotation. It can take place during the day, but also throughout the year. University buildings, for example, are empty for at least a month and a half in summer. What do you do with them? Elsewhere, during weekends, fleets of vehicles do not get used, how could that change? This idea of rotating activities, in my opinion, may allow us to avoid, each time we have an idea or a new function, building an isolated building on the outskirts of a city. Cities are said to be spreading...
Cities are places where interactions are maximized, and we must work on the intensification of uses. For the moment, I am also talking about humans, but we need to consider interactions with non-humans. The city as a place of serendipity, a place for meeting, communicating, living.

Alain Bretagnolle
This requires a certain availability of spaces, and of the mind.

Luc Gwiazdzinski
This is the idea developed by the philosopher Henri Maldiney: existing involves being ahead of oneself in meeting others.
In suggesting hybridization, first of all, you must have confidence in other people. Hybridization is not an easy process, you need to trust people. Such trust makes serendipity possible. In other words, 1+1 = 3. Something else is going to happen, a third space; third parties are inventing themselves, and fruitful marriages do exist.

The exhaustion of the modern project now raises the question of its legacy. How can we inherit this modernity, founded on expansion, in our limited world? How can we redefine our relationship to resources? How can we redefine resources as a common good? How do we build, when human activities relating to construction are responsible for 40% of global greenhouse gas emissions? How do we emerge from a purely consumptive relationship to resources and reverse this state of affairs?

An agri-neighborhood

Lucé, France

We have been working on the *Plateau Nord-Est* project in Chartres for several years. In this context, Architecturestudio was called upon by a farmers' cooperative wishing to question the future of a nine-hectare agricultural wasteland within an urban environment as well as its purpose, while considering the need for the agricultural sector to adapt to new forms of cultivation more adapted to the challenges of tomorrow.

This site, which used to be surrounded by fields, used to store the harvests of 150 farmers in the region and helped to feed the world. Today, the large, decrepit silos no longer store wheat and barley grains, but the equipment for storage—humidity sensors, underground heating galleries, and conveyor pods—raises important questions. These interconnected silo-monuments form a sort of network with the rest of the transport equipment, including trucks and wagons, still present on the site.

How can the meaning of such an agricultural infrastructure be reactivated today? How can we devise new functions for these silos, inherited from the recent past? Can this transformation of the site respond in an experimental way to the agricultural sector's quest for alternatives? Indeed, while the industry has been destabilized by the limits of the extensive farming system subject to the globalized price of cereal crops, society is starting to become eco-conscious and aims to reduce the carbon footprint of the food industry. Can the encouragement of new farming methods (without using pesticides or synthetic fertilizers), the promotion of short food supply chains, the diversification of cultivation methods, and even the integration of a new social, educational and economic value chain linked to these modern practices, define a new roadmap for the agricultural forms implemented by the cooperative?

Designed in cooperation with the farmers, the project is based on the regeneration of the site. On the one hand, by proposing to clean up and regenerate the soil, for the benefit of vegetable crops and public spaces open to neighboring districts. On the other hand, by upgrading the industrial architecture of the silos to a place for experimenting with new forms of high added-value greenhouse crops, such as aromatic, perfume or medicinal plants—thus creating possible synergies with the Chartres-based Cosmetic Valley. In a circular logic, the project also proposes to process and distribute the products of these new crops on site. This agricultural diversification hub project allows for the dissemination of the catalyzing services of a new agri-neighborhood around public spaces.

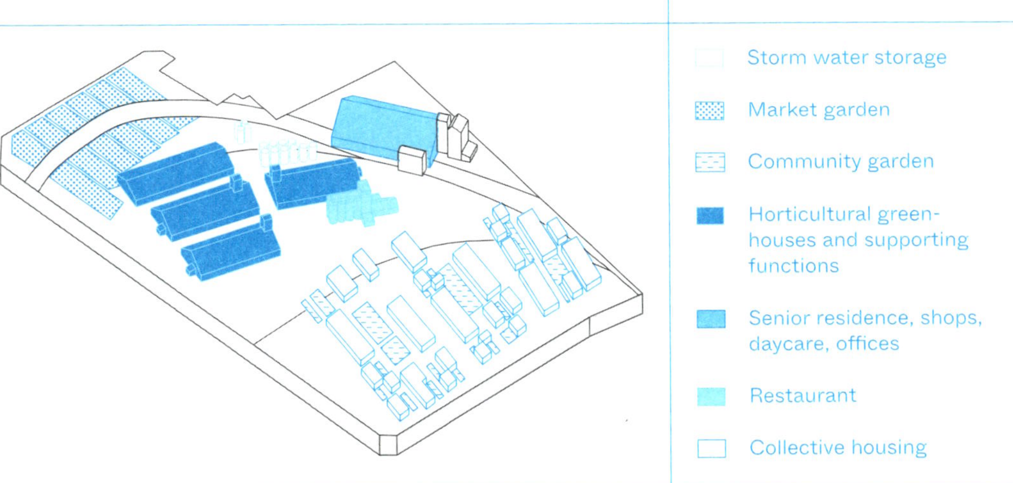

Storm water storage

Market garden

Community garden

Horticultural greenhouses and supporting functions

Senior residence, shops, daycare, offices

Restaurant

Collective housing

From an architectural point of view, these difficult questions call for the definition of responsible action, from the perspective of both the localized act of building and its implications at economic, political, and ecological levels. Resource scarcity weakens and unbalances our world, at the scale both of our everyday environments and of our planet, and undermines the logic of trans-territorial solidarity rather than reinforcing it. Ecological awareness, a major factor in geopolitical instability, calls for a new sharing of resources alongside their regeneration. Does the notion of the Anthropocene not invite this? A celebration of the birth of a terrestrial community, all moving towards the same destiny, rather than bio-regional retreat? The twenty-first century, we know, will be the century of great global migrations. The urgency is twofold: we must commit to the adaptation of impacted territories, and to the generosity of resource-rich territories.

Alain Bretagnolle
We were saying earlier that we could not wait for a revolution that would bring down capitalism to change our social model. I tend to agree from a pragmatic point of view. However, there are symbolic issues at stake, as capitalism is associated with an existential form of materialism. I would like to talk to you about the awareness that we share this planet with other living beings. Does a cosmological question not arise, as well as symbolic issues beyond the technical and economic ones?

Romain Boursier
And I'd like to add: how can we think about and consider this materialism in terms of scales and territorial approaches? Some researchers are talking about bioregions...

Grégory Quenet
One of the great strengths of capitalism is that it erases scalability, and makes it possible to implement the same solution at different scales and replicate it by dis-embedding and de-contextualizing. The question is not simply one of materialism versus dematerialism, but rather one of embedding versus dis-embedding. Let me explain: the debate is not for or against the use of cars, for or against the use of bicycles. The issue is not the object itself, but the way it fits into a territory, and how it is contextualized. The definition is important here. Etymologically speaking, territory has two meanings: it has an apocryphal meaning, which is the territory referred to as *Terror*, i.e. power: the territory as a space for the projection of power. And it has a second meaning, which is territory as land, as soil. The dialectic between the two meanings is very important in answering the question you are asking. We can, to start with, consider the territory as land, and say that we are going to build bioregions that will be self-sufficient, that will take care of their soils as they used to. Indeed, if we consider the relationship between the territory we live from and the territory we live in, to use Pierre Charbonnier's categories, there has been a very strong shift with globalization: territories have started to live not from their own production, but from imports. We can relocate, of course, but a second question concerns the territory in which power is projected: which authority controls the resources of the bioregion? The self-sufficiency of a bioregion is all very well, but in this case it means that resources no longer circulate between territories, and what is to be done with those that are not able to feed themselves? Today, the issue is no longer that of Western countries. A large part of the world's emerging countries are not able to feed themselves. Egypt is 95% dependent on imported grain, as are South-East Asia and West Africa, in which case, if we say that we are going to build

"Positive Food" neighborhood

Herblay, France

Close to one of the largest retail areas in France, the *Patte d'Oie d'Herblay*, lies a surviving agricultural enclave whose arsenic-polluted soils only produce with the help of intensive agriculture, which heavily relies on synthetic fertilizers. Located on the Beauregard plateau, the site is bordered by the historic road linking Paris to Rouen, and overlooks the Seine valley.

This enclave bears witness to the historic market gardening vocation of the site, where vines, featured on the town's coat of arms, were cultivated on the slopes, while food crops, which are still present today on the outskirts of the site, were reserved for the plateau. Under real-estate pressure, small, heterogeneous buildings have developed over the last few decades. In recent years, the agricultural enclave has been consumed by an urban front of tightly regulated projects facing the fields, which cannot avoid urbanization.

In this perspective, each of the stakeholders involved in the making of the city can project their desires for future facilities, housing or new shops. The landscape diagnosis has made it possible to raise the question of the value of degraded soil—which in the eyes of all, has lost its original meaning. What approach can be implemented to reveal the initial purpose of a site, with regard to development aspirations? How can we take care of both land and people?

To do so, we suggest studying the prototype of a "Positive Food" neighborhood. To this end, we have estimated the current yield of the soil under alternate cropping (year n wheat; year n+1 barley) in Kcal/ha. This data was then compared to the profitability levels of different cropping systems, also expressed in Kcal/ha. Vegetable crops, orchards, tunnel crops, and soilless crops. All of them show significantly higher yields. It is therefore possible to invest in the creation of a market garden following soil remediation, in order to recover the "iso-caloric" productive equivalent of the previous system on a smaller surface area, without using pesticides, and based on a short food supply chain, while creating local jobs and opening the place to the public. Depending on the agricultural scenario chosen, different urbanization scenarios can be envisaged (subject to the terms of application of the zero net artificialization objectives). These studies have made it possible to approach the question of agricultural urbanism, thus making it possible to consider the reactivation of rural activities in a peri-urban environment. They also raise the question of new financial models capable of integrating the investment cost of these productive infrastructures, while regenerating the soil, sparing resources and encouraging new environmental, social and cultural value chains.

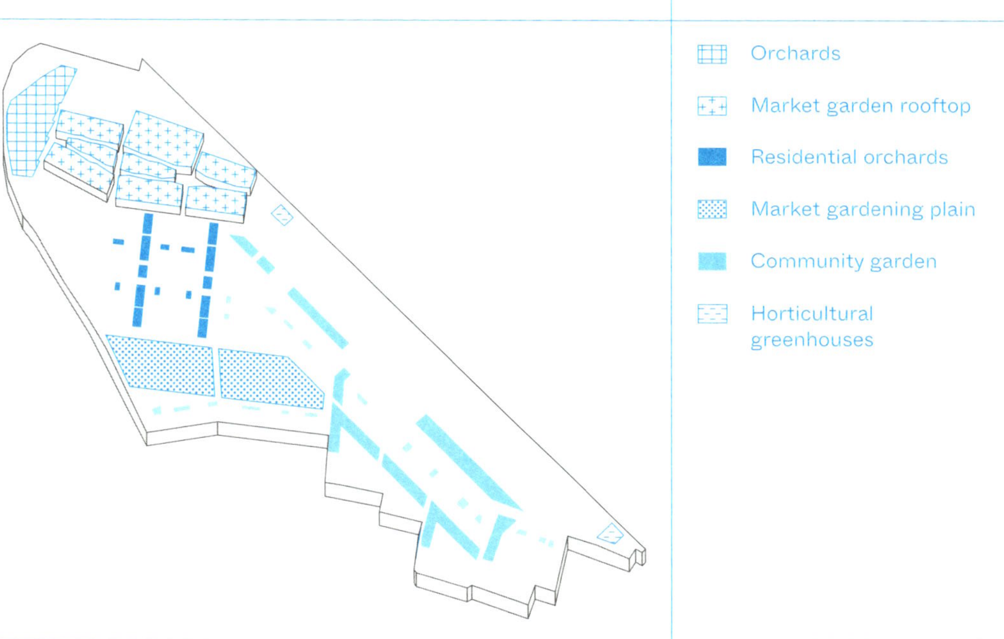

Orchards
Market garden rooftop
Residential orchards
Market gardening plain
Community garden
Horticultural greenhouses

bioregions that will be self-sufficient, this means that we are changing the conditions of power and circulation. We cannot think in terms of bioregions, but from the point of view of the circulation between land and power, between these two meanings of the word "territory."

Alain Bretagnolle
We must consider a point somewhere between globalized flows and local territories. Designing territories that would be their own resources, or be autonomous if you like, is also about giving power back to the inhabitants over their own territories. What you're saying is that this is legitimate from a certain point of view, but we must not lose inter-territorial solidarity in a national or inter-regional equalization scheme, for example.

Grégory Quenet
This is one of the limits of the term "commons." The word "commons" also has two meanings in English: it means both collective rights and collective property. The two are often mixed together, even though they belong to different levels. What we need to see is that commons, as a "collective right," have the primary function of denying access to resources to those who are not part of the group. This is the great ambiguity of the sustainable management of commons. The idea of an oasis sounds good, but we must realize that in such systems, sustainability is based on the fact that outsiders do not have access to land and water. It therefore involves a form of obstruction.
The other important issue that ecology has not been able to address is the question of the scales of a territory. It's not just a matter of questioning whether it is global or local, not that political ecology knows no in between. The political culture of generality, to use Pierre Rosanvallon's term, is what allows us to link the different scales together. Nothing would be more dangerous than to build sustainable places, closed in on themselves, to the detriment of such forms of solidarity. Unfortunately, I fear that this is what is happening. Take permaculture, for example. If you look at its effect, which is great—and I do think it's great—it transforms life, and not just the content of a plate. But if you consider how permaculture is implemented locally: a few enclaves that do not change anything to the intensive agriculture it is totally surrounded by. How do we integrate the different scales? How do we link them together? This is a deeply political question.

François Gemenne
The way in which we conceive the organization of society seems to involve two opposing models. There is the model of bioregionalism, which I am also quite critical of, not only

From this observation, at the scale of our professions, two major hypotheses or avenues of research seem to be emerging. First, the resource-space is no longer to sought after through *extension*, **now impossible, but rather through** *intention*—**that is, by doubling our attention to that which supports our human settlements: the land. Secondly, and along the same lines, resource-time can no longer be conceived in the inertia of linearity but rather in the movement of the cycle, in repetition and beginning anew. Space and time, land and renewal: towards a rational use of resources for the future.**

Nice, France.

for the reasons mentioned by Grégory, but also for others that I will come back to, and this model is opposed to the model resulting from the Anthropocene.

We know the geological definition of the Anthropocene. When we think about it in terms of cause, we can see competing concepts, such as the Capitalocene, the Androcene, the Oliganthropocene, either to emphasize that capitalism is the cause of the disruption of the planet's fundamental equilibrium, or to highlight that patriarchy is to blame... All these criticisms of the concept itself as well as its causes are obviously perfectly legitimate and audible, and that debate is important. But it seems to me that we are missing the essential point of the concept, which is not to designate the cause of these ruptures, but rather to invite us to reflect on how to govern this new Earth. I see the Anthropocene as a mode of government, and as a profoundly cosmopolitical mode of government. The concept of the Anthropocene is often criticized for placing all human beings on an equal level of responsibility. But in reality, there is something very powerful about this notion. If we consider the Anthropocene as a principle of government and not as a cause of the situation we are in, it means that we consider that we have an equal responsibility towards all humans, and I would even extend this to all living things, which inhabit the planet. For me, the Anthropocene is an invitation to consider above all our earthly identity—as inhabitants of Earth—as an identity marker.

Basically, bioregions, even if their demarcation line is no longer political or national, but more natural or landscape-based, contribute to this idea that communities exist, and that these communities are self-sufficient. The bioregion concept is the negation of the Anthropocene as a principle of governance and as a principle of responsibility.

Grégory Quenet

Wouldn't we prefer common responsibility to equal responsibility? That is actually what the Kyoto Protocol involved, and the question we have never managed to answer: that of common but differentiated responsibility. That is to say, common responsibility towards all human beings, but different in terms of impact.

François Gemenne

This is not only the principle of the Kyoto Protocol, but also that of the Montreal Protocol, the success of which we are celebrating today, coincidentally, since the UN has confirmed that the ozone layer will have recovered in about forty years.

Herblay, France.

Productive edges

Réau, France

In this vast peri-urban area of Essonne, on the edge of the Francilienne ring road, stands a somewhat forgotten aeronautical infrastructure whose history marks the pivotal events of the twentieth century. Created in the 1930s, the Villaroche airfield was successively occupied by the French army, the German air force, and then the U.S. air force. After the liberation of France, it became the testing and experimentation center for aeronautical and aerospace research. Today, 7,500 employees work there, although the runways no longer represent its core activity. In this new context, it was decided in 2007 to develop an economic pole around the aeronautical activity thanks to approximately 500 hectares of available land.

Fifteen years later, very few activities have been established, and we have been asked to examine the purpose and future of a site that is seeking new sustainable transformation pathways. What meaning can be given to an aeronautical infrastructure in a context of transport decarbonization? Can this infrastructure reconnect with its immediate rural territory, composed of villages and farms? How can the large scale of giant aircraft hangars and kilometer-long runways be articulated with that of vernacular farms, age-old landscapes and discreet hamlets? What new amenities can be imagined between these two worlds?

To create a symbiotic link between these two contexts, the agency proposes the creation of an intermediate landscape, which filters the views towards future industries and re-establishes a continuity with ancestral productive landscapes composed of channels, walls and shrubby hedges. The diagnosis should reveal historical pollution of the cultivated land with synthetic fertilizers over decades, which requires the implementation of a soil management strategy to respond to the challenge of restoring potentially valuable land.

These landscaped areas are therefore used for the phytoremediation of polluted land, and then for the development of agroforestry crops. This thirty-meter-wide productive edge of the future economic site will be able to produce hemp for the local eco-construction industry, which will soon be needed for the *Grand Paris* construction sites.

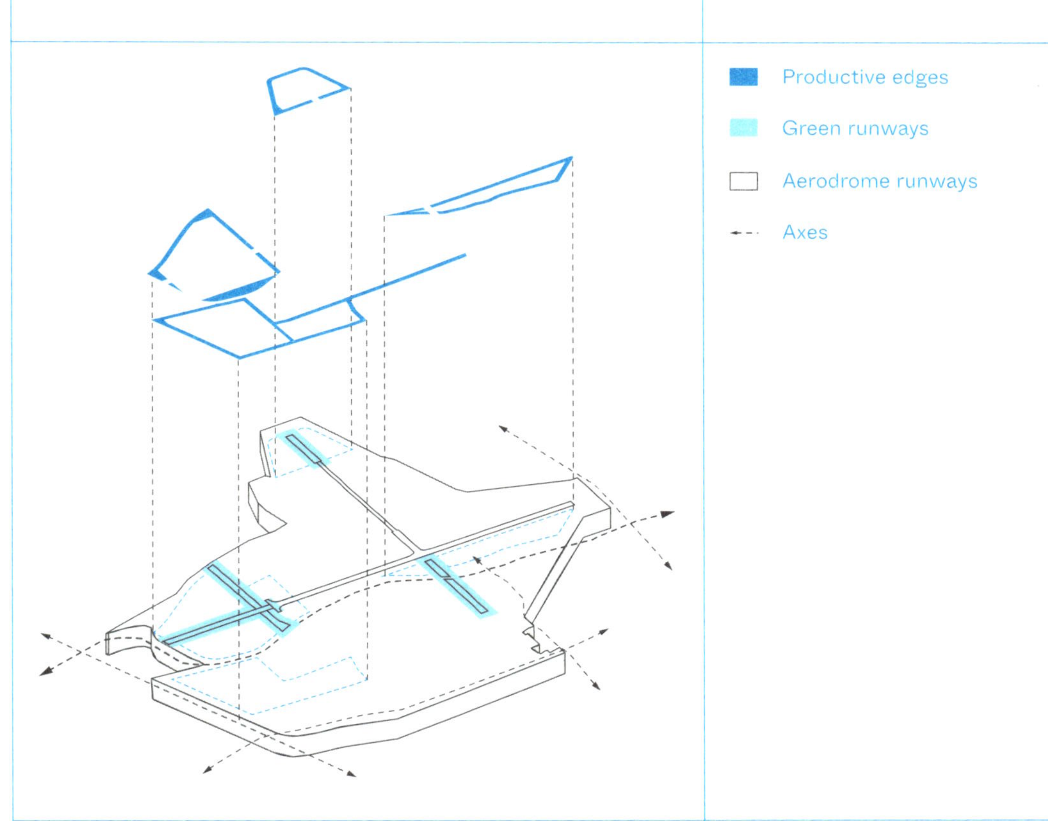

Regenerating the Soil, Regenerating Architecture

What is the territory of architecture? Is it divided in two, between nature and culture, the untouched and the built? Is there not an interface missing between these two territories, between the wild and inhabited? For a long time, in fact, architects have seemingly forgotten to consider places of transformation for themselves. This third sector—productive and primarily agricultural, a territory serving the served territories—remained on the sidelines, as if excluded from our ways of thinking and our fields of action. It is modern folly.

Grégory Quenet
The weak spot of ecology lies in the way it is considered as outside history, because ecology in its American matrix was originally built on the idea of a paradise lost. That is to say, the idea of a world without human beings—which remains the matrix of the United States as it was built—of the American settlers who arrived thinking that this was a virgin land occupied by human beings who did not have an impact on their natural environment, which is obviously false. This theological matrix is very strong and prevents us from considering these commons, and therefore the different responsibilities they involve, as they should be.

Romain Boursier
That's perfect, we're reaching the heart of the debate with the political implications of the Anthropocene. François Gemenne, as co-author of the sixth IPCC report, you were present at the COP 27 climate conference in Sharm El-Sheikh, Egypt. If we consider the evolution of climate change, as you have done in your previous works, how has this geography of impacts evolved? How, as co-author, have you been able to observe these developments, these dynamics, in recent years?

François Gemenne
We are aware of the fundamental injustice of climate change, which is both generational and geographical, since the physics of the climate means that those who are primarily responsible for the problem will suffer the consequences to a lesser extent than those who are not, or are only marginally responsible for the problem. This is true at a generational level: there is approximately a gap of about one generation between our actions and their consequences. It is also true at a geographical level: the most vulnerable countries are generally Global South countries, and within a society the most vulnerable strata are generally the poorest, most disadvantaged members of the population. Those who have to reduce their emissions are therefore not the ones who will directly suffer the consequences of their action or inaction. This is probably one of the reasons why we are so unable to act on climate change.
It is important to understand and realize the extent to which this COP 27 marks a significant inflection point in negotiations. Note that the climate negotiations opened in 1995 with the COP 1 in Berlin, which was chaired at the time by Angela Merkel, Helmut Kohl's young Minister for the Environment, and at the time there was no discussion regarding the consequences of climate change. The subject was nearly taboo. Both because there was that illusion that we would manage to act radically enough to reduce the level of greenhouse gas emissions, and also because there was a fear that any discussion about

City infrastructure

Nanterre, France

The emblematic Nanterre-la-Folie intermodal station for both future line 15 and the Eole RER line, and later for future lines 18 and 17, will be a structuring pole of the *Grand Paris* network. The station will be built on a former rail freight site, set back from a neighborhood undergoing major changes. It is therefore a station where part of the civil engineering structures will not be excavated, but built from the natural ground, then covered by the public spaces of the future *Les Groues* neighborhood.

As part of this work involving the simultaneous design of superstructure and infrastructure spaces, how can the station serve the ambitions of the neighborhood and of a unique travel route? How can it create an underground space that benefits from the qualities of above-ground spaces, and thus become part of a continuity of routes and uses? How can it create a sensory experience, which may allow passengers to feel outdoor weather conditions, or to find their way intuitively?

The station was designed so that passengers may benefit throughout their journey from a natural light supply of 200 lux during the day, equivalent to that of a construction that would have been designed with artificial light, as is usually done. The design work, in iteration with the environmental engineering approach, made it possible to confirm the desired amount of natural light by sizing a window of some sixty linear meters.

This large Scope brings daylight into the infrastructure spaces and thus materializes the large southern façade overhanging the rails. This structure lies under a public promenade, which spans the station, and leads pedestrians along a belvedere of more than one kilometer on the edge of the future neighborhood.

From the platforms, travelers rise to the surface through a large, luminous space, from which the Scope acts as a periscope, by showing the urban surroundings of the station. In the depths of the construction, compensatory lighting connected to a weather station can amplify or nuance climatic phenomena. Further down, "weather ceilings" propagate the variations in light intensity of climatic phenomena recorded on the surface into the platform areas.

From the rail car to the neighborhood, travelers follow an intuitive route, guided by the infinite nuances and variations of light and climate.

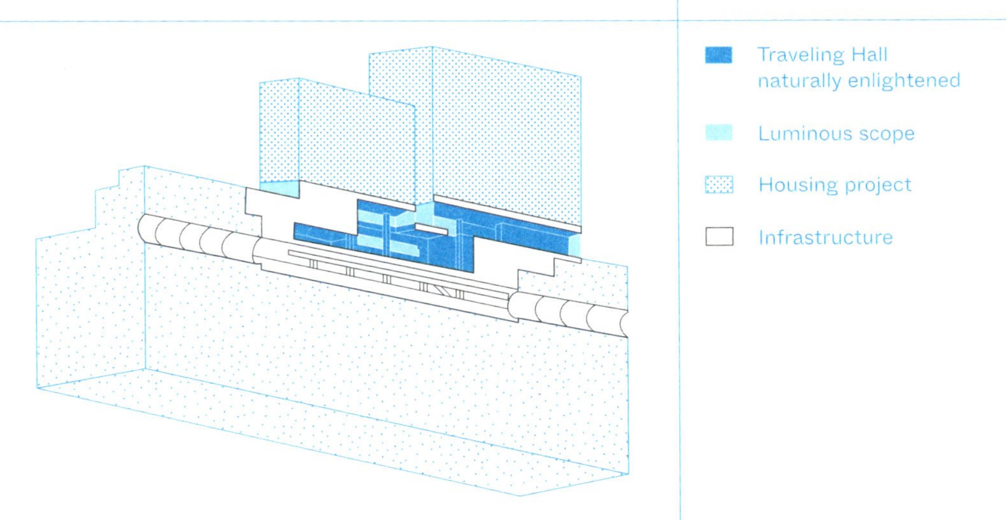

Traveling Hall naturally enlightened

Luminous scope

Housing project

Infrastructure

The soil, however, as a prerequisite for any settlement, is synonymous with fertility, with nourishing earth. It is the first condition for humanity's existence. Architecture has always been more interested in places of consumption than in places of production. These territories of production remain remote and inconspicuous, either rural or industrial, and in service of the urban, visible, and architecturally designed territories of consumption. Today this functionalist schematization reveals white areas, to be explored as new terrain for projects. It wasn't until recently that architecture and the productive city were brought into discussions[6] around alternative types of collaborations and alternative spatial relations between agricultural and urban territories. The issue of better sharing land, as a resource at the base of any possibility of inhabitation, is a precondition of *Tracé Bleu*.

6. See the two Europan editions dedicated to "Productive Cities."

the consequences, i.e. any talk of resilience or adaptation, would provide an easy excuse for governments not to reduce their emissions.
Unfortunately, these impacts materialize primarily in Global South countries. The Kyoto Protocol is a protocol between rich countries. Global South countries are formally a part of it, but they are outside looking in. From the early 2000s onwards, we began to discuss adaptation, and this became a second negotiating track in the international arena. Funds started to be mobilized. The discussion on adaptation and resilience is in itself an admission of defeat in relation to the resolution to reduce our emissions. We can see that in some places direct losses and damages cannot be addressed by adaptation solutions. There is nothing we can do but cover the cost of this direct loss and damage. Global South countries will demand that this be taken into account as well. This is why the agreement reached at the COP 27 is extremely important, because for the first time industrialized countries are formally acknowledging their responsibility for these impacts, they are acknowledging it based on Article 13-182 of the French Civil Code, and are committing to compensating the countries considered as victims. This is a very important step because it opens up a third negotiation pathway. Even if negotiations on loss and damage are once again an implicit renunciation of adaptation and resilience.

Romain Boursier
This is indeed a great step forward. But if we look at it the other way round, are the most developed societies the most prepared for the impacts?

François Gemenne
Certainly not, precisely because they became aware of their own vulnerability much later, and for a long time lived under a sort of illusion of invulnerability, as if the impacts were for Global South countries, and they only had to worry about the causes of climate change.
We have become acutely aware of this with events such as the summer of 2022 in France, or the summer of 2021 when Belgium and Germany were hit by terrible floods. We are vulnerable and unprepared. A surreal situation took place in Belgium when the Belgian army realized that the boats they had at their disposal did not have enough motor power to cope with the flood current, and they had to call on the local jet-ski club!

Alain Bretagnolle
Since we are talking about negotiation, I wanted to examine the notion of living organisms. Grégory Quenet said that the notion of environment refers precisely to the notion of surrounding, i.e.

Inverted skyscraper

Jinan, China

In 1954, with the first five-year plan, Mao set up a heavy industry based on the Soviet Union model. In 1957, Jinan, the capital of Shandong, on the banks of the Yellow River, opened an iron mine that would be exploited until the very beginning of the twenty-first century. It was the transformation of the mine's two main access shafts and its network of galleries that was in question in 2019.

Our proposal centers on using the mine as a dual resource: a source of building stone, and a place to live. In Jinan, the summers are long, very hot and humid, and the winters are very cold. The inertia of the earth provides a response to these extreme conditions, which will be further exacerbated by climate change.

Conical excavation and programmatic layering create a new cave dwelling, two inverted skyscrapers linked by an underground funicular, whose terraced gardens gradually sink into the ground. The upper rings house a mining museum, hotels, shops, housing, offices, market gardening, and horticulture. The lower strata include a sports and wellness center, a spa hotel, leisure facilities, gallery tours, an aquaponic farm, artificial light horticulture and fungiculture, a power station, storage facilities, and a data center.

A panoramic restaurant, bridging the gap across the main well, is the main event. The atmosphere of this microcosm varies between the shade of the earth cavities and the coolness of the underground water, the hanging gardens and the luminous facade that harvests solar energy.

This gravitational inversion opens up a new view onto the sky and proposes an alternative interpretation of the earth's resources. A return to the primitive archetypes of human housing, in a way. The architectural outlines of this ambitious development project revisit the archetypes of local culture to adapt them to the conditions of a new communal dwelling, which future inhabitants will then better define and manage through an active co-design process.

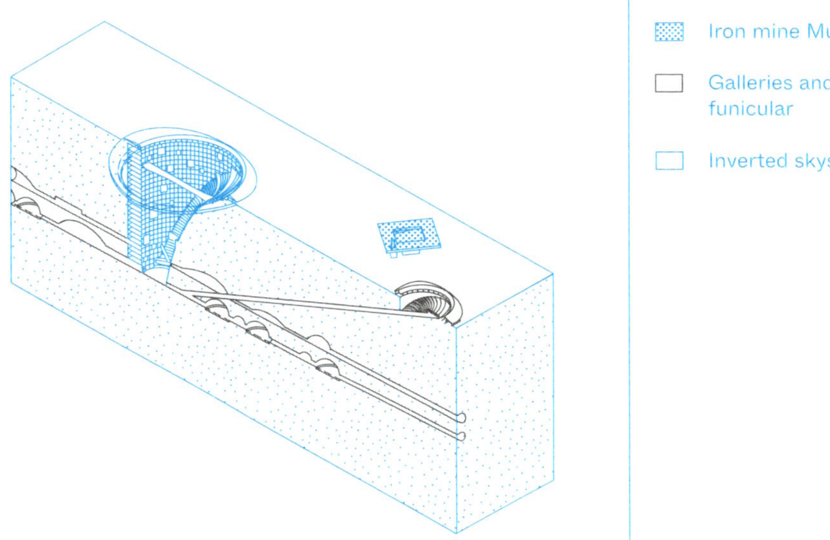

Iron mine Museum

Galleries and funicular

Inverted skyscraper

↑ → Tirana, Albania.

the creation of limits. Limits whose establishment presupposes a form of negotiation. How do we negotiate with living organisms? How do we give a voice to beings who do not have one in our decision-making processes?

Grégory Quenet

Listening to François Gemenne, I was wondering whether accounting could be one way of doing things. Accounting as a way to give a voice. In these international negotiations we keep an account of the causes, but also an account of the consequences, and establish equivalences. One small concern remains, however: we should not be establishing an equivalence between protecting and destroying, but if we look at the last few decades, the two actions have been taking place at exactly the same time, because accounting makes it possible to compensate. In France, for example, the *Conservatoire du littoral*[4] is an extraordinary way of taking care of all living things, a model that is absolutely unique in the world, which was created by the DATAR,[5] i.e. the same people who were covering the coastline in concrete, building ski resorts and promoting motorways. They said, "Since we are 'artificializing,' we must also protect." The same thing is happening to emerging countries today; these negotiations are a very good thing, but if they neglect the essential question of their historical trajectory, we'll remain in a form of temporal schizophrenia, and accounting will be facilitating this. Another example: when we look at the latest World Bank report, the conclusion presents two measures, two recommendations: firstly, we must finance the adaptation of these countries because of their vulnerability in the next fifty years, and secondly, we must develop international seaside tourism. Because it takes five years for a luxury hotel to become profitable, and adaptation takes forty years. So the two go very well together.

Let's set aside this idea of accounting, and think of other ways of taking things into account. I don't believe that, when it comes to caring for the living, we should talk as if we were a mountain, a river, or a horse. Moreover, we are probably the only species in the world that has not only domesticated all these species but also wants to see and think for them. This is a very nice form of anthropocentrism, but it has its limits. What is needed is to observe and describe living things.

We need to develop our capacity for description and investigation. This word may seem very common, very trivial,

4 The Conservatoire du littoral is a French public organization created in 1975 to ensure the protection of outstanding natural areas on the coast, banks of lakes and stretches of water of 10 square kilometers or more.

5 DATAR: "*Délégation interministérielle à l'aménagement du territoire et à l'attractivité régionale*", i.e. Inter-ministerial Delegation of Land Planning and Regional Attractiveness

Architecture and planning are now responsible for developing strategies of balanced coexistence between these three territories—the agricultural, urban, and natural. This requires an understanding of projects in the long term, but the possible actions exist: depollution, sustainable agriculture, circular material economies...

From a city entrance to a new metropolitan element

Nice, France

Parc Méridia, due to its geographical location and history, is a key part of the development of the metropolis of Nice.

The site, shaped by its horticultural past as well as by the successive damming of the Var river, has undergone an urbanization process over the last few decades while lacking in overall coherence. Set between the hillsides and the Var river, the project induces a structuring development dynamic, starting with the new tramway line.

Our thought-process, both urban and landscape-oriented, is based on what is "already there," in this case the agricultural heritage of the Var plain. The landscape figure of the agrarian furrow, the agricultural technique of the valley, is very present on the site, to the extent that it has influenced the shapes of the plots of land and the crops that are still being grown today. We have decided to exploit the concept of an "inhabited furrow." These furrows take the form of environmental, visual and physical continuities which constitute the urban grid of the project, capable of hosting a great diversity of constructions (mixed residential, public services, manufacture) and landscape themes (aromatic, fruit trees...). This conceptual structure, which carries blue-green infrastructure, guarantees the coherence of the project over time while allowing for its flexibility and evolution.

Access to agricultural practices is encouraged in the heart of the block and on the roof terraces of the buildings. The urban design allows the natural ventilation of the spaces and, along with the planting, avoids heat islands. Soft mobility routes take the form of alleys, walkways, and streets. They offer shaded paths and meeting places. The network of squares and plazas encourages a diversity of uses. The large park, the green lung of the project, constitutes a vast area for sports activities and regulates the flooding of the Var river.

Thanks to its proximity to the city's public transport network, *Parc Méridia* anticipates the transition from private car use to alternative modes of transport by means of a network of roads that give priority to cyclists and pedestrians, and the installation of shared, reversible car parks, which absorb the flow of cars and distribute the flow of users across peaceful islands thanks to the alternative mobility services integrated into their bases.

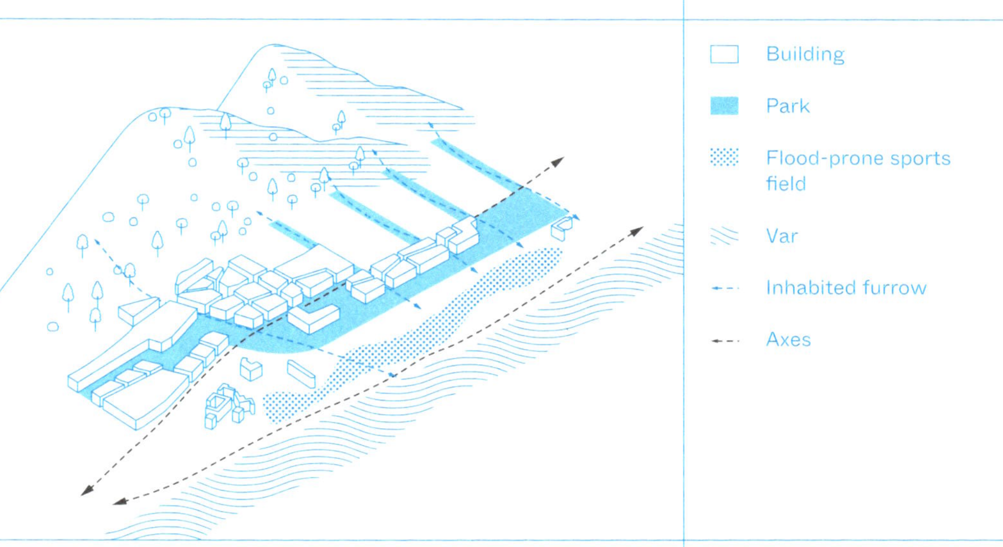

Building
Park
Flood-prone sports field
Var
Inhabited furrow
Axes

but it actually is not. Just look at the training of elites: I taught at Science Po[6] for ten years, and my students, who studied environmental issues, never left the classroom. Never. They were not taught to describe the world, they were taught to think about the world abstractly and based on norms. To speak, to make all living things speak, and not to speak through them, by a sort of ventriloquist's trick, but on the contrary to develop a form of investigation and ability to describe the world. This is our great weakness, and I think that we could also question the training of architects. As a young architect, how are you trained in botany, geology, hydrology, in understanding air flows? For a long time this was the norm. Arcisse de Caumont's course in Caen in the 1830s, which gave rise to his treatise on civil and military architecture, dealt with geology, botany and natural history, which he practiced as an enlightened amateur because he did not conceive a built form independently of all this.

Alain Bretagnolle
The dynamics of living environments are indeed essential. Gunter Pauli said that "any protection measure is programmed for failure, we must give nature the possibility of taking back control of its own evolutionary dynamics." This implies moving from a static representation of cities or architecture to a temporal representation, dynamic in its relations to what it is actually related to.

Grégory Quenet
The Chair that I hold has not been designed based on the notion of ecology. It deals with the ecological challenge, but not with environmental issues. We do not deal with pollution, international negotiations, climate, etc. It has been organized into three years: time, places, commons. And why did we start with the question of time? Because today we are faced with the need to think about a common temporality between people and their environment, and also between disciplines. That is the difficulty. Natural sciences take on environmental change, and the science of culture takes on social change; how do we consider both of them together? Harald Welzer, in "Climate Wars," used a beautiful metaphor: he said that it was like two trains traveling on parallel tracks. The train of social change and the train of environmental change. The problem is that when you look at one from the window of the other, nothing seems to be moving. We are faced with a real challenge which is conceptual, practical, and operational. We need tools and do not quite have them yet.

6 The *Institut d'études politiques de Paris*, also known as Sciences Po, is a public research university that offers courses and conducts research in political science, history, economics, law and sociology.

The geological dimension of the Anthropocene formalizes the generalized artificialization of the Earth's surface. The Earth's soils today are composite, without exception. The opposition between natural and artificial is obsolete; we live in the era of hybridity. The natural is rendered artificial by human activities and, conversely, all artifacts are rendered natural by the effects of time. This results in a new type of relationship. New territory is opening up both in support of and as a resource for new projects: spaces of brownfield sites, of neglected zones, and of urban interstices where related processes of biological regeneration, of ecological restoration, or of agro-ecology unfold. Land is a common good, one that exists prior to any project and that through construction—or non-construction—should be shared.

From a motorway junction to a mixed connected neighborhood

Créteil, France

The French State's land mobilization plan for housing construction (2012-2016) anticipates the construction of 41,000 housing units in the Île-de-France region, and gives the Créteil l'Echat site the opportunity for a major redevelopment near the new Grand Paris Express station.

The perimeter of the site is an unusual urban figure that follows the curves of an A86 motorway junction occupied by the DIRIF[1] head offices. These large, loose, single-use and underused areas allow a silent landscape to develop within them, seemingly set apart from the world.

How can these inherited forms of a city designed for networks be revisited and overturned in favor of opening up the surrounding neighborhoods, and welcoming new users and inhabitants? How can the place of nature and its various functions be increased so that it may consolidate the present ecosystem and the quality of the living environment? How can we also pacify spaces constrained by noise and traffic thanks to a protective form of urbanity that encourages beneficial social interactions? How can we anticipate tomorrow's living and working needs, especially in the vicinity of the Henri-Mondor Hospital and the Grand Paris Express Créteil l'Echat station?

The project suggests transforming the numerous constraints of the site into opportunities through an attentive and vigilant approach to each element included in what is "already there."

Existing vegetated areas will be restored to their former state within the project by a diversity of landscaped spaces: linear garden, wetland water retention area, planted sports ground or green spaces at the heart of blocks.

Public spaces are developed for the benefit of all users, giving priority to pedestrians through a variety of recreational, sports, leisure, and social facilities.

The built-up areas are intended as quiet environments. The reversible design of the street-level floors offers flexibility in the use and programming of the ground floors.

1. DIRIF: Direction des routes d'Île de France

↑ Santiago, Chile.
→ Créteil, France.

Land as a common good is a major ecological issue. This primary resource is fundamental to the protection of inhabited environments. How can land be shared with living beings? How can we enjoy the benefits of nature on a daily basis and, at the same time, protect it?[7]

To make a project from the land, to make it a support for mobility and hospitality, a place of a community's political expression or of economic potential, to make it a reservoir of biodiversity or a filter capable of decontamination: it must be saved. This is the contradiction, that to increase land's viability it should be impacted as little as possible. This means periodic intensification rather than sprawl in order to support the collective project of its use. If we want to develop our human settlements in a sustainable way, spreading outward cannot be the dominant modality.

7. See for example Catherine Larère, *Penser et agir avec la nature: une enquête philosophique*, Ed. la Découverte, 2015.

Romain Boursier
This raises questions about new temporalities. It also raises questions regarding systemic approaches.

François Gemenne
And about schizophrenia too…

Grégory Quenet
The word "environment" is thus interesting in its etymology. The environment, in reality, initially refers to the fences that we build around a house. It's what you surround yourself with. What the word says is that, at the beginning, there is a form of negotiation of limits.

Romain Boursier
Today, we can see that architecture and our cities will have to deal with otherness on all levels. Especially if we consider the climate migrations to come.

François Gemenne
Indeed, we often talk about it as a future risk that could still be avoided, whereas it is already a reality, and has always existed: the geographical distribution of the population on the planet is largely due to environmental factors. Either because certain areas were colonized as they offered a temperate climate or abundant natural resources, or because certain environmental changes or degradations have driven populations into exile over time. What is striking is how many absolutely significant events in human history have been linked to exile, to the displacement of populations for environmental reasons. For example, about 8,000 years ago, the Egyptian people moved from what is now Sudan to present-day Egypt because of the desertification of the Sahara. This is what led the Egyptian people to move up and found a civilization whose importance in human history is well known today. Another more recent example is the earthquake in Lisbon on November 1st, 1755, which initially caused the entire population of Lisbon to be displaced for several months in refugee camps. A whole series of discussions, poems and correspondence, particularly the famous one between Voltaire and Rousseau, have given rise to a new vision of natural disasters and to concepts such as vulnerability. Then more recently in the United States, the great migration of the Dust Bowl, a terrible drought that hit the center of the United States in the 1930s and led tens of thousands of farmers from Texas, Arkansas and Oklahoma to migrate to California. This migration is described in Steinbeck's "The Grapes of Wrath" or in John Ford's film of the same name, and has made California the most populous and wealthiest state in the United States today. We can find many migration, exile and displacement

An eco-neighborhood in a military fort

Issy-les-Moulineaux

The city of Issy-les-Moulineaux decided to build an eco-neighborhood in the former nineteenth century military fort when the army left the site in the early 2000s. The new Fort district has been designed based on the notions of openness and inclusion with regards its surroundings.

Its urban structure is composed of three entities. The Bastions are linked by the curtain wall promenade, which runs around the entire periphery at the top of the fortification walls. The vaulted blockhouses of the curtain walls have been converted into a restaurant and a community center. They contribute to community life and reinforce links with neighboring districts.

The Villas are small elliptical buildings, randomly distributed, like pebbles, on the former central esplanade, which has been converted into a large landscaped park, protected from car traffic.

Finally, the Belvedere building is built around a vast public square that houses services and shops, while opening up the structure of the fort onto the wider landscape: *La Défense* business district and the Seine valley.

This composition has made it possible to create a diversified urban space, which optimizes the opportunities offered by the pentagonal structure of the fort. Access to the district is ensured by two gates, which serve a loop route along the curtain walls and give access to the car parks beneath the buildings. The park and belvedere square are thus preserved from car traffic. Soft mobility routes cross the entire site.

No fossil fuels are used to heat the flats. A heat pump system fed by boreholes in the deep aquifer provides low-temperature underfloor heating. The municipal swimming pool, built nearby, benefits from that system. A set of digital services allows the efficient management of activities and services such as carpooling.

The landscaping, composed of shared gardens and orchards, enhances the different urban sequences. The park houses the children's playground, and the belvedere square is embellished with a reflecting pool parallel to the Seine skyline.

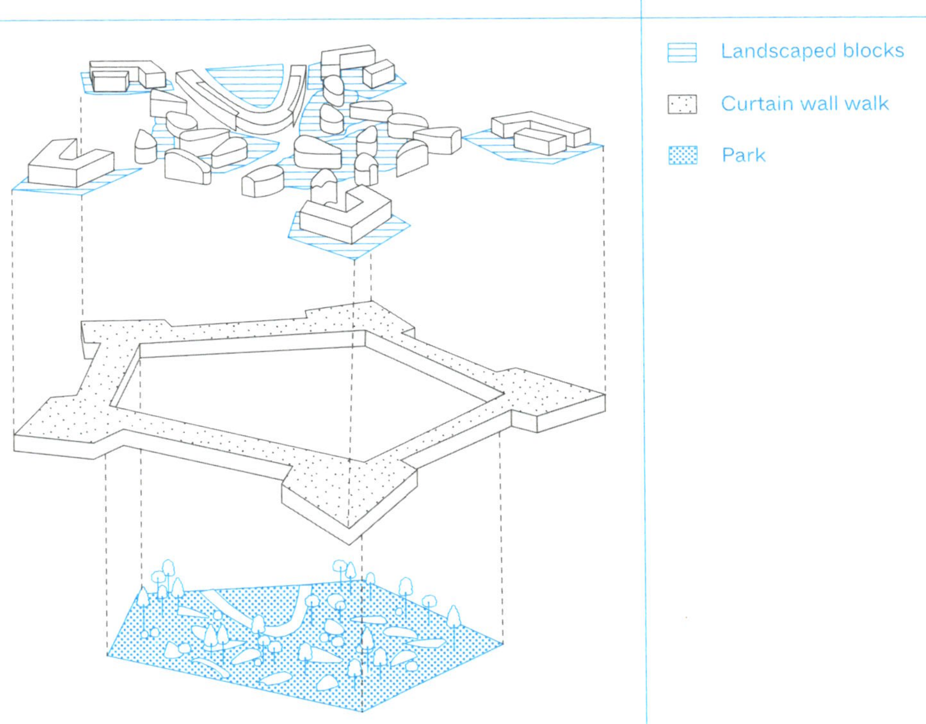

Landscaped blocks

Curtain wall walk

Park

We know that by maintaining the rhythm of technological human expansion, we are threatening the very presence of humans on Earth. The idea of development cannot be sustainable, so long as it is inherently equated with expansion. This paradoxical situation invites for reflection on other modes of development, or an "intensive expansion," as stated by Jean-Luc Nancy.[8] Intensification means limiting the extent of land use so as to manage it in the long term, in an appropriate and differentiated way.

8. Jean-Luc Nancy, preface by Benoît Goetz, *La Dislocation*, Éditions de la Passion, 2001.

events linked to environmental issues throughout history. However, at the end of the Second World War, when the migration and asylum regime was defined, only two main reasons for which people could migrate were considered: political persecution and violence, which would guarantee them international protection, asylum, and which was formalized in the Geneva Convention in 1951, or economic reasons, to improve their income, to find work, and it was up to the country of destination to decide whether or not it wanted to accept them, and under what conditions.

Our entire political and legal architecture has been structured around this dichotomy, between political or economic migration, and the role of the environment in migration has been totally neglected. Climate change is making us rediscover the importance of this factor, which in fact has never ceased to be important, and is now forcing us to reconsider our way of thinking.

Finally, there is also a tendency to see things as separate categories, as if environmental motives were separate from economic and political, or cultural and demographic motives, when in fact they are profoundly linked. When you consider, for example, that in sub-Saharan Africa, half the population depends on subsistence agriculture as their primary source of income—this figure even rises to 70% in the Sahel—and that subsistence agriculture is extraordinarily vulnerable to climatic variations. This means, to put it bluntly, that as soon as it gets hotter or rains a little less, half of the people, 70% in the Sahel, lose their main source of income. In much of the world, economic resources are intrinsically dependent on the state of the environment.

Grégory Quenet

What I find very comforting in our debate is that we can see the importance of ideas, of categories. We can see that in what François Gemenne describes: the very strong effects of categories, how to identify them, how to overcome them. They have impacts, and I find that very comforting, such power of ideas.

François Gemenne

That is the power of complexity. But how are we going to quantify the loss and damage? I'm part of a working group whose mission is notably to put a figure on the cost of migration. What does that include? How much does migration cost? A cost for whom? For migrants? For the society they are leaving? For their destination society? How do you calculate the intangible costs, the trauma linked to uprooting? These are all very important questions for calculating how much we owe the countries affected.

Issy-les-Moulineaux, France.

To think about a resource is thus to consider its reserves, and a certain notion of density—one which is now more programmatic than built, more spatial than temporal. Soil in this case is considered as a support for layered urbanization, serving the counter-intuitive idea that development, if it is to be sustainable, doesn't expand but rather intensifies. From this point of view new territories, long invisible, are appearing today. Brownfield sites, major infrastructure, large and now obsolete equipment, and monofunctional zones—whether they will be residential, economic, or commercial in the future—all hold potential that can be concretized by another shared division of the soil. In making these viable and by adapting them to new uses to contain urban sprawl, to preserve space for agriculture, and to reserve other space for nature, ecosystems can coexist at geographic and territorial scales.

Romain Boursier

We have reached the third part of this discussion, which is perhaps more foresight-based, and concerns the society of the future. Luc Gwiazdzinski, how do you think time feeds the imagination?

Luc Gwiazdzinski

I believe that room must be left for the imagination. If you remember your best childhood or even pre-adolescence memories, they often occurred in unfinished places. In buildings under construction, in wastelands that were falling apart, in the woods, where you could let your imagination run wild, but also go and do your thing, bring things back home, build stuff. How do you leave room for possibility, for the imagination? Earlier, I was talking about adaptation rather than transition. Since you are envisaging this idea of improving the habitability of the world, or worlds, well, it seems to me that in order to inhabit it, we need to be able to construct imaginary worlds, and therefore leave options open. When I hear talk of transition, I always sense that it's going to be a slow process, and that I'm going to be taken by the hand and led towards something. Basically, that I'll hear: "Listen, Luc! We're going to take the situation in hand, ask for your opinion, and cross over. And things will be better on the other side." But that is not what's going on. The reality is the notion of uncertainty, and how to constantly be managing a systemic crisis. There is a quote by Woody Allen which says: "We are all interested in the future because that is where you and I are going to spend the rest of our lives." I think this is great food for thought. I too want to spend my life in it, and I think that to do so, all the more so as we no longer have narratives, as we are no longer experiencing progress, modernity, as the past is becoming heavy, particularly in France with a heritage that weighs heavily on us... I truly believe that we have this capacity, a bit like the kings of Portugal or Spain a few centuries ago, to send vessels towards an elsewhere, towards a future, thus investing in tomorrow. I remember the work that was carried out at the Venice Biennale with *Encore Heureux*, around the *Lieux Infinis* (Infinite places) project. I liked it a lot, and share this approach, but it requires us to have a vision of the world that is not continuous. It is spatial, it is temporal. When we continue to look at things from above, as an institution, we do not look at what is happening. A lot of ships are being launched, but not by the State, nor by Europe, as they do not need approval; many young and not so young people are trying things, experimenting.

From a linear plot to an inhabited promenade

Buenos Aires, Argentina

Built around a planted promenade linking two dynamic city arteries, the project proposes an innovative model of co-living, thus allowing for the porosity of urban areas and opening up new social interactions. The project is located in the Barrio Norte neighborhood, one of the most densely populated areas in the city of Buenos Aires. It occupies two interconnected plots of land between Billinghurst and Bustamante streets, opposite the district's hospital, which it connects by creating a pedestrian environment that benefits both the city's residents and those of the high-rise flats. Located in an interstitial space, on a deep plot of land hitherto unknown to the urban network, this passage gives rise to a certain porosity of movement and use, through a succession of spaces organized along a new urban promenade.

On either side of this green lane, the project includes the construction of housing units grouped into several blocks of flats, of services and collective spaces including a planted deck crossing the block. The deck contributes to the high environmental quality of the site, which is designed as an island of freshness. It is able to absorb the region's sometimes torrential rain by planting adapted and luxuriant vegetation. The diversity of uses that it offers inhabitants makes it a central and porous place, which provides a new way of living. With a variety of facilities, it aims to develop a high quality living space with a wide range of amenities. The dwellings, with balconies and terraces opening onto the gardens below, are spread out as numerous typologies capable of accommodating a multitude of users, and thus contributing to the development of a family-oriented and multi-generational neighborhood.

The whole project is part of the gradual transformation of the city, which is seeing the construction of numerous architectural projects designed to offer the best possible living environment. The project is contextual, and acts as a prototype of diverse co-living forms and as a new architectural icon in a rapidly changing city. It responds to the growing need for housing through innovative and sustainable architecture.

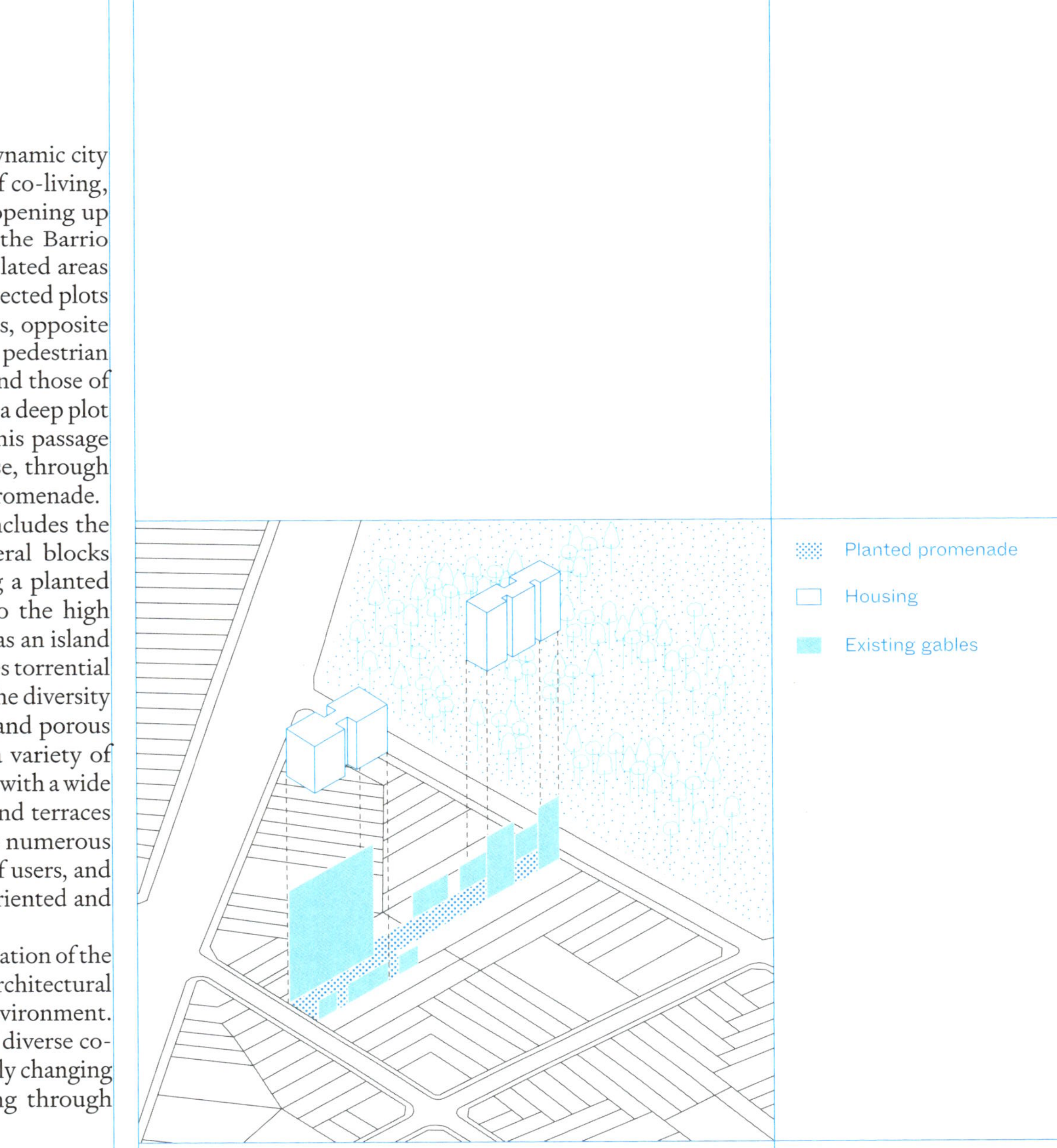

Planted promenade

Housing

Existing gables

↑ → Paris, France.

MIROIR
FRAGILE
CHEMINEE

Re.source: moving from static resource management to a dynamic approach. Considering the intertwining and complementarity of scales, the superposition of programs, and the cyclical functions guaranteeing the autonomy of any balanced ecosystem. Re-source: considering the chronotopia of inhabited environments.[9] Re.source: make even time itself a resource.

9. The chronotope, from the Greek χρόνος and τόπος is a concept invented by the philologist Mikhail Bakhtin to signify the solidarity of time and spatialities of a place.

Romain Boursier

According to you, we need to rediscover the diversity of time-scales in the city.

Luc Gwiazdzinski

Yes, maybe I need to clarify my approach. I am not in favor of acceleration, nor am I in favor of slowing down. Because people often tell me: "You're part of the slow movement." To which I answer: "No, it's the question of pace that is being raised." There are times in my life when I feel under pressure, with the questions you're asking me for example, and I like that tension. And later on, I may feel more relaxed. And I don't want to be the resident snail all the time either, that's not really who I am. And that's true of cities, where there must be places of acceleration where you can connect, as well as areas where you can breathe. That's what the notion of pace means, like in buildings, like in neighborhoods. A city for me is a place where I will find myself under pressure, it includes places I know with people I know, and places where nobody knows me, where I am entirely free. From a spatial and temporal point of view, it's about how you juggle with that. Today, there is the bad city that keeps accelerating, that is saturated, that is killing us, pretty much the vision of futurists in the 1930s, on the one hand, and on the other hand, a slow pace. This point of view is binary, which is a shame, and calls for imagination again.

Romain Boursier

Doesn't imagination also require long periods of time? Doesn't it imply more profound transformations, which go beyond our scale?

Luc Gwiazdzinski

Yes, I haven't forgotten this long-term perspective. I consider myself to be very Braudelian: I read Braudel a long time ago, he made quite an impression on me, and I chose to study geography because I believed in geography and urban planning, as interesting keys to citizenship. This question of the long term, of the territory to be developed, that was what land-use planning was about, the search for a better distribution of people, activities and wealth, for the well-being and the fulfillment of the population, and that was Eugène Claudius-Petit's work. I was fortunate enough to take part in regional foresight studies in Alsace, Franche-Comté, the Territoire de Belfort, in different places, and I have always found that we are constantly reminded of a sense of urgency. Talleyrand said: "When it's urgent, it's already too late." To which I reply: "Let's have faith, and try new things." But this does not prevent us from working on exercises of foresight. That is to say, maybe not over the next thirty years, but perhaps try and ask ourselves what we will be in

Intensifying a school complex

Saint-Étienne, France

Rather than a renovation, the *Cité Scolaire Honoré d'Urfée* project is a transformation based on the notion of grafting. Extensions are developed directly onto the structures of 1950s and 1960s buildings.

Organized according to a linear structure that extends across the site from east to west in order to favor north-south solar orientations, the grafting of the new constructions actually involves building right up against the old buildings. They allow the creation of new hybrid constructions, whose aesthetic choices are the markers of the process:

- → To the south, the original buildings retain the simplicity of the facades of the post-war educational buildings; their walls are white.
- → To the north, the new buildings present complex facades, designed according to a three-dimensional folding process that echoes the design of the landscaped park. The openings randomly unfold behind a facade of dark brown wooden slats.
- → At the junction of the two complexes, a building forms a metallic line that crosses the entire site.

The two entities of the Cité Scolaire—with the middle school to the west and the high school to the east—share the same architecture but are kept separate. While both entities have their own entrances, play areas and classrooms, the canteen, gymnasiums and multi-purpose hall are shared and dispersed in different parts of the large park which, following a regular north-south slope, constitutes the green setting of the complex.

In the same way as for the buildings, the large park is a combination of existing spaces, planted with magnificent mature trees, and recent landscaping that allows the creation of new places and differentiated atmospheres through the promenades that criss-cross the park's flowerbeds.

At the bottom of the site, a large retention basin leads surface runoff into the urban water network.

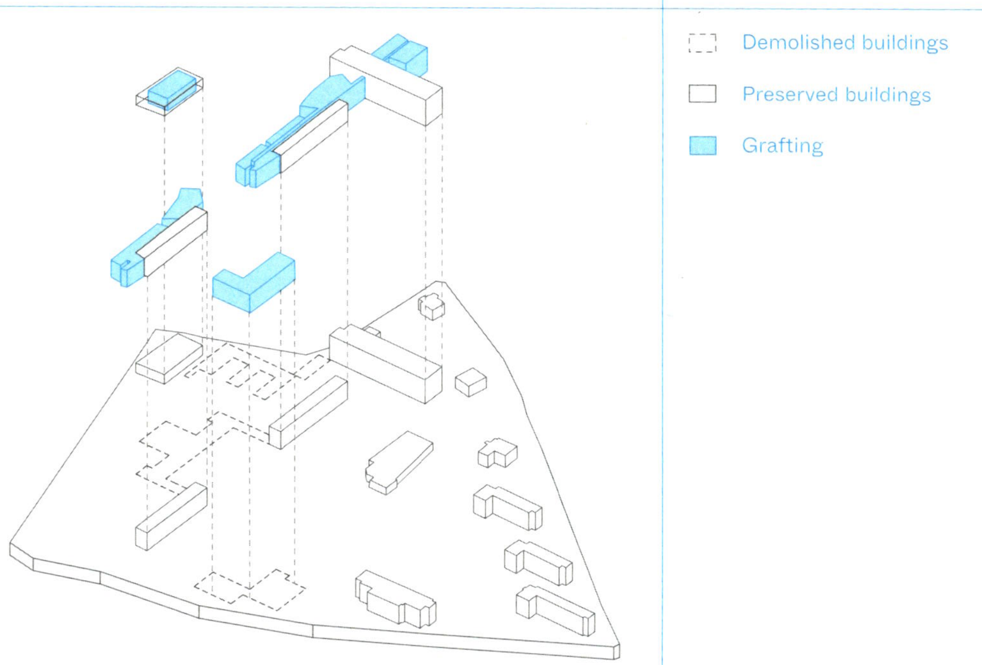

Demolished buildings
Preserved buildings
Grafting

Temporality is, in effect, a compensatory resource that must be activated. To consume less land and less energy in either construction or in management means the reuse and recycling of materials, the adaptive reuse of built heritage, the reversibility of new buildings, the pooling of uses... this intensification of modes of building and living makes time the resource common to all resources, either material or spatial. This is now a path forward to consider for the sustainable transformation of environments. It is this consideration of cyclical resource-time that allows us, today, to move from design projects to projects of transformation.

ten years? And get geographers, town planners and architects to contribute, but also designers and film-makers. I find that cinema does not offer us many positive inspiring imaginings, although it should! Because artists are the ones who express time and movement well, and who represent it well. I think that in the learning mechanisms of collective intelligence, the artistic dimension is really important. And it offers a strong basis for creating objects, figures, programs, mediations, and ultimately imaginary worlds that will change things.

Romain Boursier
François Gemenne, since your last book *"L'écologie n'est pas un consensus"* (Ecology is not a consensus), you have appeared in the media advocating a new social pact. What kind of future does this new pact describe for us?

François Gemenne
In my opinion, it's a question of desire. One of the reasons why there is a certain form of ecological distress today is largely due to the fact that we still see the fight against climate change or, more generally, environmental issues as a kind of constraint to which we must submit as a sum of efforts, or even sacrifices, to be made. We have a fairly clear vision of the world we would not like to see, a world devastated by the impacts of climate change, where biodiversity has largely disappeared. This world is described in most scientific reports and projections. But we still don't really have precise visions of the world we would like to move towards. We're feeling our way along, between techno-futuristic imaginings such as Elon Musk's, or images of an almost prehistoric candlelit world. What would a 'modern' decarbonized world look like? We do not know. And I think that this is where architects, urban planners and designers have a very important role to play, to show what the world we would like to move towards could look like in concrete terms, and which could mean that we no longer see environmental issues through the prism of constraint, but through the prism of the project.

Romain Boursier
Shouldn't we also call on artists and their ability to suggest possible scripts?

Alain Bretagnolle
Grégory Quenet, you were the scientific advisor for the exhibition of Laurent Grasso's work at the *Cellège des Bernardins*, "Anima," which is still showing. In a way, "Anima" seeks to make the invisible part of the world visible. Is it because you think we need new fictions to help us change our civilization model?

Densifying and inhabiting the "concrete slab"

Paris, France

The rehabilitation of the eastern part of the Jussieu campus marks the completion of the major renovation project of this university complex designed by Edouard Albert in 1960. The original architecture of this modern building possesses qualities and a sense of poetry that needed to be preserved and enhanced. However, it was necessary to question and adapt the characteristics of this generic architecture, built on a concrete slab, detached from its context. The work on the existing building also made it possible to reexamine the potential of the built surfaces, in order to generate new uses of spaces that had previously been little or badly used.

The transformation was carried out with respect to the original architecture. The superstructure required numerous adaptations to integrate the chemistry, biology, and physics research laboratories into a framework that meets current safety and comfort requirements. On the other hand, a major transformation of the base has radically changed the relationship of the campus to its environment. The architecture of the slab was largely redesigned in order to introduce a direct relationship with the natural ground, and streets were cut into this thick base, bringing light and natural ventilation to the functions located at ground level. The uses of the base have been transformed in depth. The generic aspect of this building, designed based on a grid that could be extended ad infinitum, was also questioned. In the patios, singular objects of architecture have been built to house transversal functions: libraries, cultural center, amphitheater. They make it easier to find one's way around the university and are the basis for campus life, by allowing the different disciplines to meet.

Beyond the response to strictly programmatic issues, the campus redevelopment has made it possible to implement the concept of space saving. The forecourt of the Zamansky Tower has been transformed into a garden conducive to rest and social interactions, which provides the vegetation that was sorely lacking in a very mineral environment. The effects of the wind have been greatly reduced by these landscaping arrangements. Some patios have been covered by a light and transparent roof, thus allowing air to pass through but providing shelter from the rain for spaces that were previously inaccessible to users. That is the case for the patio overlooking the large research amphitheater, which has itself become an informal amphitheater, a place for shows, parades, conferences, and a relaxing zone for students, well beyond the functions initially assigned to it.

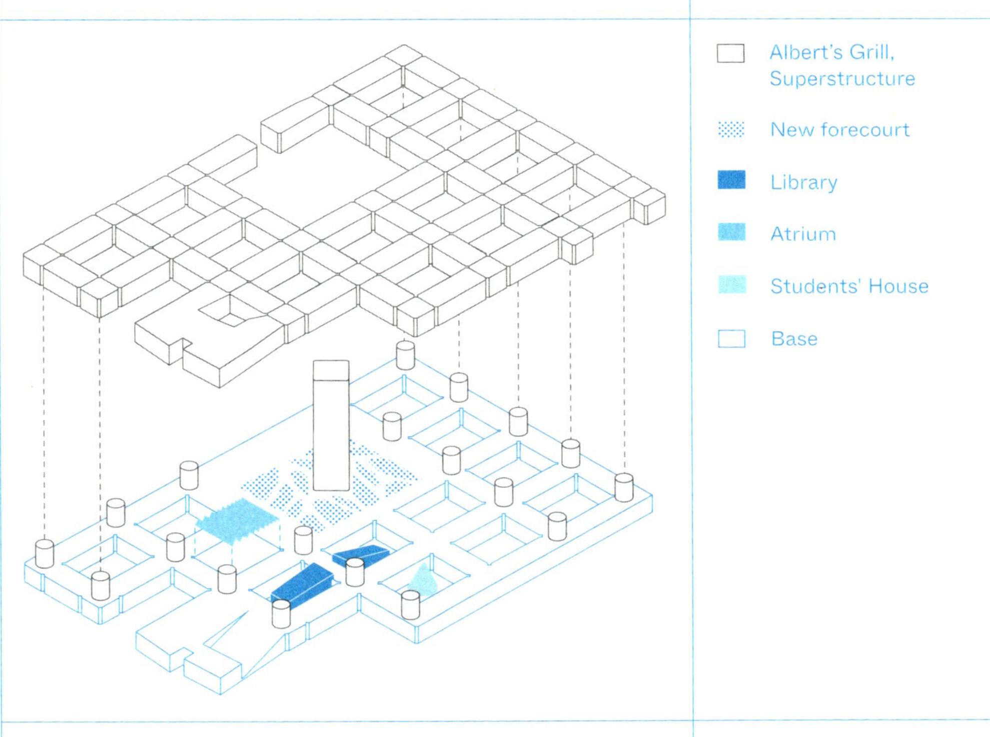

Albert's Grill, Superstructure
New forecourt
Library
Atrium
Students' House
Base

Jussieu University
Campus - East Area,
EPAURIF,
Architecturestudio,
Michel Desvigne,
Atelier TESS.

Paris, France, 2015.

Transformation works over the long time frame of sustainable development. As part of a transformation, the design project aims only to accompany the evolution of a situation, based on its potential. For the philosopher François Jullien, if a project implies a certain violence to the existing, its transformation is only an accompaniment to what is unfolding. This gentle evolution of the project can only take place by playing close attention to reality, and its silent transformations.[10]

10. François Jullien, *Les transformations silencieuses*, Grasset, 2009.

Grégory Quenet

There is always a risk in the relationship between researchers and artists, that of using art to convey a message and vice versa, artists importing scientific work that has already been stabilized. What we did with Laurent Grasso was to put him in direct contact with the speakers at the Chair's seminar: Bruno Latour, Philippe Descola, with theologians, anthropologists and geologists.

In the end, a society is made up of the material and symbolic forms it inherits and which must be inhabited differently by setting them in motion. That is why such meetings are important. At a time when, in the field of research, we come up against something that we cannot yet conceptualize, an artist may invent a form that does not need to resolve the tensions and that thus makes visible elements that, conceptually, are still invisible. With his work, Grasso has created a kind of time machine that stages this time that we are not yet able to name, that has neither beginning nor end, where the past is our future, and the future is behind us. It is an immersive film, in which there is no longer any difference between interiority and exteriority. Thanks to the use of Lidar, the type of camera that allows you to go inside rocks, there is no longer a top or a bottom, and through this experience, viewers experience the sacristy of the *Collège des Bernardins* in a different way. It is a place that was conceived at a time when climate change and environmental issues did not exist of course, in the thirteenth century. What fascinated Laurent Grasso was the beauty of the Gothic nave, the pillars, through which the force of the Earth can be felt. The clamor of the Earth... By positioning himself in this nave, he set it in motion and revealed something that our eyes did not want to see, which is the force of the Earth.

Through the work of art, we can change this, draw an analogy and give meaning to our world. We are inside a work of art which has not been designed to deliver a message, which has not been designed to tell us what we should do, and a society actually has every right to destroy itself—we do it very well individually too, for example. In this sense, a society makes its own choices.

Being forward-looking basically means thinking about this simple question: "What is a better life?," which sounds like a rather ridiculous, silly question... I'll take a very simple example of this, a better life, which was clearly demonstrated by Marshall Sahlins in the 1970s. He revealed something quite astonishing about the affluent societies of the Stone Age, which for a long time were considered to be poor. He explained that in these groups, people worked very little, four or five hours a day, no more, because they spent most of their time doing what was most important, i.e. performing rituals, negotiating with the gods, as well as building family ties, so they sat down

Reinvesting roofs and courtyards

Paris, France

The brief for the 38 Kléber project was to bring a 1930s building that had already been renovated fifteen years earlier up to standard in architectural, environmental and usage terms. The challenge was to use the current revision of the city of Paris' zoning code and its new guidelines to maximize the project's potential. The planning permission was issued the day before the start of the building work.

The 1930s architectural style and its rigorous geometry are highlighted by light boxes in the bay windows, the lighter faience of the inner courtyards to improve the luminosity of the spaces, and the ground floor completely open onto the avenue. The upper floors terraces are planted and the courtyards demineralized, the curved glass attic provides views of the Eiffel Tower while integrating photovoltaic production, and the top terraces are freed of their technical function to create amenity spaces overlooking the Parisian rooftops.

In place of the former entrance courtyard, a horticultural production greenhouse with orange trees forms a vast entrance hall (the first harvest during the renovation works led to the production of delicious jam). Japanese-style gardens completely reconfigure the second courtyard, which has been excavated to provide new meeting spaces with natural light. The office floors have been redesigned based on controlled aesthetics and noble materials in the common areas: wood, brass and glass paste. The technical systems have been reviewed for better energy performance.

The renovation project was a success, as it created over 600m² of floor space at a prestigious address, bringing the building up to environmental standards, restoring an architectural style consistent with the original building, and creating high-quality working conditions for the new HSBC France headquarters.

In the end, this is the story of an encounter between urban regulations that give designers more freedom to adopt an innovative approach to current climatic challenges, and a project management and construction team that was able to make its ambitions a reality.

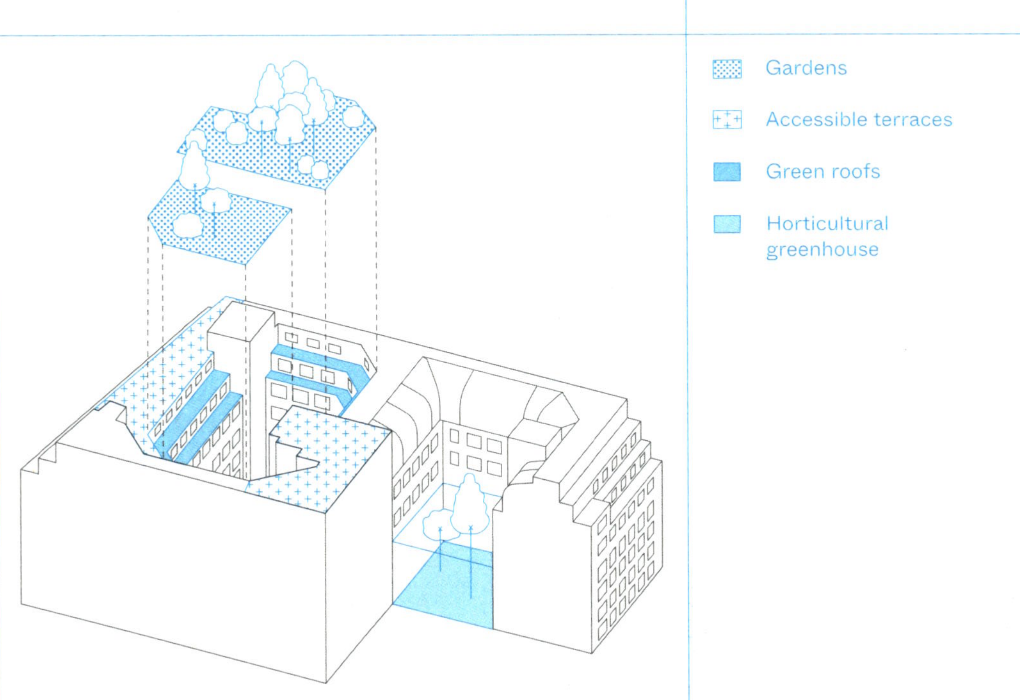

Rehabilitation of the Office Building at 38 Avenue Kléber, COVEA immobilier, Architecturestudio.

Paris, France, 2019.

Architecture participates in this evolution of environments, in a dynamic understanding of ecosystems. The complex movements that animate environments are only perceptible in the long term, although science today reports these perfectly—as in the IPCC reports, for example. The urgency is to make architecture a privileged tool for creating harmony between the cultural and the natural.

and talked. Which means that a better life is a form of life that is collective. Think about this incredible statistic that came out during the World Cup. When we get together, energy consumption significantly decreases. The World Cup final represented a drop in energy consumption equivalent to five nuclear reactors. That is absolutely incredible. So for a better life, let's finance the places where people live collective lives!

Romain Boursier

We also need to talk about the public and private freedoms that are at stake in these lifestyle changes. François Gemenne, you say, for example, that the personal carbon allowance appears to restrict freedom. Yet the German Constitutional Court is now asking for details on the carbon trajectory beyond 2030, in the name of the preservation of future public freedoms. Which implies that the absence of ambitious targets would deprive future generations of the freedom that we enjoy today.

François Gemenne

When we discuss the measures to be taken to reduce our greenhouse gas emissions today, we very often see them in terms of freedom deprivation, in terms of giving up individual freedoms. What the German Constitutional Court ruling says, which I think is an important ruling in terms of law, that I hope will be remembered as one of the greatest constitutional rulings in the future, is an invitation to reconsider the way that we conceive freedom. Today, we have a very individualistic conception of freedom. It is almost an atomized conception of freedom. I believe that if we want to establish the terms of a new social contract, we absolutely must redefine a more collective conception of freedom.

And this must involve a greater awareness of the carbon footprint of each of our actions. In other words, highlighting what each of our actions or behavior implies for others. Actually making visible or audible the impact of these actions for the community, so that each of us may also question our own behavior and what it represents for the community.

Grégory Quenet

I agree that this notion of freedom is collective, and is inseparable from the idea of history as a community of common destiny. This is actually very paradoxical, at a time when we could be reaffirming the idea of a community of destiny as a common historical experience—which is a common historical experience of the transformations of the Earth—we are instead witnessing a significant fragmentation of society. In my opinion, this is because two things have been profoundly damaged in the very thing that made politics possible. Firstly, language: it is important to note how words have been perverted. And then

Amplifying modern heritage

Paris, France

The restructuring of the Maison de la Radio et de la Musique[1] is the perfect example of a building within which we found the resources for its own regeneration. First of all, we were driven by a strong political and social will: there was no question of rebuilding the Maison de la Radio elsewhere.

The building, emblematic of the heritage of the 1960s in Paris, designed by Henry Bernard and inaugurated by General de Gaulle in 1963, despite its original roughness, held the promise of an unprecedented renewal. We used this heritage, rich in possibilities, in order to transform it.

We began by transforming the original asphalt car parks into a generous vegetation-filled urban forest, the first identifiable sign of change. Over 425 trees were planted. We took the radio studios out of their fortress and opened them onto the city. We reorganized and transformed the routes so that they may be adapted to the new needs of the public, journalists, musicians, etc. A nave, a veritable indoor street beneath a glass roof, was created, and takes users to the central agora, bathed in sunlight. The tower, originally dedicated to the archives, now houses new double-height offices connected to the peripheral premises by several walkways.

Studio 104 has been adapted, while retaining its identity, to accommodate electroacoustic concerts. Finally, we deconstructed the former studios 102 and 103, which had become obsolete, to create the Grand Auditorium, the highlight of the renovation process, a symphony hall with 1,462 seats designed for the four musical orchestras of the Maison de la Radio et de la Musique.

We were keen to carry out this transformation while preserving the image of the *maison ronde* (round house) so dear to Parisians, and by bringing about a functional and aesthetic renewal from within. We restored the original emblematic spaces: foyers, halls, galleries, making sure they—as well as their associated works of art—were restored to their original splendor. The new spaces, resolutely contemporary, meet this heritage and give new life to the whole project.

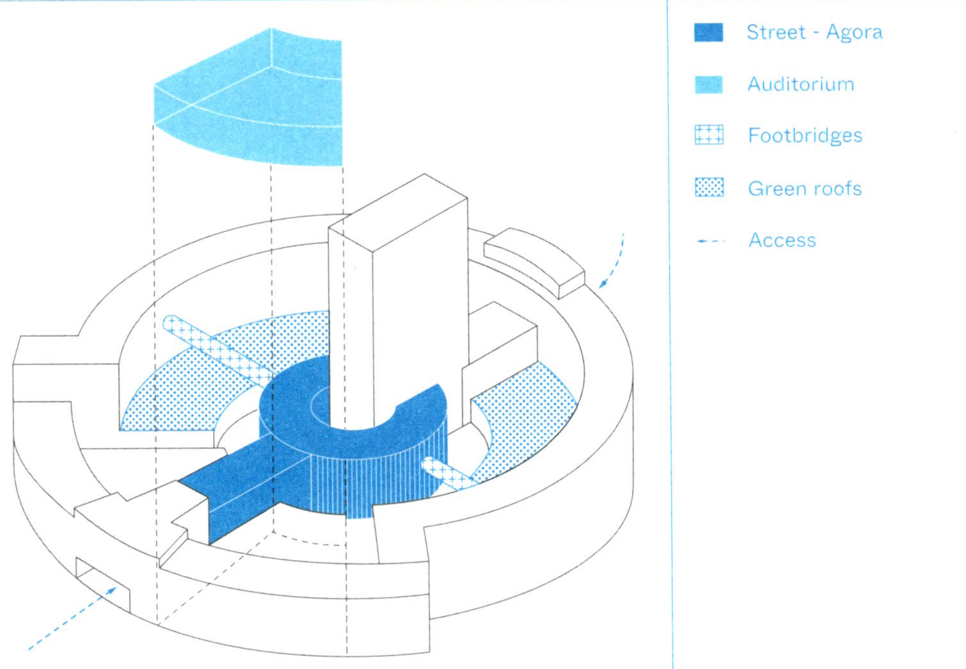

1. Headquarters of Radio France, the French national public radio broadcaster.

Restructuring of the
Maison de la Radio et de
la Musique, Radio France,
Architecturestudio.

Paris, France, 2023.

The Gaia hypothesis, put forward by Bruno Latour (but formulated before him by James Lovelock in the 1960s),[11] defines the Earth as a vast autoregulating system, populated by organisms capable of solidarity and even of defending themselves as a whole. If the Promethean quest for technology created the illusion of superiority, even of humans as all-powerful over nature, this hypothesis now invites them to fall into line and to work collaboratively as part of a system. The architecture of environments engages a gradual transformation with the forces of life. It operates through resilience and alteration, through regeneration and through degradation to adjust and to reconnect to Earth's system. It encourages the development of new natural-cultural relationships to stimulate the synchronization of human and social cycles with all terrestrial life cycles.

11. Based on the work of biologist Lynn Margulis: *La Terre est un être vivant, l'hypothèse Gaïa* (1979); *Les Âges de Gaïa* (1990); *Gaïa. Une médecine pour la planète* (2001), *La Revanche de Gaïa* (2006).

the body, the political body, both a body that speaks, as Latour said, and a body that has a collective dimension. These two aspects need to be totally reinvented.

Living together as a society is not simply a matter of social relations, as Durkheim thought, it involves considering a set of existing elements, which are held together and assembled. It means reinventing these assemblages. The question of forms of organization, once again, is extremely important because I think that we are at a turning point with, on the one hand, the temptation of a sort of clean slate, that of a society incapable of reinventing itself and which fantasizes its own destruction. We call this "collapsology." Let's remember another time in history when this happened. In the two decades preceding the French Revolution, the great pictorial theme in fashion was volcanoes. People painted volcanoes, climbed Mount Vesuvius, had picnics with poultry cooked in lava, and created artificial volcanoes in their own garden when they had a lot of money, like the Prince of Goerlitz in Anhalt-Dessau. This was a society which, as it thought itself incapable of reforming or transforming itself, dreamt of its own destruction in order to rebuild itself. And then there is another voice that consists of investigating, making an inventory of the forms we have inherited, inhabiting them differently and setting them in motion.

Alain Bretagnolle

Thank you very much to our three guests. Let's keep the only question that matters, "What is a better life?" and keep working at it!

Augmenting architecture

Douala, Cameroon

The architectural heritage of the 1970s and 1980s occupies an important place in the heart of African cities, and its renovation is an important issue. The current restructuring of the Charles de Gaulle building in Douala, in the administrative district, is a convincing example of augmented architecture, both in its uses and in its habitability.

Built in the 1980s, this former sixteen-story housing complex belonging to the *Caisse nationale de prévoyance sociale*[1] had been uninhabited for several years. The project exploits all the potential of this concrete-built modernist architecture, for the benefit of a new hotel complex, which offers several types and lengths of stays while being more open onto the city and better adapted to the local climate.

Sheltered from the tropical rains and providing passive solar protection, large balconies constitute outdoor living areas in the continuity of the rooms and flats, and redesign a new façade with fluid lines of a kinetic character. In another formal register, dominated by the vertical lines of its solar protection screens, a four-story elevation which houses suites, a lounge, and a restaurant crowns the whole project and acts as a landmark in the city.

The new life of this modern era building confirms the relevance of a reinvestment of twentieth century heritage through which architecture, while responding in a more specific way to climatic issues, itself becomes a resource and support for revitalizing the city.

1. National Social Security Fund in Cameroon

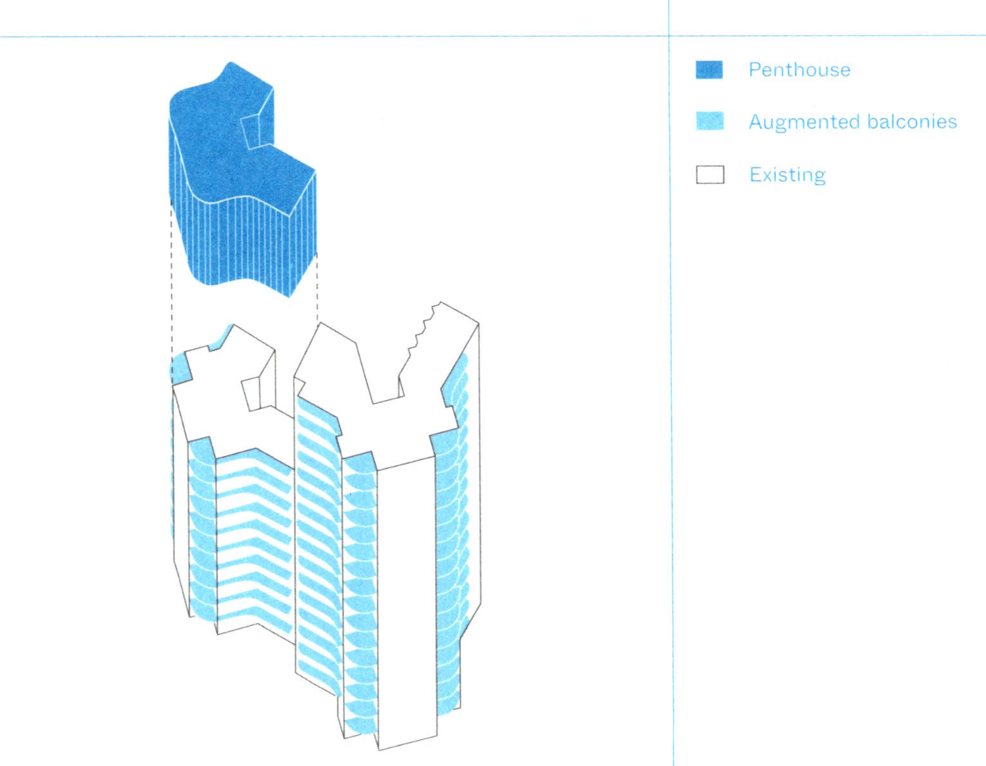

Penthouse
Augmented balconies
Existing

Abidjan, Ivory Coast.

Transforming a UNESCO heritage site into a post-carbon model

Pingyao, China

The Chinese city of Pingyao, a UNESCO World Heritage Site, has been the subject of an international consultation to establish the main guidelines for its preservation and renovation as part of an energy-saving approach. Located in the heart of the Shanxi region, at the heart of coal production in China, the energy transition of this historic city has a symbolic value for the renewal of Chinese cities.

In its European definition, sustainable development includes four different notions: respect for the environment, a sustainable use of natural resources, social and economic relevance, and respect for local culture. The project involving the restructuring of the city of Pingyao integrates proposals along these four lines, in order to improve the comfort of its population while limiting energy needs.

The reintroduction of nature into the city helps to reduce the effects of global warming and to offer new uses. Green spaces of different scales have been reintroduced or reinforced: agricultural spaces around the former fortifications, a central park, planting along the streets, and domestic gardens in the courtyards and on existing roof terraces. The green spaces around the fortifications also offer the possibility of creating an open-air sanitation system, as well as water retention basins.

The city consists mainly of traditional houses organized around an inner courtyard and oriented according to the cardinal points. The energy renovation of the buildings is based on their consistent orientation. A solar thermal roofing system has been proposed: the tiled roofs have been maintained, they serve as solar catalysts to bring heat to a network of pipes located underneath, in a low-tech and inexpensive process.

The insulation of the buildings is reinforced in accordance with traditional construction methods: the mud brick walls protected by a clay plaster on the outside are lined with an insulating complex on the inside, made of a sprayed earth-hemp mixture. In the main rooms, the historical system of the bed-stove, which used to be the central piece of furniture in the room and to be irradiated by the heat of a masonry heater, has been reinterpreted, and is fed by the solar thermal heating system of the roof.

The challenge for the city of Pingyao is to carry out an exemplary transition process towards a post-carbon urbanity on a remarkable heritage site.

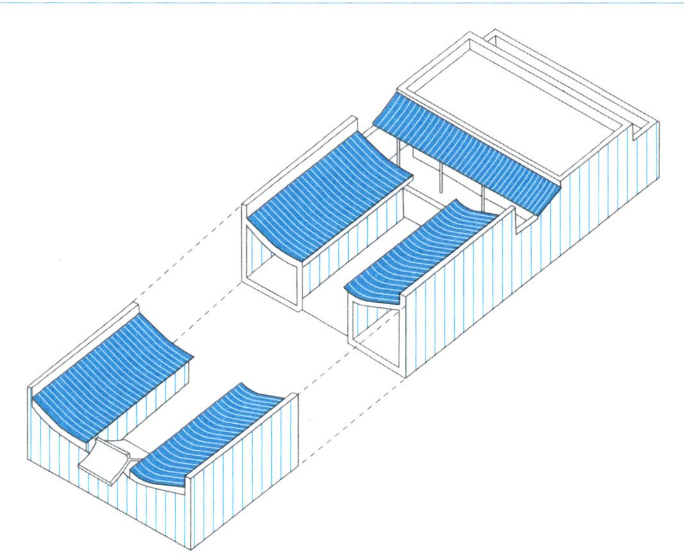

Solar thermal roofing system

Mixed earth and hemp insulation

Douala, Cameroun.

To transform rather than to project the new is to propose a shift in the activity of architects, whose production itself becomes a resource for a bigger project—one of rebalancing the Earth's system. This notion of architecture, that of managing inhabited environments, implies a new relationship between the collective and nature. As stated by the pioneer of political ecology, André Gorz: "Reforming our relationship with the environment requires a reformation of our society, and vice versa." And this in turn requires a new form of governance, one that is more open and more inclusive, one that invites new actors to the table and that raises new questions on the ethics of action.

ESSEC 2023 Campus, ESSEC Business School, Architecturestudio.

Cergy-Pontoise, France.

A shared campus

Dijon, France

The ESTP/ESEO Metropolitan Campus is located by one of the main entrances into the city of Dijon, and thus defines a new centrality. The project responds to the ambition to enhance the local academic education available by hosting the *École Spéciale des Travaux Publics du Bâtiment et de l'Industrie* (ESTP) and the *École Supérieure d'Électronique de l'Ouest* (ESEO)[1] by associating interconnected and adjoining buildings. This "smart building" is intended to interact with a wider "Smart City" context through the opening of large shared common spaces and the "On Dijon" showroom, the city's major digital project.

This hybrid project aims to bring together two schools around a theater-like atrium, a place for new educational practices, in a single building that can be shared and opened up to third-party uses.

Can the sum of the needs for living and meeting places for each of the constructions be fully met? How can we make this opportunity into a greater, stronger and more meaningful commonality? How can we create a new address for everyone, open onto the city? How can we manage these cross-use demands throughout the year and in real time?

We placed the large modular amphitheater at the heart of the project: it is thus visible from the surrounding area and accessible from the two schools. We then distributed the hybrid common spaces around it, such as the large tiered atrium, the panoramic gallery and the educational terraces. These spaces promote new educational practices and encourage serendipity.

The building's post-and-beam structure allows for flexibility of layout and reversibility of spaces over time, as the city retains ownership of the facility.

This first hybrid and "smart" higher education building has been awarded the R2S certification, and allows for improved shared use of its spaces and services in real time, thus becoming a new metropolitan common.

1. Both ESTP and ESEO are French engineering schools

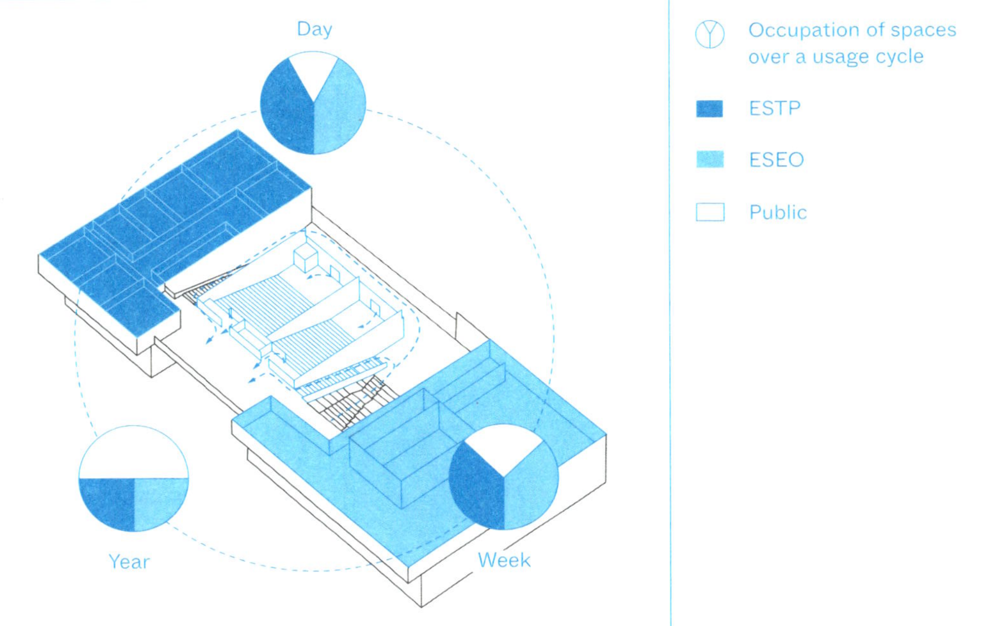

Herblay, France.

A Cité des Arts open to all commons

Montpellier, France

The Cité des Arts, designed to accommodate 2,200 students, brings together the music, dance, and theater conservatories formerly scattered around the historic center of Montpellier, on the site of the former Grasset maternity hospital.

The entrance pavilion has been preserved and renovated in keeping with its early twentieth century architectural style and houses the administration and resource centers. Forecourts and a square have been specially developed, and are open to new public uses in the heart of the Boutonnet neighborhood, in relation to the cultural program of the facility.

The morphology of the Cité responds to the Mediterranean climate with the passive features of a naturally bioclimatic architecture: a vertical village made up of independent volumes that shade each other and create patios, terraces and hanging gardens in their spacing, through which air circulates and where refreshing vegetation grows.

The large dance halls occupy the top floor on the green terrace, with splendid views over the plane trees that border the site: the roofs of the conservatory, amidst the trees, have become a dancing area.

Natural light is omnipresent in all the corridors, where views of the gardens enhance the itineraries. The large glazed halls of the avenue are protected by brise-soleil slats whose colors reflect those of the surrounding plane trees.

The chronotopic use of the Cité's facilities—the large 400-seat auditorium, the modern music room, the choir rooms and the early music rooms in particular—was conceived from the outset so that the public and associations may have access to them outside of the conservatories' opening hours: in the evening, on weekends, and during school holidays.

While giving shape to an ambitious project, we have created a real living environment which supports teaching excellence and is open to a cultural program for all the audiences of the city. In short: an architecture at the service of the development of new communities, on different scales and over different time periods.

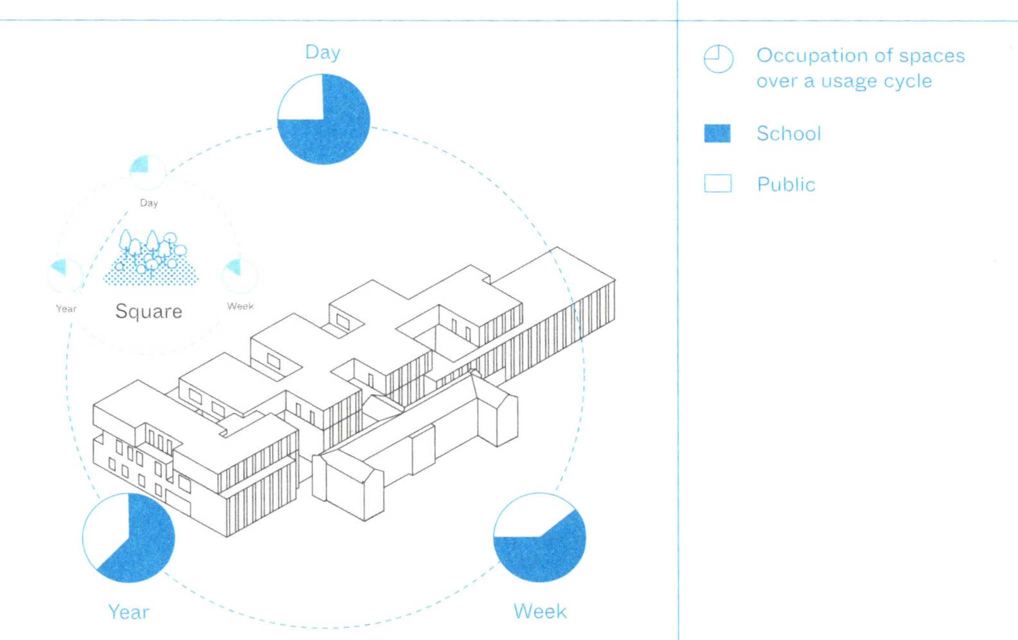

Cité des Arts,
Montpellier Méditerranée
Métropole, SA3M,
Architecturestudio,
MDR Architectes.

Montpellier, France, 2021.

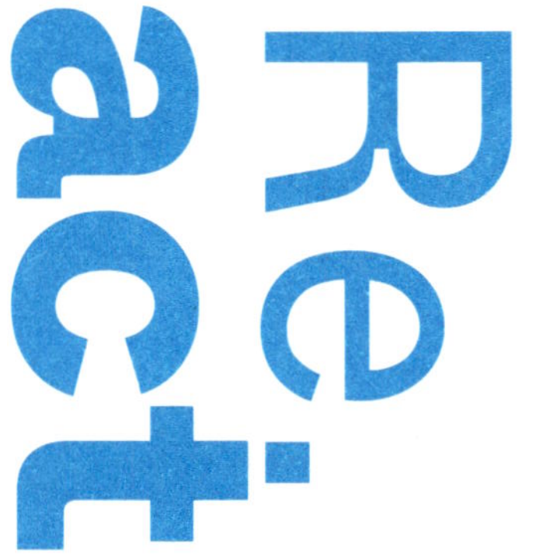

What set of actors can define the commons?

Franck Boutté Founder and President of Franck Boutté Consultants – Grand Prix in Urbanism, 2022

Emmanuelle Cosse President of L'Union Sociale pour l'Habitat, former Minister of Housing and Sustainable Habitat

José-Manuel Gonçalvès Director of CENTQUATRE-PARIS, Artistic Director of Grand Paris Express

AS Explore, moderated by Alain Bretagnolle and Romain Boursier, Partner Architects/Urban Planners, Architecturestudio

Architecturestudio interrogates our capacity for resilience through the notion of the commons. How can we collectively decide on what we share, on our access to and use of resources, all while respecting the conditions of life on Earth? How can this new paradigm reinforce our capacity to live together in a better equilibrium?

Tomorrow, how will the actors involved in the transformation of territory be able to define a good use of the commons? Following what objectives? By reducing the logic of the exclusive appropriation of resources, especially of land, while aiming towards collaboration and sharing. By forming new collective narratives built around new ways of life, ones more sustainable for inhabitants.

The aim of this round table is to question different actors involved in the production of housing on their representation of this notion of the commons, in a way that is particular and/or shared. Within a context of institutional complexity and social demand for shared decision making, shouldn't we seek out a new governance of the commons, to adapt our territories to the transformation of our ecosystems?

99. **Projected Territories**

SUPPORT FOR DECISION-MAKING
- **Simulator** | Santiago, Chile
- **Conceptual framework** | Metropolitan Area of Greater Paris, France

TAKING CARE OF OUR TERRITORIES
- **Hybrid landscape** | Kabul, Afghanistan
- **Regenerative architecture** | Al'Ula, Saudi Arabia

113. **Invited Research**

INHABITANT CO-DESIGN
- **Prospective inhabitants** | La Celle-Saint-Cloud, France
- **Social empowerment** | Poitiers, France
- **Residential consultation** | Toulouse, France
- **Female governance** | Lomé, Togo

EXPLORATORY PROCESS
- **Inhabited view cones** | Chartres, France
- **Sensitive envelope** | Bordeaux, France
- **Modeling light** | Amiens, France

139. **New Models**

METROPOLITAN LABORATORY
- **Circular triangle** | Paris, France
- **Site energy** | Issy-les-Moulineaux, France

AUGMENTED PROGRAMMING
- **Rolled-out ribbon** | Saint-Malo, France
- **Open stage** | Angers, France

151. **Shared Narratives**

- **A shared laboratory in Venice** | Venice, Italy
- **Stimuli for Paris** | Paris, France

New Aspirations

The fragility of inhabited areas and the depletion of resources call for a greater resilience of territories, for a reactivation of the evolutionary dynamics of nature. The commons, these collective resources—natural or societal, material or immaterial—are once again at the center of our socio-ecological questions. As their name indicates, common goods create society as soon as they are accessible to and/or managed by the collective. They imply a shared interest and raise the question of caretaking by the collective, in an era of exacerbated individualism. Architecture has always played a role in the management, provision, and transmission of common goods. Nevertheless, a crisis is sweeping through the profession. How can we hold onto this collective project in an increasingly fragmented world? How can we safeguard general interest when the logic of individualism is continually gaining ground? More simply: how can we *act*, collectively?

Santiago, Chile.

↑ Abidjan, Ivory Coast.
→ Marrakech, Morocco.

The profound modification of the planetary ecosystem calls for an evolution in the distribution of planning roles. The nature of architects' and urban planners' design activites has changed since the start of the century, and our approach to governance has also shifted. From the organization of decision-making processes to the aim of our urban and territorial politics, the environmental crisis has considerably altered the expectations of citizens as well as the processes of planning. Particularly in the early phases of a project, the inclusion of various actors is a first response to the complexity of themes that have emerged over the past twenty years in our profession. What are the mechanisms? How can this mode of governance become more inclusive?

What set of actors can define the commons?

Romain Boursier

How, starting from a reflection on the commons, might we respond to the three major ecological crises we are going through today? This is the question I would like to ask our guests. First there is the climate crisis, which forces us to adapt our territories and to integrate uncertainty as a driving force within our projects. This is followed by the biodiversity crisis, and the need to once again place our focus on living things in order to manage the place these occupy within inhabited environments. Finally, the resource crisis, which leads us to reduce our consumption of energy and of materials and to define a frugal, efficient architecture. In other words, can we shift the paradigm and move from a logic of resource exploitation, one based on a linear model of economy, to a logic of managing resources that relies on a circular model of economy? Secondly, we will consider how these resources define natural commons such as air quality, biodiversity, and cultural commons. Finally, we will reflect on how to mobilize these commons, and for which ambitions and projects. The question of governance will therefore be crucial. As noted by Elinor Ostrom, winner of the Nobel Prize in Economic Sciences in 2009, proper management of the commons is the only guarantee of social and ecological justice. How, then, might we adapt the governance of our territories in order to plan their transition?

Alain Bretagnolle

What are these commons, seen from today's perspective? With whom do we define them, who do we share them with? For what social project? My first question is for Franck Boutté. We are currently working in conditions of ecologic solutionism. By this I mean that our notion of ecology remains strictly performance-based: compliance with RE2020,[1] a satisfactory carbon footprint, sustainably sourced construction using wood, straw, earth... and all this should allow us to save the planet. Do these solutions, which in the end are more quantitative than systemic, seem to you appropriately scaled to the current climate challenge?

Frank Boutté

You used several terms that I would like to come back to: "systemic," "performance-based," "quantitative." Let's go back to the origins. In 1975, a book titled *Le Macroscope* (The Macroscope) was published, written by Joël de Rosnay,

1 The RE2020 is a national regulation on energy consumption for all new buildings in France, in effect as of January 2022.

Simulator

Santiago, Chile

In 2014, as part of a multidisciplinary team, we took part in the development of Santiago 3Deseado, a 3D simulator of the Sustainable City – a digital decision support tool for urban planning in the city of Santiago, Chile.

After a series of unsuccessful tenders aimed at covering the Panamericana—the urban motorway that generates a social and spatial fracture in the urban fabric of the city—Carolina Tohá, then Mayor of Santiago, chose to use this innovative approach to highlight the challenges of her territory. By modeling the existing city, our task was to show how it was possible to transform a territory marked by this urban barrier, a symbol of inequalities in the heart of the capital, into a more democratic, open and sustainable space.

The approach, co-developed with local stakeholders, was structured around 11 keys for the Sustainable City including social equity, the use of resources, and quality of life. The survey of the territory highlighted specific issues for each of the keys through the analysis of some sixty mapped indicators.

Nine urban scenarios were designed and evaluated to cover the motorway, including:

→ The creation of a continuous green belt and heritage enhancement
→ Four new business and intermodal clusters
→ The creation of new urban ground for development

After 18 months of work, two of these scenarios were selected, enabling us to reconfigure the fabric of Santiago by generating a new city dynamic focused on ecology, sociability, and resilience: the Promenade des Places and the Boulevard Continu. These projects generated:

→ 80,000 m² of buildable land, thus ensuring the economic viability of the development operation.
→ 56 ha of public green space, enabling Santiago to cross the threshold of 15 m² of green space per capita recommended by the WHO.
→ 4 intermodal hubs around existing metro stations, thereby increasing soft and electric mobility options.
→ 25% of additional pedestrian spaces.

Ultimately, the projects reduced car traffic and associated noise pollution by 35%.

On October 23rd, 2016, Carolina Tohá lost the municipal elections and her successors abandoned the project.

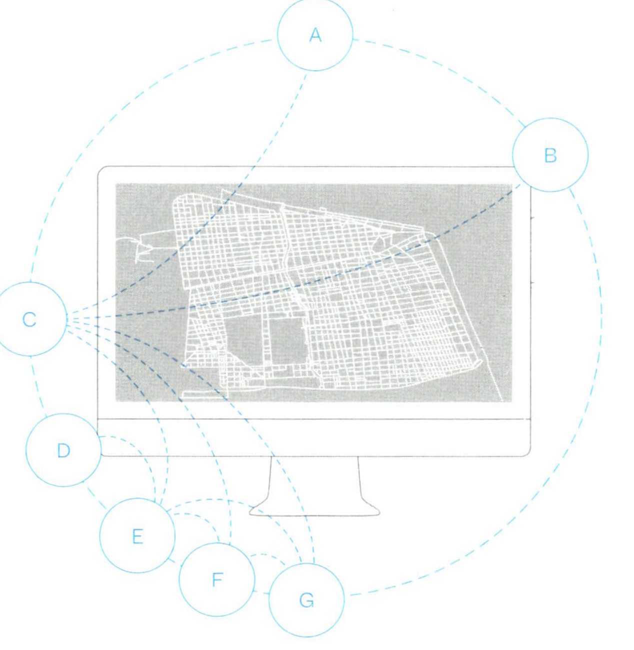

Ⓐ Municipality
Ⓑ Government (Ministry)
Ⓒ Architecturestudio
Ⓓ Associate Architect
Ⓔ Engineer
Ⓕ Operator
Ⓖ Modeler

who was at the time considered the father of systems theory in France. In this book he articulates the idea of a new tool, the macroscrope, in the following way: "We invented the telescope to see and understand the infinitely big, infinitely far away; we invented the microscope to see and understand the infinitely small, infinitely close. Today, we must invent a new tool, and it is not a laboratory tool, but a tool that is at the same time philosophic, conceptual, political, methodological, and operational. The macroscope, therefore, to see and understand the infinitely complex." This wish, thus formulated in 1975: we could make it ours today.

With this definition he laid down the basis of systems theory, which is to recognize that things are complex, whereas for more than twenty years we have been applying the principles of sustainable development with a clear propensity for simplification. This is solutionism: ready-made solutions, considering things separately. We invented the low-energy building, and with that thought we had solved part of the problem; after the low-energy building we invented net-zero and net-positive buildings, after net-zero and net-positive buildings we invented the Smart Grid, and then we invented the Smart City, and so on. These "innovative" concepts are all digressions, all fatal errors in judgment. Without a holistic approach we cannot adopt a complex, comprehensive point of view, and we cannot enter into a system of secondary effects, of correlated effects.

We know today that a small event, somewhere on the planet, can have much more severe consequences on the other side of the world. There are leveraging effects, amplifying effects, chain effects, effects of synergy, induced effects, contrary effects, and so on, and this is what we have to be able to understand. I've just gone back nearly fifty years with Joël de Rosnay, but the questions that drive us today were already asked in the report of the Rome Club in 1968, the first international conference on the environment. We can see that we find it difficult to advance, and when we do advance, it is unfortunately by addressing each criterion individually. All those who are interested in the environment, and perhaps even more those interested in ecology, have the goal of finding ideal equilibriums between different criteria. Ecology is the science of equilibriums. Quite the opposite of a maximalist approach! A couple of terms from French illustrate this nicely: *aménagement*, or planning, and *ménagement*, or management. The "a" in *aménagement* is not necessarily a negating "a," but today we speak more about the management of an environment—*management d'un milieu*—rather than the planning of a site. From "site" to "environment," from "planning" to "management:" the search for ideal equilibriums involves new words and new definitions. Architecture and urban planning are

Though the commons, it is now a question of supporting forms of community to come. Of working on possible futures, on the possibilities of architecture. For this to happen, we need new visions and a renewed sense of delight. The task is before us and it is immense: to open up to the desirable a world destined for great collapse, to build a mode of collective, ecological cohabitation, and to project new, collective imaginaries—somewhat exciting, if not lively. What narratives is architecture writing today?

Conceptual framework

Metropolitan area of Greater Paris, France

Greater Paris is a recurring figure in the history of urban planning, from the invention of the capital city at the turn of the nineteenth century, to the polycentric developments of the twentieth century, to the early twenty-first century challenges that this world city must face, in a context of socio-territorial imbalances and multifaceted ecological crises. In 2010, six years before the metropolitan governance project, the State gave impetus to the creation of a new metro transport network through the law relating to Greater Paris, thereby enabling the construction of housing to address the shortages which were estimated at over one million.

In this context of metropolitan project management, we conducted a systemic study to analyze and define the programming and constructability potential around the Grand Paris Express stations across twelve sites. Our mission was to support this dialogue between the Société du Grand Paris and local authorities, transport operators, planners, promoters and designers at the interface of the station-hub projects, to tease out a shared vision around each future place of life and mobility.

How can the ambitions of a major metropolitan transport equipment project be articulated with those of a hundred local urban regeneration projects? How to define a coherence in the methods of implementing such a large project, according to the political, social, urban, and local landscape specificities? In practice, how can we overcome the added constraints of each of the stakeholders, in favor of a culture of shared co-design with complex intervention perimeters?

After studying a dozen sites, Architecturestudio proposed a conceptual framework defining the methods of co-construction and co-design of prospective real estate transactions to requalify the future mobility spaces of Greater Paris. This tool aims to facilitate the collaboration between the various institutional and operational stakeholders. Its framework offers a historical perspective on the place of services and programs associated with stations, according to their urban position. It identifies the different stakeholders involved and the issues raised by each one of them, as well as the different programming topologies related to the stations, and the different urban and architectural strategies that are appropriate.

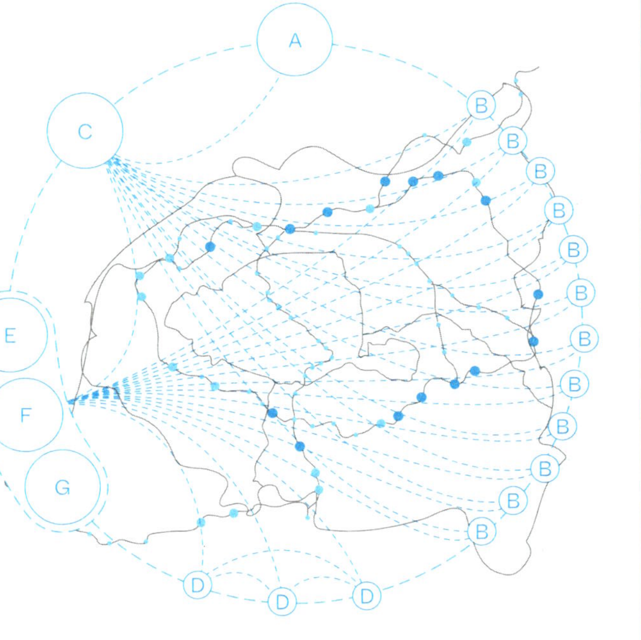

(A) State
(B) Municipalities
(C) Project manager
(D) Third party operators (real estate, transportation, developers)
(E) Architecturestudio
(F) Urban programming
(G) Real estate development

Créteil, France.

The Commons, Reactivating General Interest

The Earth is our Commons; to act for its future is necessarily to act together. Ecology, as a science of equilibriums, highlights the need to go beyond our segmented and individual disciplinary visions and to move towards a systemic approach—the only approach able to account for the complexity of reality. Gone are the days of narrow-minded maximalist methods that serve the interests of a select few: this cannot be maintained. As stated by Franck Boutté, the unpredictability of the world is such that "today no one can provide an answer from their sole point of view, from their sole discipline, their sole time, and their sole place of existence."[1] In this context, it becomes urgent to bring together all actors for collective and inclusive action, starting with scientists and politicians,[2] to finally connect the evidence of observations to the effectiveness of reaction.[3]

1. Franck Boutté, As Explore, "What Set of Actors Can Define the Commons?", November 8, 2022.

2. Bruno Latour, *Politiques de la nature, Comment faire entrer les sciences en démocratie*, Ed. de la découverte, 1999.

3. The theme of the film *Don't Look Up* by Adam McKay, 2021.

defined today by the search for these equilibriums.
If we look back at the past twenty years, we have worked almost exclusively on energy, and almost exclusively on the new. Energy, within new construction, is clearly not the problem. New construction barely uses any energy. This single-criteria approach is a bit ridiculous. In addition, new construction, at least in France—my discussion here absolutely does not apply in developing countries—new construction represents only 1% each year within the renewal of existing building stock. In other words, we have spent almost twenty years and 99% of the resources on only 1% of the problem. Once we realize this, we say that we obviously must change gears. And then it's not just energy. In any case, it's not just white energy. White energy is the energy of flux, that which we consume in the form of heating, air conditioning, etc. We now add embodied energy, or stored energy, material energy. And finally we can also speak of carbon, which produces a type of equation that is a bit more global, a bit more holistic: it's not so bad. To be a bit positive, we are starting to evolve on these issues. We took twenty years to understand that we needed to look at the existing, that we needed to look at something other than energy, that we needed to look at other actors and other living beings. So much for solutionism.
Another important change linked to this paradigm shift: today no one can provide an answer from their individual point of view, from their individual discipline, their individual time, and their individual place of existence. Phenomena are so complex that we are obliged to move towards multi- and transdisciplinarity. This is fundamental. All of this evidently and significantly calls into question our practices of planning, urbanism, and architecture in which we have often stayed within the logic of factions. It is necessary to work in teams, to respond to the complexity of phenomena by incorporating other contributions in our considerations: those of researchers, of scientists, and of civil society, even in the broader sense, to collaborate on a collective project.

Romain Boursier

The public health crisis has revealed the great fragility of our systems and has clearly called into question the resilience of our territories in critical times. The Climate and Resilience Law and the application of zero net artificialization (ZNA) together contributed to changing our view of land, to moving beyond the usual logic of consumption in order to consider it as a reserve, able to be mobilized to serve interests of the general public. Emmanuelle Cosse, as president of L'Union Sociale pour l'Habitat (USH) since that time, you have been fighting poor housing conditions in addition to managing a building stock of five million housing units. You are planning 250,000 social housing units in France. How do objectives of ZNA intersect with these initiatives?

Hybrid landscape

Kabul, Afghanistan

When we were selected for this urban study, funded by the Japanese government, we believed that we had been entrusted with a very specific problem. Because of its human and environmental challenges, the study has proven to have a universal dimension that extends far beyond the Afghan case.

There is no doubt that the context was unique. After the fall of the Taliban in 2002, approximately three million expatriates returned to their country. Kabul's population rose sharply from 700,000 in 1980 to 3.5 million by 2007, resulting in high levels of overcrowding and an alarming deterioration in living conditions. This situation, combined with strong population growth, led to a projection of nearly seven million inhabitants by 2030.

Environmental issues were not only important to the city and its people, they were quite simply existential. These issues included energy sobriety in a country that produces almost nothing, in the context of extremely harsh winters; the water cycle, at the crossroads between overpopulation and desert areas; the health of the inhabitants, with air pollution from burning tyres and old diesels and soils infected by the absence of sewer networks; and the nutritional problems of a growing population. The situation called for decisive solutions, which our project strove to provide by means of a global urban proposal for Kabul, with a mirror initiative including its extension on the site near Deh-Sabz: the only way to solve the inextricable technical problems within the capital and change the paradigm.

Given the discrepancies between the mass military investment and the funding available for the reconstruction of the country, the most important thing was to outline a shared horizon for a heterogeneous, if not conflictual population. The project proposed a new common urban good by promoting access to education, culture, public services, worship, sport and employment. We integrated the essential needs associated with the resources available on the chosen site into the design of the new city of Deh-Sabz—mountain water, agricultural areas, topography—creating a hybrid which tended towards self-sufficiency.

Although geopolitical events took a radically different turn from what was conceivable at the time, we are still consulting on this project, with aerial photos to observe the evolution of human settlements in Deh-Sabz. They seem to have appropriated some of the traces of what had been a political project.

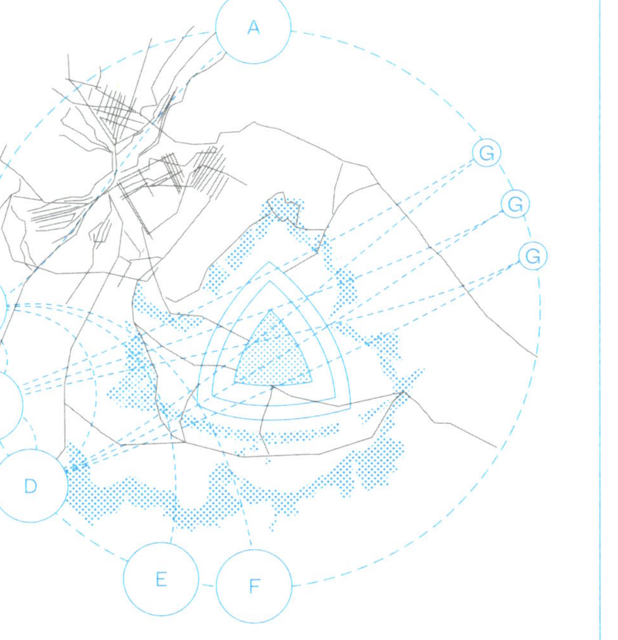

(A) Government
(B) Architecturestudio
(C) Ethnologist
(D) Humanitarian association
(E) Landscaper
(F) Hydraulic engineer, energy and airport consulting
(G) Residents

← ↑ Kabul, Afghanistan.

Our culture must evolve. We need to challenge our idea of the limit, through a systemic approach, and establish new frontiers—new boundaries. For Régis Debray, the boundary takes on two contrary functions: it separates and it connects.[4] It invites us to consider together what we know and what we don't know. Our societies are based on a system of absolute ownership, applied to both objects and ideas. This situation leads to an impoverishment of intellectual debate and to a privatization of reality that everyday deepens social inequalities, destabilizes our democratic systems, and contributes to natural disasters.

4. Régis Debray, *Éloge des frontières*, Éditions Gallimard, 2010.

Emmanuelle Cosse

One of the current difficulties, when it comes to environmental and ecological issues, is the temporality—which has changed quite drastically, as Franck stated. When I started becoming interested in ecological issues, we didn't think we would be where we are now in 2022. There has been an acceleration of climate change and in the consequent upheavals. We knew this was going to happen, but we were thinking of 2050, 2100, even as we signed the COP 21 agreement in 2015.
What's crazy—and this is the reason we have to think and act differently than we did ten years ago—is that the acceleration is to the point of being politically damaging. Currently, most armed conflicts are connected to ecological issues: water, natural resources, raw materials. We have even less time than we thought. This doesn't mean that I take a pessimistic view of things. On the contrary, all of this should propel us into action, more quickly and more intelligently, to try to make up for lost time. This is what we're currently doing. Acting against climate change means gaining time against the devastation that is currently unfolding.
The second thing I wanted to mention relates to an assumption inherent to the debate proposed here by Architecturestudio. This is that one of the solutions to resolve the problems you're bringing forward is to return to something collective, perhaps even something of public interest. We might later come back to this point to consider what we mean by these terms, but in any case, at no point did you consider that it was through individual approaches, each in their own silo, that we would succeed.
You put forward the collective mobilization of a community that wishes to move towards something else. This is an assumption that suits me very well, of course. It is in itself already a way of changing current ways of thinking.
The third subject, which I would like to broach right away as I don't want to miss it, is that there will be no progress on environmental and ecological issues if we aren't fighting social inequalities, if we don't question the place of humans within this change. We can invent as much as we like, but the reality is: where are humans within all of this? Because the great plight that follows climate change is the worsening of inequalities. Between wealthy countries and those less wealthy, but also within prosperous societies such as our own, we can question how social inequalities will be linked to climatic and environmental issues. If we don't address the ecological and the social together, we won't succeed. The example of land is a strong illustration of this point. My stance is that we have to completely reduce the consumption of land and move towards a principle of zero artificialization, even if, at the same time, we must build more and more social housing. This means that we aren't constructing only new buildings, that we are

Al Ula, Saudi Arabia.

We are no longer listening to ourselves. The way we have appropriated the world, through exclusivity and competition, renders us blind to the commons: to that which without ownership (a beautiful idea) is for the benefit of all. The interdependence of human beings between each other and of human beings with the rest of the living world can only be weakened by this notion of separation. On the contrary, we need to think about what holds us together.

emphasizing programs targeting what is already built, and that we're focusing on land that is already built up. We must also come up with solutions that are outside prices of the real estate market in France—which, by the way, is essentially a mirage. When we consider the asking prices in this sector, it becomes clear that the aim of many real estate operations is not to seek to house people but rather to carry out financial transactions. Many French people, salaried workers who will earn the minimum wage or slightly above minimum wage their whole lives, have no options for building a livable home beyond going to find a lot in nature in the suburbs, or buying a slightly older house of fairly poor quality. This is the reality of the market today. So what possibilities can we propose for them? Land regulation is essential, and very difficult. Especially as it doesn't only concern issues of housing or of economic activity. Today, the debates we have on the relocation of subsistence agriculture or on reindustrialization demonstrably involve the use of land close to means of transportation. We are now faced with this issue of land, which holds considerable sway in the transformation of public policies.

I recently participated in a debate on ZNA at the conference of the Fédération Nationale des Agences d'Urbanisme (National Federation of Urban Planning Agencies) in Toulouse. I was with Dominique Alba, and I'd like to quote what she said because as always it was very pertinent. She compared the arrival of the debate on zero net artificialization in the public sphere to the same scandal around the article 55 of the law on solidarity and urban renewal (SRU), when in 2000 we said that all cities had to consist of 20% or 25% social housing. Twenty years later, you know how difficult it is to enforce this law, but also it remains essential for maintaining balance between regions. Regarding zero net artificialization, I don't quite agree with how the law is written and decrees around implementation, but in the end the legislature states that we have used too much land. It's true that we can draw a line between those who were told their land no longer has value, and those who will see it increase. With the ZNA, there are people making financial maneuvers like never before. This is neither limited nor regulated. All of this is still imperfect but progress is real: aiming to stop the spread of parking lots and of unused, empty commercial areas is essential. Some people experience this as a stripping away of freedoms but the reality is that we no longer have a choice, and that it is better to act rather than suffer. In certain regions this even means questioning the livability and sustainability of current development schemes. In certain cities in the south of mainland France, what will we do when temperatures reach 45° for periods of several months? The question is therefore simple: what do we do? Do we adapt, or do we let these regions decline?

Regenerative architecture

Al'Ula, Saudi Arabia

The region of Al'Ula in Saudi Arabia, which is the size of Belgium, offers an exceptional natural and historical heritage: a fertile valley (wadi) surrounded by red and ochre rock formations with fantastic silhouettes sculpted by time, a cross between Nabataean, Dadan and Arab civilizations, Nabataean tombs dug into the rocks, petroglyphs, a historic city built of mudbricks on the edge of the oasis...

At the same time as the development of the region is being considered on a territorial scale, the modern city of Al'Ula is undergoing a regeneration process aimed at requalifying existing buildings and introducing new building rules whose objectives are: an architecture that is integrated into the wider landscape, offering an adapted response to climatic and environmental constraints, and generating the new identity of the modern city based on a contemporary interpretation of the architectural heritage of the historic city of Al'Ula.

In close collaboration with our teams, the Royal Commission for Al'Ula and the French Agency for Al'Ula, we developed a new way of making the city and building its identity. The new requirement of architectural quality is therefore imposed on any new building, within the framework of the building permit, in consultation with the owners and their architects, in order to raise awareness and promote new practices.

The modern city in Al'Ula is one of those twentieth-century cities where the public space and its attractions have long been forgotten. Priorities now include the creation of a lively public space, devoted to pedestrian pleasures, adapted to the local climate and rich in various stimuli. By shading a market square, livening it up with a café, an exhibition pavilion, and an open-air cinema in the evening, we can turn it into a meeting place for the inhabitants, in parallel with the restoration and reactivation of the historic city.

It is a way of building the habitat and the city together with its inhabitants, preserving an oasis for agriculture, the integrity of ecosystems for biodiversity, and the beauty of the sites and landscapes for all.

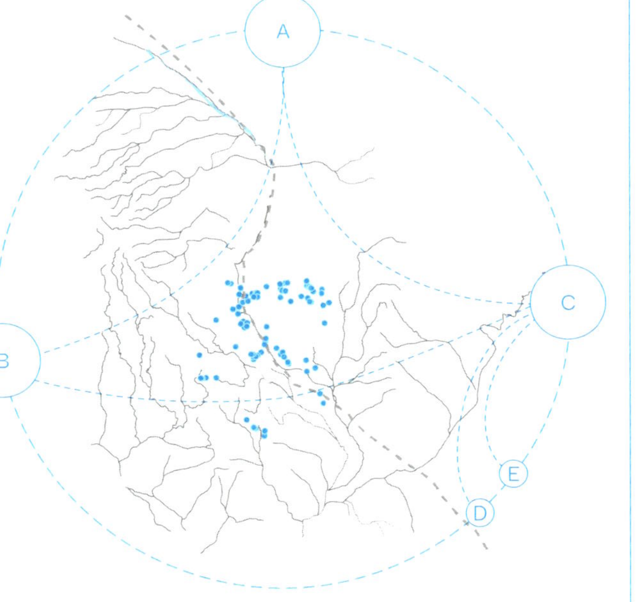

The commons represents a point of leverage as well as a challenge. *Res-communae*. The practice of the commons is a co-production and a co-management of what is unalienable. It involves collective decision-making. But how can action be coordinated? How can we agree—and with whom—when the scale of ecological issues extends beyond established political boundaries?[5] Ecology calls into question the scale of our governing systems. We need to cultivate a trans-scalar perspective and invent new chains of actors. The problems of the twenty-first century are immense and call for serious, constructed answers: the artificialization of soils, access to housing and land, economic uncertainty, climatic migration, natural risks, the collapse of biodiversity[6]—solutionism is not the solution! We need to build an environmental ethic of action. We need to think in the long term.

5. Gaël Giraud, *Composer un monde en commun : une théologie politique de l'Anthropocène*, Seuil, 2022.

6. Emmanuelle Cosse, As Explore, "What Set of Actors can define the commons?", November 8, 2022.

Alain Bretagnolle

In a holistic approach, it is important to integrate the cultural dimension. José-Manuel, you are the director of 104 Paris, and as such you work with different communities to propose cultural strategies of appropriation and to imagine new narratives to support the changes underway. Could you tell us what concrete forms this takes, and what you get out of this in terms of experience?

José-Manuel Gonçalvès

Most of the time the actors involved—often the leaders of regional authorities, either political or administrative—come to us to solve a problem. This is often tied to a space which is available, or which is neglected, with the intention of giving it new value through a cultural activity. To start, we explain the different between a cultural and an artistic activity by saying that there are already many cultural activities, and that the question is to know what kind of activity we want. Along the same lines, what artist do we want? Our work therefore consists of bringing in artists and creative individuals as late as possible, and by doing so encouraging elected officials to bring some complexity to their thought processes. The idea, as you mentioned Emmanuelle, is to bring in expertise in the field, and above all to depart from the expertise of experts who each remain in their own profession. There are experts on territory, meaning the people who experience it. The question is, therefore, how do we bring the voice of inhabitants and local actors into the project, with as little demagoguery as possible? The first thing, as Franck said, is to refuse to simplify, to accept the complexity of approaches to territory and to say that it must go even a bit further, especially when it comes to pooling expertise. Next, it's a question of encouraging new actors to consider this way of approaching territory.

The presence of communities is important, especially in "third places," tertiary spaces, which are often a theme within architecture or planning schools. All of these groups bring in complexity, in the good sense of the term; in other words, they contribute to shared expertise. It is a question of bringing them into the project, with their vocabulary and their different way of approaching territory. This is extremely important. In doing so we start to open up the lexical field, to bring new people to meet elected officials, and, by playing the mediator and facilitating these meetings, to counter any fear of dispossession of land. Because the issue, in the end, is always the control over (and vision for) land. We cannot blame elected or administrative officials for having a vision. On the contrary, this is a good thing. What we can suggest to them is make it slightly more complex, to take into account the various flows across the region in question.

Prospective inhabitants

La Celle-Saint-Cloud, France

In 1954, not without some setbacks, an association of resident-builders carried out an operation for 500 dwellings intended for growing families, with the ambition of sharing common goods (meadow, castle, and services). Located on the edge of the forest, this former estate is marked by the presence of a castle which has been transformed into a third space open to the public, and by former stables which have been converted into daily service areas.

This Anglo-Saxon style archetype of the garden city, organized around a large shared meadow, offers an exceptional living environment thanks to the quality of the landscaping arrangements. Seventy years after its creation, aware of its heritage and the strength of its collegial governance, the local residents' association hired Architecturestudio to implement its culture of dialogue and collectivism in the service of a community of 2,500 inhabitants. The mission should make it possible to imagine a concerted prospective with the residents, in order to rethink the future of the domain by 2040.

How to restore the ideal of the historical project in an ongoing project? How to integrate resident expertise in a co-design process? How to showcase the skills of the architect in the direct service of the inhabitants? How to project ourselves into the short and long term with all the users of the site?

To address these issues, we proposed a custom-made approach to co-design. This response, enriched by the co-design method developed at the agency as part of an R&D program, allows for the greater involvement of citizen-users in architectural and urban design.

This empowerment of the inhabitants and their involvement in the culture of the project requires the architect to "switch perspectives," supplementing his or her conventional knowledge with subjective modes of perception of the site, for the present and the future. This approach was broken up into stages, from the co-narration of sites during the assessment, to architectural intervention during the orientation phases (which involved living on-site), to the commented walks during the intentions phase. This process produced a first result, the "Esquisse pour 2040," which was rendered with large illustrations to enable us to pursue our reflection and exchange ideas.

This approach ensures that all stakeholders will be fully represented, including those, such as future generations, who do not yet have a say.

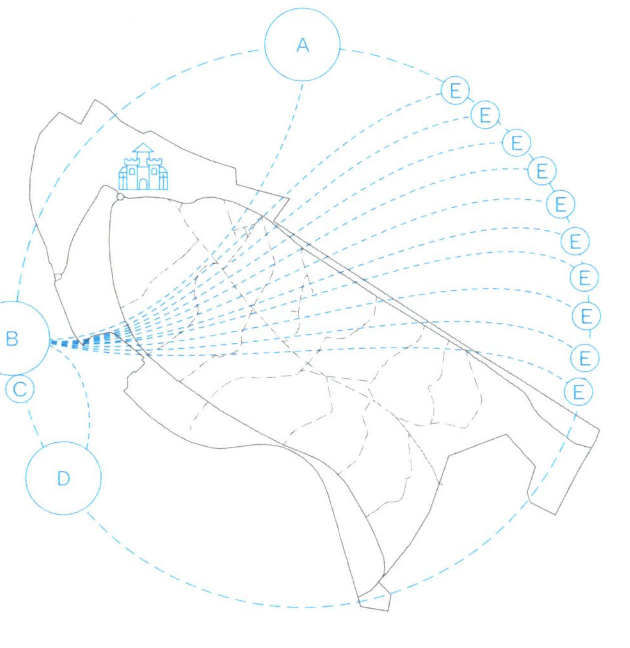

Ⓐ Residents' association
Ⓑ Architecturestudio
Ⓒ Doctoral student
Ⓓ Landscape designer
Ⓔ Residents

Al Ula, Saudi Arabia.

115

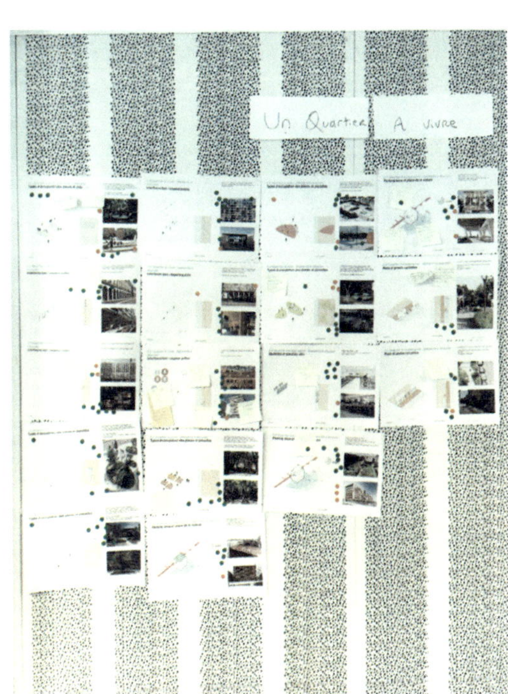

↑ Shanghai, China
← Nice, France.

Governance and Ecology

The ecological crisis has led to a profound change in terms of the actors involved, and has brought new ones to light, in each of the three areas of planning. In project management and construction management, the past few decades have revealed a need for new and expanded skillsets, open to interdisciplinarity. Architectural knowledge has meanwhile expanded towards that of landscape while the social sciences and life sciences have been subsumed into project *processes*, **along with other changes needed to respond to society's current demands: new forms of mobility, Smart Cities, respect for biodiversity, cultural factories, decontamination and remediation, urban agriculture, safety, transitional urbanism, communication, etc.**

Another aspect of our task concerns those who own or who manage public assets in a region. Here too it is a question of getting them to consider how their responsibility must lead to complex thinking. France is the country in the world with the most cultural facilities, all disciplines considered. Let's say there are more than 350 of these in the suburbs, and if you add Paris there are between 700 and 800, if you add movie theaters then we have 1500, maybe 1800, in the region of Paris alone. This is significant. At the same time, however, we might realize that the use of these spaces is monothematic, and that the consideration of territory remains mono-centric, because the use assigned to these facilities is to quickly enhance the region in question. What we are trying to do is to get actors to consider the time and spaces available in terms of artistic activity, which would allow the city to take hold of and to have another use for these spaces.

It's in this position that we are trying to situate ourselves today, and to ensure that these times and spaces are imagined with potential users. For example: a theater or an opera or a movie theater where the primary function is to be a place of consumption in anticipation of meeting the artist. Today these spaces might be dedicated not only to the so-called intended activity, but also to connection with the city and a use of the city. This question is fundamental. We must change our approach to a population and its contact with culture. Entering into a room to consume one spectacle or another, this is of course still important. But in these places it is also an opportunity to offer a shelter, an aesthetic shelter within the city, that presents the city in another way, because people will take hold of it in another way. This is a bit of the work we're trying to do with the cultural engineering part of 104.

Romain Boursier

Emmanuelle, during the HLM[2] conference that you chaired in October, you highlighted that HLMs, faced by the numerous crises that make their inhabitants more fragile, are an essential cog in the construction of a more ecologically just society. How can we recover the notion of public good within the idea of affordable property? Have there been policies on major acquisitions in the past that would have made this possible?

Emmanuelle Cosse

In the past, there were periods in which there was a shared conviction that everyone had to have housing. And that everyone had the right to a place within French territory—in the aftermath of World War II, for example, especially to support industrial development. I'm not saying that everything done

2 "HLM" stands for *habitation à loyer modéré*, or housing at a moderate rent.

in the 1950s was good, but at that moment everyone found it unacceptable that there were still slums in Nanterre. Do people today find it unacceptable that there are slums in Paris? No, unfortunately. I mention this because this change in political paradigm—and it's because of this that I'm very happy you are insisting on the commons, a point of real leverage on these subjects—is threatening us. The notion that everyone finds a place, in particular through housing, this doesn't make sense to everyone and no longer create cohesion today. It's enough to see how young people are mistreated in terms of access to housing, regardless of their situation as student or young worker. And our elderly people... I bring up these two extremes because there is a dysfunction in our country, which is one of the richest countries in the world. In truth, we don't have any problems with money, or with infrastructure, or with knowledge or intelligence. We have everything in this country, and we still can't resolve the issue. If, behind these tools we're describing, there isn't an active, combative social body, we will not succeed. This also means that we have to again highlight individual issues. In the current ecological struggle, there are those who oppose social housing in the name of ecology. We're in a complex world where, in the name of biodiversity, we can disallow an extremely well thought-out social housing program. This reality is becoming increasingly difficult. And I believe we're facing difficulties of anticipation.
Contrary to what we were experiencing a few decades ago, we now have fewer collectives working towards long-term aims. This relates to what you were saying in your question: how can we create reserves of land that will make it possible to work in forty years? How can we carry out political actions that have no immediate effect or profitability, but that will be useful for future generations?

A good example of this is the issue of land remediation. There are sites that we will remediate in ten, fifteen years, and others, industrial sites, that will require intervention over several decades. Instead of leaving these as brownfield sites, couldn't we decide to wager now on what we will do in fifty years? We have the tools for this, but too often we remain prisoners of the time frame of an electoral mandate. At the same time, in relation to the financial resources of communities, we see that on the question of land, in view of prevailing values today, it is extremely hard to resist the call of the market.

Public authorities have created public land or development agencies, most notably to intervene in areas in particular difficulty. The EPA Alzette Velval in Lorraine, for example, on the former site of Micheville, is aiming to bring life back to industrial brownfields. It is thus with public money, with taxes, that we're

Hanoi, Vietnam.

Many of these areas are now being taken over by new entities: technical or scientific experts, consulting firms in cultural engineering, laboratories in sociological research, reintegration associations, or event professionals. A set of new actors has come to enrich the ranks of project management teams. At the same time, the call for improved sharing and ownership of projects by users has been heard. The recognition of user control by the other two systems—project management and construction management—has thus materialized through the establishment of various tools related to information, consultation, and citizen participation.

trying to recreate life and housing in a changing territory. There are also new tools, such as joint lease programs, which are set up with community land trusts, in which we essentially propose an increasing disjuncture between land and building. We buy the land over eighty years while the person buys their home over a normal credit period. By spreading the price of land over eighty years, in certain territories it allows a rise in social position and in quality. This comes back to spreading the cost of land over several generations of buyers. This in turn allows us to offer housing to those with an average salary, and the opportunity to find a way of entering the market. Then, and I'm not going to make many friends by saying this, but we might have to accept that land doesn't have any immediate function, and that they are in the end supported by communities, by a public land agency, by private landowners, and even by private real estate investors (with all these investment funds aiming to go towards sustainability and who don't know how to invest). They could invest in the future, in land for which we don't yet know the use but which we known will be useful for society. It is possible that in forty years it will be productive agricultural land, or that it will be used for housing. We must come back to the idea that we can have a long-term land strategy and thus move beyond the dichotomy of buildable and non-buildable space. In a natural space, we don't touch anything and for the rest we can do a bit of anything. I'm being schematic here, of course. In the end, very honestly, political time doesn't allow us to do this. However, if we think of the commons, of public interest, these can be our guides...

Romain Boursier

This raises the question of arbitration. Do tenant associations consider themselves within these time frames?

Emmanuelle Cosse

Most often not, because the tenant associations are concerned with their daily lives and their survival. With them, since several weeks my question has been knowing how we will pay for energy, with energy costs having gone up by 1000% at times! This current topic should be at the heart of our reflection on environmental issues. But, on the other hand, there are residents' associations—councils on civic life in neighborhoods undergoing urban renewal who are considering both the medium and long term. Some of the people in our social housing neighborhoods are not only thinking of the immediate present. They are trying to imagine what they would like to have in ten years. The reality is that citizens are ready to take risks that many political leaders, even local ones, won't take.

Social empowerment

Poitiers, France

In 1974, the Plan Urbanisme Construction Architecture (PUCA) launched a consultation for experimental projects in the field of housing. The future founders of Architecturestudio, who won the competition, together with their colleague Yves-Jean Laval, produced the 274 dwellings of the Grand'Goule following the principle of Shared Activity Areas (SAA) within the dwellings. These SAAs accounted for approximately 15% of the housing area and were distributed on a level-by-level basis with double-height volumes. They were complemented by outdoor sheltered animation spaces, in connection with public spaces. An active participation process was carried out with future users in order to define the contents and methods of occupation. However, after several years of functioning to the satisfaction of the inhabitants who contributed to their implementation, their governance declined and these spaces were abandoned.

Integrated into the Beaulieu district, a priority area which is subject to a major rehabilitation campaign to reduce household energy bills and improve the security and attractiveness of the site, the Grand'Goule is now questioning its future. In 2022, the elected representatives of Grand Poitiers engaged in an innovative co-design partnership with all stakeholders: residents, users, the City and the social housing provider EKIDOM, in which Architecturestudio, with the support of a PhD student, played a facilitating role (collection of photo archives, guided walks, workshops on models, chairing of discussions, etc.).

This action-research approach, which won the call for expressions of interest entitled "Committed to the quality of tomorrow's housing," launched by the Ministries of Culture and Housing, should make it possible to produce programs that can be supported by local stakeholders over the long term. Accompanied by a renewed site-wide programming with the creation of an intergenerational residence combining students and seniors and the transformation of car parks into artists' studios, the governance of the shared activity areas, strengthened in terms of the density of spaces and services, will henceforth be jointly managed by the lessor and a residents' association.

By giving substance to citizens' aspirations to develop a mixed program in which the diversity of users enriches the common experience and the sense of "working together," through the creation of the commons, this project aims to develop approaches and best practices to address the social and spatial exclusion of residents in a disadvantaged neighborhood.

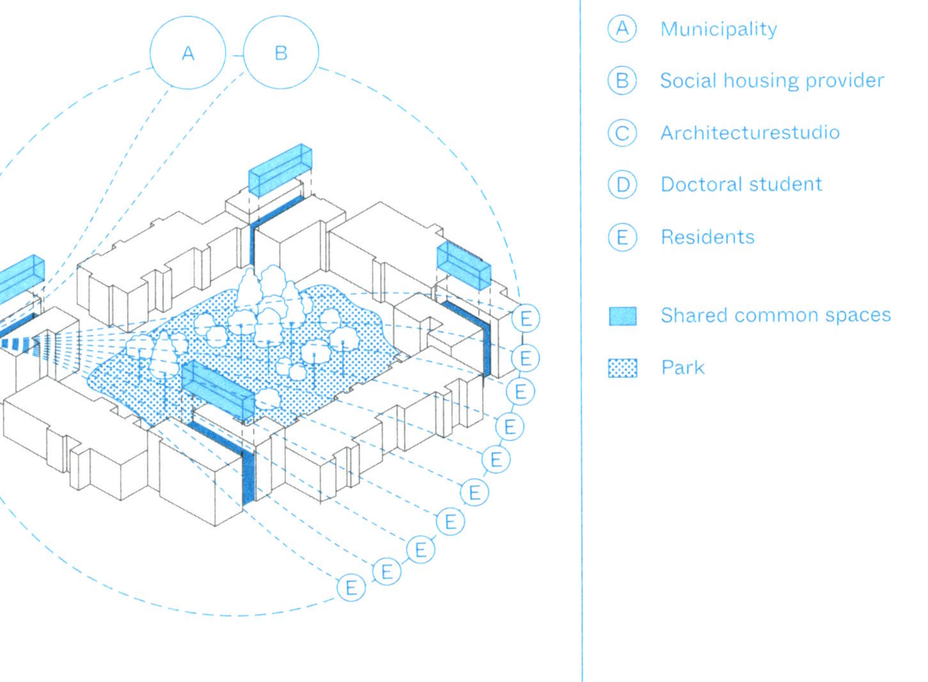

(A) Municipality
(B) Social housing provider
(C) Architecturestudio
(D) Doctoral student
(E) Residents
Shared common spaces
Park

Alongside the expanded skillsets of these three planning systems, tools for mediation have become important. Today, systems aimed towards the users of buildings—*Assistance à maîtrise d'usage*—are becoming increasingly effective and complement those of project management. This newer system, based on participatory practices implemented since the 1980s, integrates expertise coming from the social sciences (sociology, social psychology, anthropology, etc.) and connects with professionals of space (designers, ergonomists, architects, technicians) to involve users both increasingly in the planning but also in the future life of the building or the development in question. This change, along with the increased complexity of actors involved, transforms the organization of work and alters the distribution of roles in the production of the city and in regional planning.

Alain Bretagnolle

Franck, while we are talking about the commons: as actors involved in territorial transformations, we are living through a paradigm shift in which we have gone from an idea of man in his environment to an awareness of inhabited environments—that is, an awareness of other non-human living beings that are sharing the earth's ecosystems. In your opinion, what is the position that allows us to consider this new notion of the world, this new representation of the world, and that might allow us to repair what has already been partially destroyed?

Franck Boutté

I've spoken a lot about systems theory, complexity, induced effects, equilibrium, and indeed there is this question of temporality. We see these curves, the exponential growth of these curves, the great acceleration: we are there. What's happening today is going faster and faster, it's true, but it is the legacy of the decisions made yesterday and the day before yesterday, just as the decisions we make today won't have effects until tomorrow and the day after tomorrow. It's complicated, and we don't immediately see the effect of the decisions we make. However, it seems to me that we finally reaching a period of maturity. I don't know if you share this observation. I'm trying to be a bit positive after having said that for fifteen years we were in a paradigm of over-optimization. This question of temporality is a bit of a *mise en abyme* all the same. In ecological strategies, a distinction is made between those which aim for mitigation and those which aim for adaptation. With mitigation we try to reduce—reduce energy consumption, reduce carbon emissions—to prevent things from happening, to prevent the phenomenon of climate change. But climate change is here; we don't have a choice except to adapt. If we had read the IPCC reports more quickly, we would have seen that the IPCC didn't say, "If you do this, and this, nothing will happen and everything will be fine." There have always been ideas of scenarios, of trajectories, in these reports, and the trajectories can be either more or less alarming, more or less exciting. There are possibilities for action within these trajectories, but the trajectories exist. Accepting this changes things significantly for our professions. Until now we've asked stakeholders in the city to be good at taking perspective, to be "perspectivists." Today, we must be good at looking towards the future, "prospectivists." It changes everything, moving from per- to pro-spective. This means better anticipating, finally, what could happen tomorrow. The conditional is important. It means that this future cannot be entirely known, and that there is necessarily indetermination and uncertainty. Today we must know how to move forward and to carry out projects that integrate all of this. As such we must necessarily take risks,

Residential consultation

Toulouse, France

The Borderouge district, located to the north-east of the historic center of Toulouse, consists of a scattered residential area with very few facilities or services. Characteristic of fringe urban planning, it is currently in decline. The City began its requalification by means of a Priority Development Zone.

Located twenty minutes from the city center by metro and in the immediate vicinity of the motorway interchange, the area benefits from an efficient public transport service. The new district, with its 140 hectares of housing, offices, shops, equipment and services, creates an urban polarity. As a figurehead, the Totem tertiary building marks the entrance of the city and constitutes a signal, a vector of new urban and architectural intentions. The environmental and social model has been designed in extensive consultation with the inhabitants since the first study phases: interviews and workshops enabled us to take their aspirations into account and to adapt the project's morphology and program accordingly. The building's large central garden will therefore be open to the city and the ground floor will be given over to local shops.

A tall, compact building, facing the main axes, descends in open bleachers towards the heart of the block, which it protects from noise pollution. Small contiguous volumes are installed in contact with the neighboring residential fabric. The ensemble is structured around a protected central garden conducive to encounters. The terraced, wood-structure building, with two to five levels braced by the elevator shafts, frees the floors of any layout constraints and guarantees flexibility and mutability.

Planters are incorporated into the double skin of the facades. The building therefore follows seasonal and climatic rhythms, constantly changing its appearance according to the cycle of the plants. As a carrier of biodiversity and diversified spaces, landscaping is the external extension of the architectural project, promoting its integration in a wooded context.

The eco-responsible project meets current environmental requirements and has become one of the key elements in the requalification of the Borderouge district. As a carrier of new values of use, it contributes to the empowerment of each resident in terms of their living and working environment, and to the awareness of their impact on the environment.

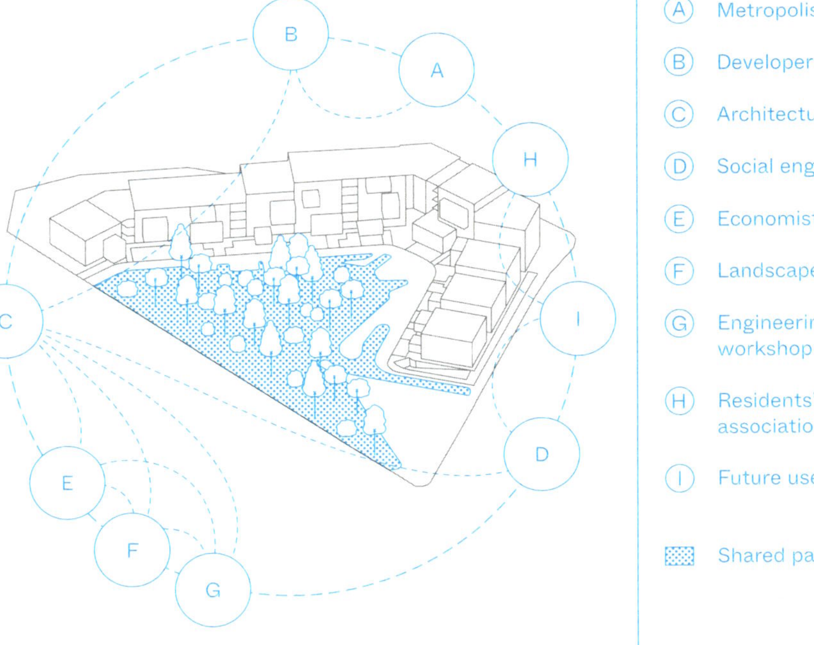

(A) Metropolis
(B) Developers
(C) Architecturestudio
(D) Social engineer
(E) Economist
(F) Landscape designer
(G) Engineering workshop
(H) Residents' association
(I) Future users
Shared park

Involving different actors, mediators, experts, future users: this isn't a novel idea in architecture or urban design, but this opening up of governance isn't motivated by the same intentions as it was in the past. Today issues of governance incorporate the importance of communication in our societies and the ecological imperative of taking care of our environment. This double characteristic shifts our relationship to governance into the field of ethics. The question of taking action is necessarily that of taking equitable action: first towards future inhabitants and known users, but also towards those we don't know yet, future generations. And towards those essential parts of our global ecosystems that cannot speak for themselves: animals, plants, minerals, elements. How do we ensure fair governance in projects while considering the non-human?

although today we are in a system of hyper-insurance. If you say to your insurance company in ten years that you are innovating, they'll tell you, "I'm removing your ability to insure." It's very complicated. Integrating external data into our discipline and being transversal, multidisciplinary, can help us to be better at creating scenarios. The word "narrative" was used. How do we manage to build narratives that engage us collectively, integrating the indeterminate as a value?
Could the notion of the commons allow this? This term interests me. It's an ancient term, existing already in Roman law.
The commons belong, along with all public things, to that which is not owned. The question is quite nice: how do we manage to intervene today on resources without owners? This doesn't mean being without active agents, which are non-human living beings. The world of animals, of plants, but also climatic phenomena and its manifestations—heat waves, wind, rain, floods—are phenomena that we must be able to integrate today.
The earth is our commons, and it is a non-human living being.
Another idea is to say that we take on only what is already built up, or filled in. That is, we aim to resolve the issue of the ecological transition through optimizing what is already built up. We ask those areas to consume less, to be less carbon-intensive, to use more sustainable resources, and we don't consider open areas—the unbuilt areas. There is little consideration of unbuilt areas which are nevertheless the site of these ecological agents, these non-human living beings. This is, for me, a real issue that we can discuss today, the question of open areas. We have just talked about adaptation and adaptation plays an essential role in these open areas, just as mitigation plays an important role in filled in areas. This is interesting. For example, we can only integrate or respond to heat waves by working with open areas, we can only work on logics of fertility—fertile spaces, non-fertile spaces—essentially through working on open areas; we can only move forward on the question of water, or water scarcity, through working on open areas. There is therefore a new challenge of working on open areas. In the end we must become actors in the management of the unbuilt.

Alain Bretagnolle

You answered my question, after a very rich detour, thank you.

Franck Boutté

Ecology mainly plays out, originally, in histories of continuity. Human interventions create discontinuity, or in other words at some point we separate, we create a limit, we set an administrative boundary, we set a cadastral boundary, and the last of these discontinuities (or the ultimate discontinuity) is that we built a wall to define an interior, an exterior. In fact,

Female governance

Lomé, Togo

The Grand Marché in Adawlato, in the heart of Lomé, developed with the trade in fabrics on the initiative of a few women from modest backgrounds, the matriarchs of the large families who now control the trade. Traditional motifs inspired by daily life, rituals, and the attributes of chiefdoms served as the basis for the creation of the fabrics. Since Togolese society is of matriarchal inspiration, the Nana Bens (Nana meaning female chief and Bens referring to the Mercedes cars that they were the first to import) are naturally in charge of business. In the wake of the fires that ravaged the market, they became our partners in developing the program and imagining the project.

The large market—150 meters long—is designed as an efficient and porous urban system, intended to connect the various axes that surround it using a contextual architectural writing. A walkway, originating in a small street and structured around a central space by ascending ramps, borders the different stalls and serves four levels of shops, culminating in the uppermost terrace. In the congested city center, this vast, panoramic public space, sheltered by a canopy which revisits the patterns and colors of the traditional fabrics in homage to the Nana Bens, hosts a garden, a craft village, restaurants, and meeting and conference facilities.

The large rammed earth walls and the lacework of compressed earth bricks bring a strong inertia to the building. Naturally ventilated, it offers optimal conditions of hygrometric comfort.

The Nana Bens' governance of the project, which is socially-anchored and uses materials from local supply chains, integrates and combines the stakes of the different communities into a single ensemble, by co-designing a program that goes beyond a strict response to a need and by creating a new place for life and exchange in the heart of the capital.

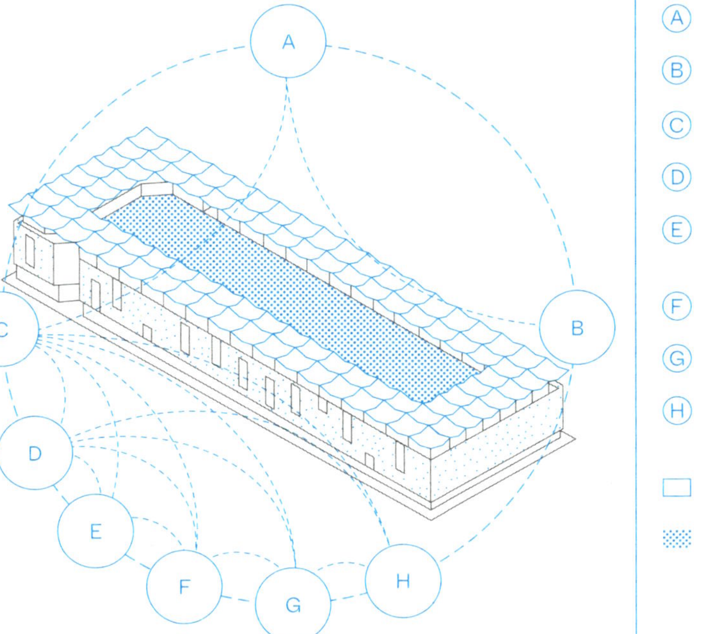

(A) Government
(B) Users
(C) Architecturestudio
(D) Associated Architects
(E) Association specialized in earth construction
(F) Engineer
(G) Developer
(H) Economist
Velum
Public space

↑ → Lomé, Togo.

Governance has taken on a new dimension in society since the early 2000s:[7] it has become more inclusive of citizens. In France this was reflected first in texts and then in practice. With the increase in ecological concerns, governance has become considerably more horizontal. It is no longer a top-down practice through which the decision-maker informs stakeholders of the project, but rather is a process both integrated with and parallel to the project, aiming at the sharing of interests between different actors. In short, it is a question of recognizing forms of expertise other than technocratic. Today, governance adopts ever more complex mechanisms to facilitate concerted actions between more diverse actors, representing interests that are more varied and connected to public life in more diverse ways—that is, actions between people with different statuses, different credentials, and especially different degrees of power.

7. For example, in the Charter of Architects' Commitment to Sustainable Development, architects are called by the Order to work in consultation (2005); in the SRU laws (2000), Town Planning Code, article L300-2 [9] and in the Environmental Code, article L121-1 [10] (2002), in the New Charter of Athens.

all major ecological issues play out in continuous phenomena. There is thus value in working to repair discontinuities.

Romain Boursier
The articulation of scales is also necessary to restore the relevance of these commons. We can find it useful to define the commons at a very small scale, and to work with other stakeholders, other actors to see how these commons are articulated and made coherent.

Emmanuelle Cosse
I also think there is the question of legitimacy. Who feels sufficiently legitimate in public space to enforce their notion of a commons? We must find more just modes of governance and regulation to build this legitimacy. Today we are very much following the dogma, or the fiction: "What does the resident think?" As if only the resident considers the city and as if the resident only has one side. There are not only residents and users; there are also businesses, public services, etc.
The interesting aspect of this revival of the question of the common and the commons, that we've seen in politics, is that it replaced and reactivated another question—"What is public service?"—when we have a public service that is increasingly commercial and monetized, and that we no longer speak about in terms of common good.
Today we talk about commons in movements of societal mobilization. I'm thinking of the campaigns in Barcelona for access to housing, which led Ada Colau to become Barcelona's mayor. The movement was called *en Comú*, "in Common," and it wasn't just a political platform but rather a mobilization of users, living in a territory, who wanted to change the status quo. They were displaced from their city by tourism and speculation. They therefore implemented measures that connected ecology and social regulation. Essentially, they achieved what politics had not yet been able to.

Romain Boursier
Franck was talking about increasingly violent climatic phenomena which bring up questions on the future of territories. How do we approach these questions? How do we prepare? How do we mobilize various actors around these questions? The coastline for example...

Emmanuelle Cosse
The coastline... I find this subject fascinating. It was only in 2015, if I'm not mistaken, that France started its project of remaking its coastlines. There are also state agencies trying to remake the coasts of all overseas territories. We've been forced to remake this coastline because we've realized that it was

Inhabited view cones

Chartres, France

At the gates of the historic city of Chartres, the Northeast Plateau, composed of large military and commercial land holdings, is one of the last territories where the city can establish its future development. In the background, the silhouette of the Notre-Dame de Chartres Cathedral, which was listed as a UNESCO World Heritage Site in 1979, reveals the exceptional landscape potential of the site.

The requalification project for the city entrance involves transforming the 230-hectare site into a new, large, landscaped and recreational amenity, increasing its reach across the inhabited area. Locally, it must redefine the borders of urbanization with the great landscape of Beauce, connect the different neighborhoods, and develop the major public spaces of future life in Chartres.

In this context, how can we rethink the composition of the public domain and the private buildings in order to create new and remarkable views of the monument? How to integrate this symbolic landmark of the territory into a reinterpreted logic of *montjoie*?

Having proposed the principle of "inhabited view cones," we specified the anticipated arrangements by calling on the skills of a doctoral student who is working on exploratory processes using optimization algorithms applied to architectural and urban design.

Throughout this work, which required us to build a generative optimization model, various successive phases made it possible to analyze the quality of views from the buildable templates towards the Cathedral, to generate blocks according to the two criteria of views and density, and then to select all the solutions that meet these criteria on a *Pareto front*.

The city is now in possession of an efficient digital model, presenting new optima *montjoie* buildable templates, which are set out in the urban regulations and to which each of the future architects can contribute an improved design with new elements and criteria.

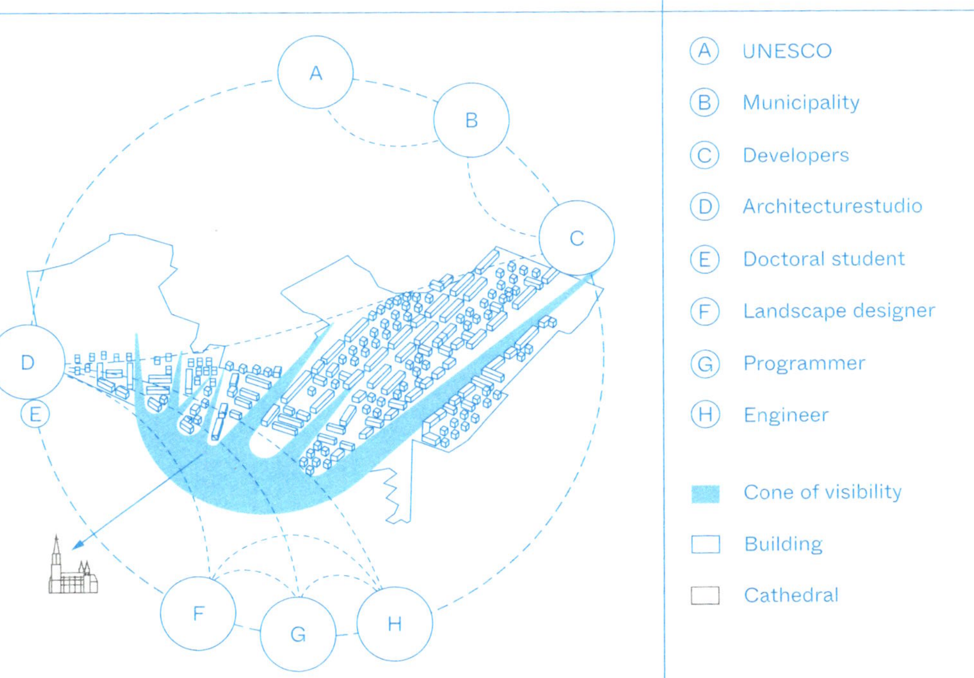

(A) UNESCO
(B) Municipality
(C) Developers
(D) Architecturestudio
(E) Doctoral student
(F) Landscape designer
(G) Programmer
(H) Engineer

Cone of visibility
Building
Cathedral

Chartres, France.

Working with elements of language means leaving behind jargon to move towards a lexical field that can be shared, towards a common and political language. This means not only making all forms of collectives "speak" without reducing or simplifying the words, but also integrating and synthesizing these divergent, often contradictory words in order to translate them into the elements of projects: programs, budgets, actions. The great difficulty thus lies in the imbalance of forces present within government apparatuses, and the difficult objective of maintaining complexity to make commonality. Hence the importance of user control and user management assistants—guarantors of a silent but clearly essential voice, that of the project's recipients. Hence also the importance of project managers and their assistance, whether public or private, in keeping the door open to a variety of actors. And hence, finally, the importance of the project manager's position in overseeing an interface where the high number of specific interests sometimes clouds evidence of common interests.

extremely worn away, and that we had to react. But behind that... you all know the story of this condominium, Le Signal in Lacanau. In the aftermath of major storms, the sea came up to the foot of building. It was necessary to expropriate people who had bought their apartment only decades before. The Barnier law was not at all suited to that situation. This hypothesis hadn't been predicted. The question also comes up in the case of Lacanau or Porge: can these cities stay where they are established or do they have to move, and when? We have already moved cities in the Middle Ages. We've also moved train stations, Gare du Nord and Gare Montparnasse for example. Today, the issue is the erosion of the coastline. We have to move territories, but where to? I don't have the answer. Ten kilometers away? Twenty kilometers away? Do we take the opportunity to no longer build in extremely fragile areas? Or do we continue to tell ourselves that we must still build on the coast, because the coast is what the French want, and that there is a market for it?

How do we bring consensus to public decision-making?

It is now extremely difficult for elected officials who try to discuss territorial plans to create a community committed to deciding this future together. These are extremely vicious, hard battles, even when the stakes are vital. We all remember the consequences of the storm Xynthia: we could see at the time that there was a disrespect for planning regulations. But with Xynthia, because there were casualties, drastic action was carried out that destroyed an entire neighborhood. Nonetheless, we haven't moved the rest of the city and so there will surely be many other territories exposed to other terrible phenomena. It's true that it's painful to explain to people that maybe their children, their grandchildren won't have a future where they are today. There aren't many public authorities to have the courage to say this. At least in France, other countries might be more mature on these issues.

Romain Boursier

You say that these are extremely difficult subjects, but is it possible to create scenarios around these transformations? José-Manuel, in the work that you carry out with cities, do you see potential for a co-construction of common narratives on these subjects?

José-Manuel Gonçalvès

The desire today to look towards the future, as Franck said, is something that we also feel in the arts, where we see extremely strong trends that allow us to study certain phenomena, in particular thanks to the digital.

The rapprochement with science brings together two sets of expertise, that of artists and that of scientists. Contemporary

Sensitive envelope

Bordeaux, France

As the region's first tertiary building with Positive Energy and the first building in the ZAC Saint Jean Belcier on the banks of the Port de la Lune, facing the Garonne, the headquarters of the Caisse d'Épargne Aquitaine-Poitou-Charentes affirms the values of the institution and takes its place in the Bordeaux landscape with an elegant architecture providing panoramic views of the river.

One of the programmatic challenges consisted in creating a permeability between the Garonne and the Halle Debat-Ponsan, the former Bordeaux slaughterhouse whose reinforced cement structure has been preserved as part of the urban renewal project. To express the desired transparency, we extruded a glass prism using the dimensions of the plot. This crystalline prism is enriched by a series of provisions intended to enhance the use of the building: patios, terraces with external connecting stairs and pockets of greenery. It is placed on a double height pedestal that houses the functions of representation and reception, as well as the meeting rooms and the concierge. The Deck that overlooks it offers spaces of relaxation for the staff: cafeteria, restaurant, kitchen and activity rooms with panoramic views of the river. The upper stratum of the prism is devoted to the offices and crowned by the boardroom.

The thermal performance of the envelope is ensured by a double-skin glass façade, which presents itself as an antithesis of low consumption 'thermos buildings," since it reverses the usual ratio between 70% opacity and 30% transparency to offer bright interior spaces and wide views of the Garonne. Parametric studies enabled us to create a more opaque façade where the building is 14 meters deep and a more transparent one where its width is 24 meters. We guarantee 70% natural light in the building's central walkways.

The façade complex incorporates ultra-reflective, automatically-controlled blinds which enable the reflection of solar inputs towards the outside through extra-clear glazing, whilst regulating the penetration of natural light in the interior spaces. The thermal buffer formed by the façade, combined with this controlled sun protection, enables the inertia of the exposed concrete slabs of all the ceilings to produce cold in summer and heat in winter, thereby significantly reducing the energy consumption of the building, as confirmed by the post-occupancy testing campaigns carried out by the CSTB.

At the prow of the building, marking the entrance of the bank with a large bamboo patio, the façades bend and generate a horizontal canopy that appears to float, supported between the two façades, 24 meters apart and without any apparent structure. The roof is covered with photovoltaic cells that fold back to form sunshades on the building's south-facing rear façade.

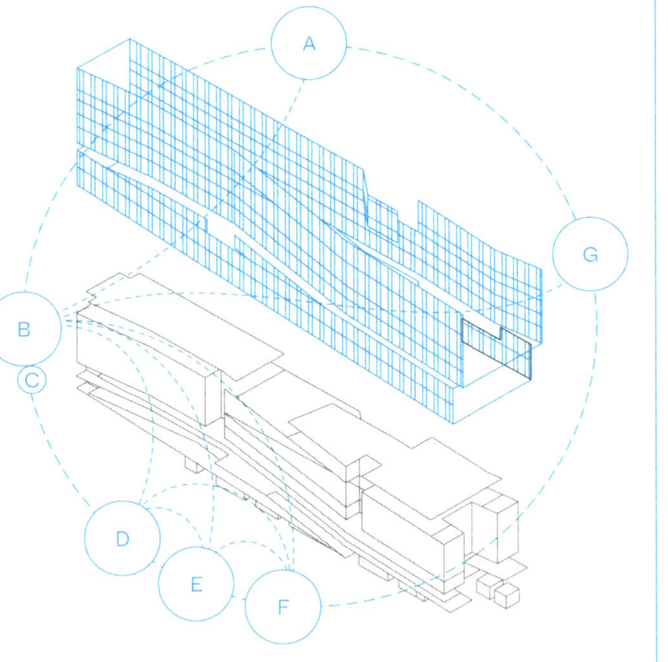

(A) Project manager
(B) Architecturestudio
(C) Doctoral student
(D) Engineer environmental
(E) Structural and fluid engineer
(F) Acoustic engineer
(G) User
Optimized variable façade

Headquarter of Caisse
d'Épargne Aquitaine
Poitou-Charentes,
Bouygues Immobilier,
Architecturestudio.

Bordeaux, France, 2017.

The commons require the constitution of shared spaces for discussion. From a philosophical point of view, ecological governance has been a consideration since the end of the 1970s. The ecological crisis, or the awareness of a limited and fragile world, thus poses new ethical problems in its engagement of a collective responsibility. The person responsible for the consequences of human actions is no longer "man" as a subject but rather "man" as representative of humanity. The problem of the ecological crisis therefore requires a planetary macro-ethic, and this constitution of humans as inter-subjects is a new paradigm in the philosophy of the twentieth century. Peter Sloterdijk and Bruno Latour reformulated this shift by asserting our exit from the modern space made up of objects at our disposition, and our entry in a new world populated by inter-subjects; that is, by living beings dependent on one another.

art is moving from an interpretation of the visible to a formalization of the invisible. Something is changing; artists are in the process of entering a future-oriented, prospective dimension by trying to make visible phenomena that are currently not visible, and by collecting data, especially from scientists. Artists have become hybrids… as soon as they have mastered a few elements of science, we immediately think that they have become scientists. Not at all. They take a number of elements that allow them to imagine forms, and from these forms they produce narratives. The new narratives of artists consist of both an understanding of reality and of an extremely strong relationship to living things. And even if we have always had futuristic narratives, or stories—especially in cinema—these were often catastrophic, or conversely overly embellished, as we see in Avatar or Dune, for example: films in which we manage to identify things because they are still in our fictional field. Today we are witnessing things that go beyond our usual representations, and that place us within new fictions. It isn't simply the digital that allows this; rather, it is the communities of experts who come together and who trust one another. I once had the opportunity to work with archaeologists, and we realized that they had produced fine works and images but we weren't at all aware of their work. We then did an exercise that we called *Materialité de l'invisible* (Materiality of the Invisible), on the forms this "invisible" might take, on the unnamed.

Franck Boutté

On this question of making visible the invisible… this is a motto in our firm. Our first publication, thirteen years ago, was titled "Invisible Virtue," which is to say that in the end there is something that prevents us from taking action. How is it that we are so aware of what is happening, but we aren't able to act? For the past fifteen years or so I have been addressing objects that are particularly invisible, and I believe this question of making visible—of naming things, of being able to render them societal subjects and thus to engage with them—this is a subject to consider. It's true that energy isn't very visible, apart of course from its production (if we put solar panels on roofs, for example). That's why, in trying to make things visible, at some point we end up making caricatures, like sprinkling buildings with solar panels. Carbon is also not very visible, unless we say, "It's wood." A second caricature. Comfort is not very visible, questions of health are not very visible, air quality is not very visible. One has to go look up the statistics to see the number of deaths linked to air quality around the world. It's difficult to take action because ecological issues cannot be seen, cannot be heard, and cannot be felt. The health crisis has meanwhile made certain things real and entirely visible,

Modeling light

Amiens, France

Architectural research on generative design enables us to express the complexity of a program through the simplicity of an active facade.

The Faire Faces Institute has given rise to the creation of the first study and research center devoted to disfigurement. This program, unique in the contemporary scientific landscape, is strategically located at the entrance of the Amiens teaching hospital.

Spread over a little more than 3,000 m^2, the research center combines laboratories, offices, a library, an operating hall, two MRIs, an amphitheater, an exhibition center, catering facilities and technical premises, to ensure the proper functioning of this heterogeneous ensemble.

A base, anchored in the sloping ground, supports a plateau which opens onto the vast landscape, sheltered by a horizontal building which is raised up off the ground on stilts. The sociability and meeting spaces are arranged on this plateau in the heart of the building, surrounded by both the research plateau in the upper floors and the teaching plateau in the basement. The design of the spaces presents a strong, direct relationship to the exterior, which showcases an extensive landscaped project; the exhibition and catering spaces open onto a terrace overlooking the green horizon of the Picardy hills.

The challenge was to give simple expression to the complexity of a medical research program. Naturally, we were motivated by the parallels between the primordial role of the face in human interaction and that of the façade in the understanding of the building. We needed no further prompting to use the architectural research program that had been set up at the agency around a young architect researcher, associated with a CNRS laboratory.

The façade, which expresses the project and houses the laboratories and offices, is characterized by large, fixed sun shields whose optimal orientation and geometry were defined thanks to a written digital program that integrated the parameters of exposure, brightness, glare and views.

We believe that the search for new forms of beauty has its rightful place in architecture. This search can be enhanced by architectural research that subjects digital algorithms to human sensitivity in generative design. In a symmetrical approach, in which the sensitivity of the human eye was analyzed by the digital tool, the artist Michel Paysant produced a monumental eye-tracking artwork which we printed on the concrete of the façade of the foundation, face-to-face with the landscape.

The agency's research program has pursued the study of the Faire Faces Institute after the completion of the building in order to refine the process, even though it can no longer be used for the project.

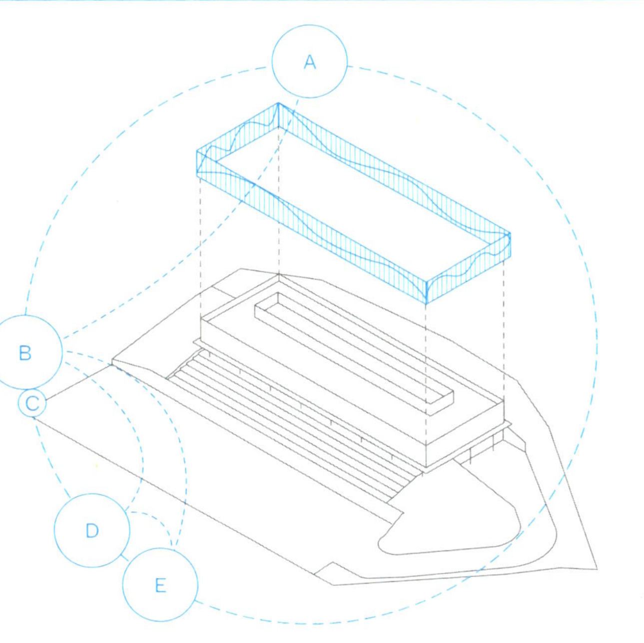

(A) Project manager
(B) Architecturestudio
(C) Doctoral student
(D) Engineer
(E) Economist

Parametric façade

Faire Faces Institute,
Amiens Picardy University
Hospital,
Architecturestudio.

Amiens, France, 2022.

A Meaningful Framework for Discourse

"Act so that the effects of your action are compatible with the permanence of genuine human life."[8] Hans Jonas' categorial imperative defined an ethic of responsibility of humans towards future generations. He thus sets out a principle of action which links an existing actor to an actor who does not exist. This text is fundamental in that it opens up the ethics of action to contemporary ecological questions. With his *Imperative of Responsibility*, **Jonas designated human beings as responsible for what the future can be. The volume's ethical principle can be formulated as follows: our actions today are responsible only in that they preserve the possibility of action, under the same conditions, for future generations.**

8. Hans Jonas, *The Imperative of Responsibility: In Search of an Ethics for the Technological Age*, University of Chicago Press, 1984 (1979).

and this was helpful for both environmental and ecological issues. We said to ourselves: "The quality of public space is important, the size of a street is important, the surface area and even the volume of my home are important, it's important to have an outdoor space, the ceiling height is important, it's important to be able to ventilate and therefore to have a building that ventilates itself." But to be able to self-ventilate, of course, it wasn't enough for a dwelling to span the building and to be able to open the windows—what is essential is that the windows could open onto a non-polluted area, and an area without excessive noise, for example. The actors shifted their views after the health crisis, and when we told them, "The first requirement is perhaps to have an outdoor space in every dwelling," whereas before it was "No," it became: "Yes, it's true, why not." Ceiling height has become a quality, etc.

The summer of 2022, which everyone will remember, also drives us to no longer produce a project without discussing its comfort levels in summer, not to mention resilience, adaptation to climate change—all this makes it possible to put regulations in place. You have to be able to imagine things to be able to implement them. We have to ensure that all these issues which are so prominently visible can be named in order to discuss them, to have a debate, and thus it because a societal issue. Crises allow this. It's dramatic, but we often learn from crises.

Emmanuelle Cosse

What is certain, for me, is that our wealth makes us completely immature. On the issue of regulations, Franck, you are absolutely right. It's the immaturity of the actors, although not the only factor, which means that you must in fact have regulations that are at times ridiculous in order to get things moving. ZNA is like an earthquake for many people. I'm not saying it's the smartest thing, but it's unbelievable that it gets people moving, elected officials, because all at once we tell them: "You can, you cannot. You might be able today, you won't be able to in fifteen years."

To be a bit provocative: I've participated in many discussions since the first lockdown on the attractiveness of a "greener" living environment, and in the end I became very weary of the simplistic nature of the reflection. Many spoke about the appeal of the average life and green spaces but very few agreed to debate the feeling of overcrowding. Residents didn't just want green space, they wanted more square meters to live in! There are people who had a fine experience of the lockdown in their Parisian apartment, 200 square meters for three people, which is very livable, with or without an exterior space. The problem is when you have five people living in fifty-five square meters… In addition, the Covid crisis also had the merit of highlighting—finally!—all the people who are holding the country together on

Circular triangle

Paris, France

The Triangle Eole Evangile, located at the Porte d'Aubervilliers in Paris, was one of the sites of the Réinventer Paris contest—a call for innovative urban projects launched by the City of Paris in 2014. To develop a social and solidarity-based project on this atypical plot, which is hemmed in by SNCF tracks, we surrounded ourselves with a multidisciplinary team: the Belgian developer Revive, which develops projects exclusively located on urban or industrial wastelands, the promoter Nacarat, the Emmaus Défi association, which develops sites devoted to reintegration, the Bellastock association, which studied the reuse of materials within the project, and the designer Ramy Fishler, as well as institutional partners: the Institut National de l'Économie Circulaire and the Université Condorcet.

This team gathered together with an ambition that went beyond an architectural project: to design a pioneering neighborhood in terms of circularity and waste control. The notion of "circularity" took shape in different aspects of the future neighborhood: food—with the creation of a local agricultural ecosystem and the presence of an urban farm; energy—with the creation of clean energy for neighborhood use through the establishment of a anaerobic digestion plant, powered by organic waste collected on site, and the reversibility and scalability of functions.

The project was organized according to a programmatic mix of horizontality and verticality: tertiary cluster, urban farm, mixed housing/office buildings, workshops, retail outlets and services. We developed the framework and the modularity of the spaces with an emphasis on rationality, the economy of the construction, and scalability: the buildings are designed according to a module of 5.5 m across. Their three-module width enables the integration of all wet rooms and walkways in the central module. The standardized distribution of ducts and cores enabled us to anticipate the future reversibility of offices to housing and vice versa. At the prow of the triangular plot, a research center for the circular economy is housed in an emblematic building that marks the entrance of the site from the future metro station.

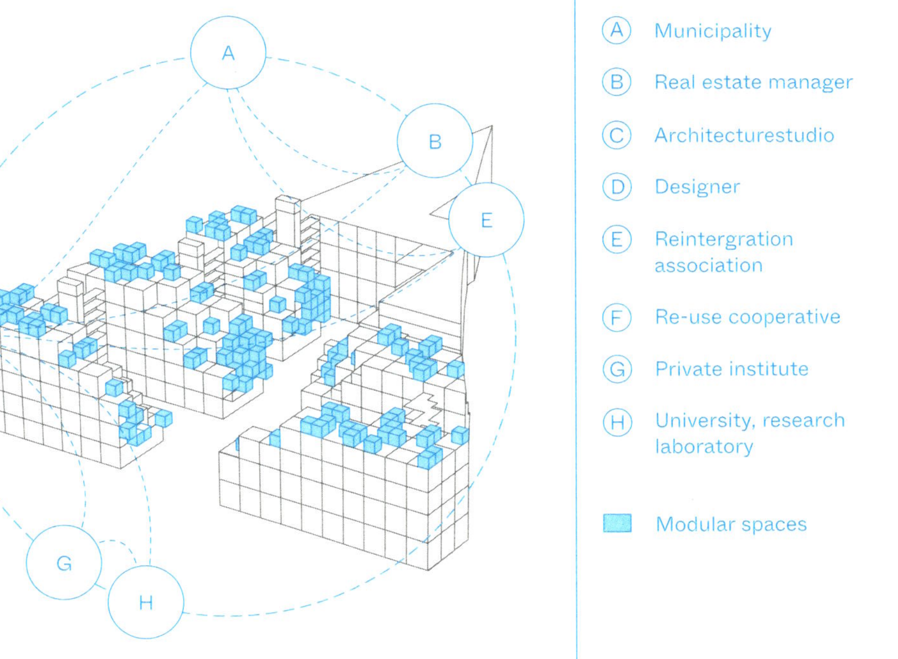

(A) Municipality
(B) Real estate manager
(C) Architecturestudio
(D) Designer
(E) Reintergration association
(F) Re-use cooperative
(G) Private institute
(H) University, research laboratory
Modular spaces

It puts forward an asymmetrical relationship: we are responsible for human beings who cannot be responsible for us. This principle can be extrapolated to the non-human: Michel Serre has proposed replacing the social contract with a *Natural Contract*,[9] while Bruno Latour wrote his *Esquisse d'un parlement des choses*, an "outline for a parliament of things."[10] Several years later (1983), Karl-Otto Apel put forward another response, a counterproposal to that of Jonas: the ethics of discourse. For him, ethical questions demanded restrained, loyal, and sincere negotiations, which he called *discourse*. He thus distinguished himself from the alarmism of Jonas, whom he accused of focusing only on crises and of proposing only an emergency solution, a state of exception, and not a valid ethical regime. Moreover, for Apel the one-sided notion of responsibility proposed by Jonas would also increase our guilt towards future generations, and so would not promote action.

9. Michel Serres, *The Natural Contract*, University of Michigan Press, 1995 (1990).

10. Bruno Latour, "Esquisse d'un Parlement des choses," *Ecologie & politique* 2018/1 (n°56): 47-64 (Original publication 1994).

a daily basis: the famous essential workers. But did we really push the subject far enough, asking: Where do they live? Why are they housed so far from urban centers? Why didn't they have the right to live next to their place of work? We are well aware of this phenomenon in Île-de-France, and elsewhere. If we are sincere, the crisis did not really change the situation in terms of rebalancing the social housing supply in SRU communities. On the other hand, you're right, Franck, it did change approaches to the quality of what we're doing: adjusting the ceiling height, having real and spacious kitchens, etc.

Previously we were talking about land and ZNA, zero net artificialization. I wanted to come back to the idea of visibility. To make things visible is an old political battle. My political engagement was born in the fight against AIDS almost thirty years ago now. And our battle was to bring out into the open something that was hidden, using methods of visibility and with a large focus on cultural intervention. The other battle of "visibilization" was the big debate on air pollution. Today we don't talk about it at all, because we still struggle to make these impacts visible. Despite everything, debates on nature, on bringing nature back to cities, finally allows us to return slightly to the question of pollution. We struggle to make this visible, also because people are afraid and this keeps them from looking. We're in an anxiety-provoking period, and eco-anxiety is a reality. This might be where it's important to return to the question of common objects; it might be a way to find ways to not be completely paralyzed.

Franck Boutté

Crises render a phenomenon hyper-real and make us react. For example, when we hear the IPCC scenarios: an increase of 1.5°, in fact, everyone finds that cool. The problem is which indicator you give in order to say, "Listen, we're talking about an average, at a certain place it's so many days above 30°." It's actually necessary to work on extremes in a representation, to an extent. You have to be measured because eco-anxiety effectively prevents any dynamism and mobilization. At the moment you're dealing with several consecutive days of a heat wave, with fires everywhere, a water shortage everywhere, a low agricultural yield, energy costs that have increased tenfold, then you say to yourself: "We really have to get moving." Except that these figures were actually in the report, they just weren't the ones that were communicated. It's for this reason there's the question: on what should I communicate to provoke engagement?

How can this phenomenon of eco-anxiety be controlled? At the same time, what won't put the crowd to sleep?

Even on the question of the coastline: if we're talking about a centimeter of sea level rise, it isn't visible, but if we project that on the Netherlands then it hurts. The scenarios of +1, +2,

Site energy

Issy-les-Moulineaux, France

At the cutting edge of the Smart City, in a vast territory of economic development with high added value, the very attractive city of Issy-Les-Moulineaux promotes the emergence of innovative urban and architectural proposals. Already equipped with a swimming pool and a school based on these principles, it is also a forerunner because of its interest in the Feng Shui philosophy, embodied by a large-scale apartment building and services. Feng Shui, literally "wind and water," is a branch of Chinese science which has been used in Asia for millennia, governing many constructions in order to harmonize the environmental energy (Qi) of a place, thereby bringing health, prosperity and well-being to its inhabitants. These principles have been integrated into the design of the project, including the orientation and organization of the spaces, their geometry and materials, up to and including the choice of the name Ôm, the symbol of the source of the universe.

The project concerns the rehabilitation of a site sandwiched between the avenue de Verdun and a steep embankment supporting a railway axis. An impasse overlooks the work of art. In the precepts of Feng Shui, the relationship to the energies released by the environment, the landscape and the botanical elements is fundamental. This strength of the site is summarized here by the embankment. This oasis of greenery and fresh air in the middle of the metropolis, which we identified in the green belt of the PLU, was our anchoring point. The construction of the site establishes a telluric object, whose fluid forms are based on the embankment and whose inhabited strata adapt to their context with open views in all directions. Ôm is also environmentally efficient thanks to innovative energy, water and waste management systems and the landscaping of the site.

The square layout of the patio, a meeting place, and the gradual slope of the rounded, south-facing terraces produce various housing typologies above a base of services that includes many shared spaces.

Ôm is a habitat common not only to humans but also to all kinds of plant and animal species thanks to the number of planted terraces and the sanctuarization of part of the green roof, designed to accommodate and preserve biodiversity. Following the principles of Feng Shui, Ôm proposes an inhabited microcosm where all living things can coexist in harmony with each other and with the cosmos.

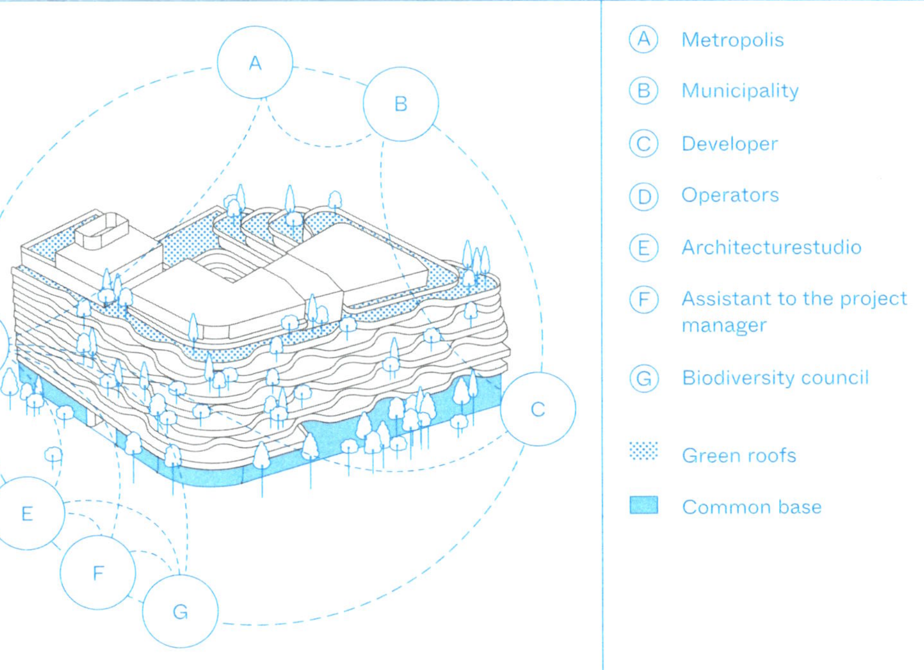

Ⓐ Metropolis
Ⓑ Municipality
Ⓒ Developer
Ⓓ Operators
Ⓔ Architecturestudio
Ⓕ Assistant to the project manager
Ⓖ Biodiversity council
Green roofs
Common base

The rules of a discourse ethics must allow us, according to Apel, to carry out a meaningful discourse—discourse respectful of the specific interests of each of the participants and guided by common interest, the only possible means of collectively reaching the right decision. These rules apply first of all to the effective representation of those in the discussion, by weighing personal interests against their ability to communicate; that is, by their *power*. After this "communicational inventory," the rules apply in respect of the structure and in maintaining collective interest. This requires the presence of a neutral person, an arbitrator—a chairperson—whose role consists of discerning specific interests from common interests by exposing discrepancies and possible contradictions between the discourse as conducted in reality and as one can expect it to ideally be conducted. That is, it is a question of finding a balanced form of taking action now, guided by an ideal collective.

+3 cm: maybe these don't say very much, but let's look at this on a coast that is extremely flat, and then it's a certain city that disappears...

Alain Bretagnolle

Through this passage from the invisible to the visible, and through the work of artists on the imaginary, in the end we realize that the imaginary itself is a possible commons. José-Manuel, in the demonstrations that you've organized, what kind of echo do you hear of this sentiment—in the population, in society at large?

José-Manuel Gonçalvès

To begin, this doesn't advance simply by way of artistic representations, but through the alliance of skills between experts, who in turn look to the future and who transfer into story-form what is in the process of playing out. How can we ensure that these visions of the future are not catastrophic? How do we avoid eco-anxiety? If a work is then presented, there is a small chance that awareness will arrive in the way we imagine. Of course, if the work is carried out in a slightly different way, in particular on questions of governance and therefore on the *process* itself, then something is happening. If we manage to include not only the population but others who are aren't experts, and if we try to build together a representation of what is given to us and to understand, in that moment, then other things can also happen. There are actions that we're currently taking, for example, on the question of social representation. As Emmanuelle said, social issues are intimately linked to environmental issues. We can't separate them; it's impossible. We have to address them at the same time. Those who also have influence—that is, those who have access to communication and who can pay a great deal for communication—they too must be convinced that just because they own the world doesn't mean it's not worth participating. Elon Musk comes to mind. How is it possible to manage an equilibrium and not find yourself in a position, or let's say almost, of neocolonialist thinking? Because really, we might start out with good intentions and want to share them, but it's difficult, there is always some sort of history of oppression behind it. How is it possible to implement processes so that this history, which exists, doesn't prevent the expression of other imaginaries or other interpretations made by the population, with the elements and information presented to them?

Again, I think that we shouldn't give up the battle, including among the wealthiest populations, and say: "There are a few less of them, it's less of a problem, we'll let them go their way with their 200 or 300 square meters, and we'll let them live. They don't interest us." Yes, they do interest us because they

Rolled-out ribbon

Saint-Malo, France

The Cultural Pole of Saint-Malo is an emblematic facility, commissioned by Mayor René Couanau to complete the urban project he had initiated on the site of the old station, in order to create a new urban polarity between Saint Servan, Paramé and the inner city.

The project thus engages a redefinition of the surrounding public spaces, as supports of new uses, which are generated and integrated into its very architecture.

The two functional polarities, initially distinct in the competition program – an art house cinema and a media library –, are united in one active ensemble. A unit marked by architecture, a Janus-like building between land and ocean whose two volumes with inverted movements are connected by a photovoltaic ribbon, but especially by the programming of coordinated events within the facility, to which the agency contributed significantly, in partnership with the Troisième Pôle. After the competition stage, the direct dialogue with the client enabled us to open up and exploit all the possibilities of the proposed project.

In this sense, architecture is an embodied and continuous programming, and what has been put in place here is a governance by the project.

With our partners, we not only designed all the furniture, created the visual identity of the Grande Passerelle and printed a fresco of poems and literary excerpts on the facades of the cinema, but also deployed the initial program, defined the contents of the media library collections and their consultation methods, established the organizational chart of operations and designed the interfaces in terms of cultural programming between the media library and the art house cinema and between the cultural pole thus constituted and the major Saint-Malo festivals. At the end of the construction, the first exhibition of photographs on the LED panels of the building's facades and the esplanade paid tribute to the construction workers.

Based on the project chosen by the community, on our initiative and with added skills in project management, the governance by the project in consultation with future users has made it possible to create a cultural facility that is unanimously supported.

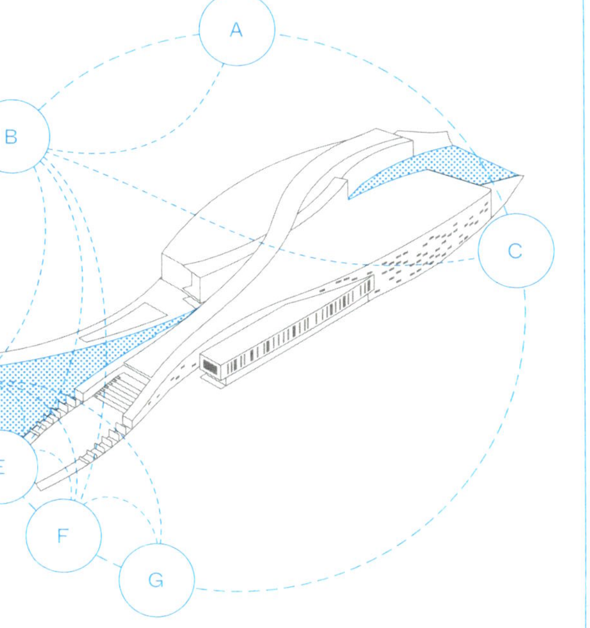

(A) Municipality
(B) Architecturestudio
(C) Cultural engineer
(D) Structural and fluid engineer
(E) Acoustic engineer
(F) Lighting designer
(G) Economist
Esplanade

Saint-Malo Film
and Multimedia Library,
Ville de Saint-Malo,
Architecturestudio.

Saint-Malo, France, 2015.

Nouveautés

The realities of project governance, as we experience it in our professions, are not so far removed from the assertions of an ethics of discourse. It is a question of reaffirming the role of the project manager, who, in order to maintain their neutrality and their defense of general interests, must ensure a new level of representation in the set of actors involved. How can the complexity of this set of actors and the emergence of new mediators contribute to redefining the relationship between economic power and general interest? How, truly, can we make decisions together and move from an exclusive governance to an inclusive one? And without proxy, for future generations? How can the interest of those without a voice be integrated into the decision-making process? Humans, and non-humans?

have resources, they have access to information, they provide resources. I'll point out that art, in particular contemporary art, is a market. It's a market, which means that there are people who pay for artists, who pay for their work, and so we have to manage to convince this market to invest in other representations of the world. If we don't do it in this area as well then we are beaten; that is to say, we'll end up with representations of oppression...

Alain Bretagnolle

A question for you, Franck. Since Kyoto we've begun using the slogan "Think Global, Act Local," and we have—in opposition to the Smart City and the networked city—some much more rooted initiatives, with off-grid communities. We've realized in this way that energy autonomy can provide a certain autonomy in decision-making. The question is a bit worn out, but I'll ask you anyways: what is the right scale for ecological governance?

Franck Boutté

We've defined the commons as an unowned resource. For there to be a commons, there also has to be a community. This is fundamental. For there to be a commons, there also has to be rules on managing this commons. Without rules, no commons, and the issue today is managing to define rules for the good management of resources. Earlier I was saying that ecological phenomena essentially play out within continuities. At the very beginning of our discussion, we talked about systems and that an event in one place can have repercussions on the other side of the planet, with very significant effects of leverage. All of this means that environmental issues call into question, or even jeopardize, the issue of scale. This also means that we won't solve environmental issues by staying within our perimeters, whatever they may be. When we see the terms of equalization between rich countries and poor countries, right now at COP27, it's clear. These questions are predominately trans-scalar.
Everything plays out at all scales, and what needs to be reconstructed is the idea of a global chain. We always inherit from upstream; this upstream is scalar or temporal. We are also always responsible for a downstream, and this is also scalar or temporal. The reconstitution of this chain of actors can help us define new rules of governance for the commons because these chains of actors, these chains of values link together ecological agents in virtuous circles.
If we say, "France, in the end, doesn't account for much in absolute value and in terms of carbon emissions, so as long as the United States and China don't take action, what good is it to hurt ourselves so much?" But then, if we change the indicators and if we look at carbon emissions per capita, we will say: "In the end, France is not so good." If we add in

Open stage

Angers, France

At the interface between the Maine, the city and its venues, the Théâtre du Quai is an urban antechamber for the performing arts. Located on the banks of the river, in the city center of Angers, the facility plays a key role in the regional cultural dynamic. The building, organized around creation, training and urban animation, houses the Center Dramatique National Pays de Loire, the Center Chorégraphique National d'Angers, the Forum, two 971 and 400-seat theaters and all the human and material support necessary for their proper functioning.

Its architecture, which favors the emergence of shows in the multiple venues made available to artists, students and spectators, is at the service of the performances that take place there. The building offers an active, original interface with the urban context. This dialogue takes the form of a peristyle which opens onto the city and the river, where the Forum is located, with magnificent views of the castle of King René. From this urban antechamber, which hosts temporary exhibitions or street art events, audiences access the galleries that lead to the two main halls by crossing a very thick concrete veil with multiple openings onto the Forum and the city.

The exterior facades of this Forum are retractable, disappearing completely in the summer months in order to incorporate the public space and its cultural activities. A technical grid in the ceiling enables all kinds of scenic arrangements. The wind currents that follow the river penetrate into the volume thanks to horizontal louvers which are integrated in the glazed facades, naturally refreshing the interior spaces. In winter, on the other hand, the built envelope acts as a thermal buffer, offering a transition with the outside in intermediate temperatures. On the roofs, adjacent to the dance halls, the panoramic restaurant and the public terrace provide views of the castle.

This theater interface strengthens the links between show time, pedagogical time, and the time of the city.

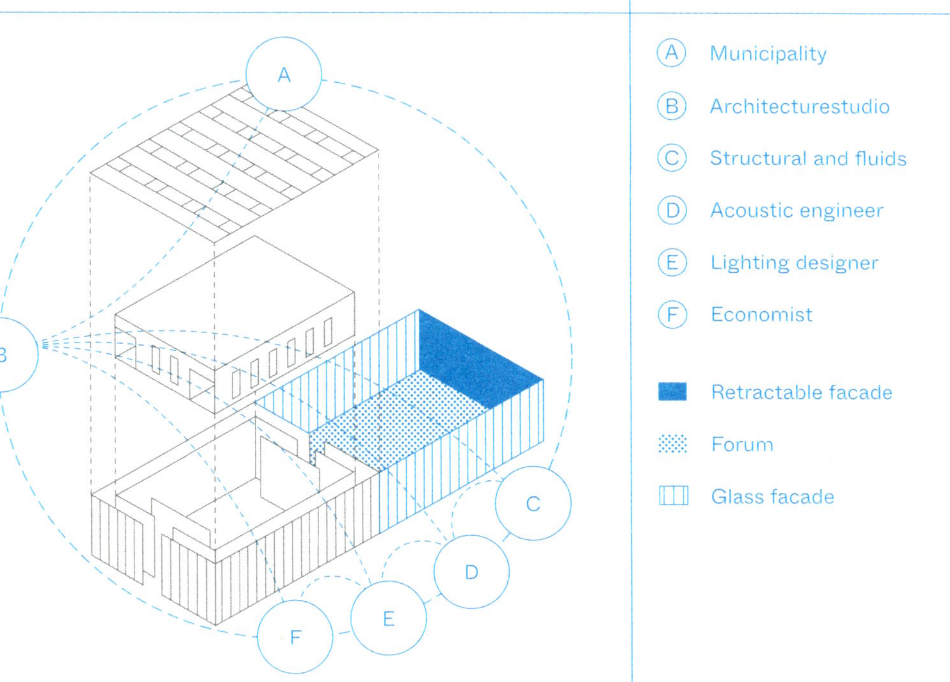

(A) Municipality
(B) Architecturestudio
(C) Structural and fluids
(D) Acoustic engineer
(E) Lighting designer
(F) Economist

Retractable facade
Forum
Glass facade

Théâtre du Quai,
City of Angers,
Architecturestudio.

Angers, France, 2007.

The Ecology of Action

Faced with the moral, social, ecological, and financial failures of our time, it now appears urgent to move beyond governance by norms and towards other, shared forms of decision-making that are more egalitarian, more equitable, and above all more anchored in reality. Architecture and urbanism are disciplines that work towards sustainability, social cohesion, and better ways of living together. The aim of our professions is to build, to transform, and thus to act within the unpredictability of the world that is ours. That governance guided by an ethic of action allows for a better sharing of decision-making and a consensus on objectives is already a significant step forward. Unfortunately, this does not ensure proper execution of the said action. To borrow a question from Edgar Morin: what can we expect from action in a place where there is uncertainty?

the emissions that have been externalized, then we talk about reimportation, because today this constitutes 45% of France's carbon footprint, which isn't negligible and means that 45% of our carbon emissions have been externalized in other countries, including China. As soon as we start to think about these equalizations, we see that there are problems of international solidarity at play, and that the question lies there. This is the first COP where these questions have been put on the table. How do we say to these countries, "You too, you also no longer have the right to produce emissions"? We should above all try hard, here, to allow them to develop. We can't forbid this; when we are ourselves a product of remarkable development, how do we say to them: "It's done for everyone, for you too"? While they are just at the start of a process. It's fundamental to think of new international solidarities through the lens of ecological issues, because the question of sovereignty, of enclosing oneself within one's borders, all of that, it won't work. We won't solve anything.

Alain Bretagnolle

Thank you, Franck. Can I ask each of you what you've learned from our discussion? For my part, I saw the trusted linear process of project management, planning, design, production, operation, and maintenance fall apart before our eyes.
We will also have to question our own practices. Emmanuelle, José-Manuel, and Franck: a word of conclusion?

Emmanuelle Cosse

When we say, "Think global, act local," the question is above all that everyone is aware of the impact of their own actions. What is very interesting about the current moment is that the environmental crisis is shaking up a lot of things in the right way. It's disrupting the logic of the market, it's disrupting economic and political orders, it's calling into question issues of power. We are all in the same boat, even if some will suffer more than others, it's clear. But things will have to change, it is inevitable. Today, I am certain of two things. The first is that there are no foregone conclusions; even if the situation will certainly deteriorate further, all action is useful. The second thing, which is very hard and disturbing to accept for some, is that we can't continue to live as before. We spoke about engagement, and this is a term that I like, but not everyone wants to or has the capacity to be engaged. It's incredibly destabilizing in the sum of our life views, no matter what our age and our role in society. But I believe it's an opportunity to create a collective and to change things, to make the world more acceptable. This forces us to be more intelligent and to find solutions that might be a bit more refined or less lazy than in the past. This is quite wonderful.

A shared laboratory in Venice

Venice, Italy

In 2008, we created the CA'ASI in Venice, a "Shared House" which is also an art and architecture gallery, designed to showcase the creations of young architects with whom the agency comes into contact in the course of its international activities. The CA'ASI is a laboratory of ideas open to the world which has progressively become a reference venue for the fringe events of the different Biennales.

The exhibitions showcase the works of young architects from around the world, selected by an independent jury. Over the past decade, these events have enabled us to discover the productions of young Chinese, Arab, African, Latin American and European architects. They convey the emotion provoked by the design of creative solutions in specific conditions, the emergence of architectural quality in geographical and socio-cultural contexts as diverse as Chinese megacities, remote African villages and the favelas of Rio de Janeiro.

The human habitat is the leitmotif of the themes under discussion, exhibition after exhibition. The one in 2023, devoted to the *Tracé Bleu*, focuses on the profound paradigm shifts caused by the climate crisis and mass biodiversity extinction which architects and urban planners must now contend with in their practices, with a view to conserving inhabited areas. By means of a participative laboratory, it gives a voice to the citizens of the world who pass through Venice, in order to outline the new commons of a weakened habitat.

These exhibitions aim to reach an audience beyond specialist circles. Scenographers, graphic designers and artists lend a hand, facilitating visitors' communication with the events. Rereading the content programs developed by Architecturestudio at the CA'ASI enables us to retrace the stories of these exhibited elements which have often been displayed in other places: at the Academy of Architecture in Paris, at the Arc-en-Rêve in Bordeaux, in Madrid or Buenos Aires. Tracé Bleu will be exhibited at the Centquatre in Paris before moving on, in turn, to other shores.

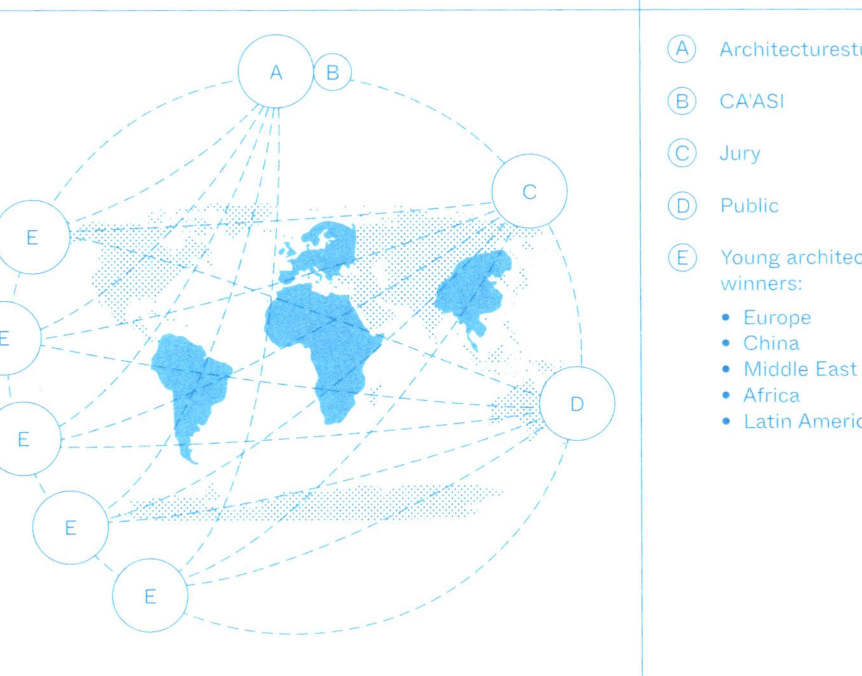

Ⓐ Architecturestudio
Ⓑ CA'ASI
Ⓒ Jury
Ⓓ Public
Ⓔ Young architects winners:
- Europe
- China
- Middle East
- Africa
- Latin America

The conduct of action in a homogenous environment and in a changing or uncertain environment have nothing to do with each other. In the first case, the result of the action is in accordance with its intention; the action remains one and united from its decision until its realization. In the second case, Morin observes: "All action escapes the will of its author by entering the game of inter-feedback in the environment in which it intervenes. This is the principle belonging to the ecology of action… The ecology of action is, in short, taking into account the complexity that it presumes—hazard, initiative, decision, the unexpected, the unplanned, awareness of drifts and transformations."[11] And this difference in the stability and consistency of action changes everything. The ecology of action thus poses a serious problem for governance by showing us that its results sometimes evade the will of actors.

11. Edgar Morin, *Introduction à la pensée complexe*, Éditions Seuil, 2014, p. 107 (1990). Translated from the original French: "Toute action échappe à la volonté de son auteur en entrant dans le jeu des inter-rétro-actions du milieu où elle intervient. Tel est le principe propre à l'écologie de l'action… L'écologie de l'action c'est en somme tenir compte de la complexité qu'elle suppose, c'est-à-dire aléa, hasard, initiative, décision, inattendu, imprévu, conscience des dérives et des transformations."

José-Manuel Gonçalvès

We need to rediscover certain freedoms. I believe our society must once again acquire a taste for trying, for prototyping, for testing, and also for failure. From the moment our relationship to things consists solely of efficiency and profitability, we crystallize fears. This concerns all involved, all actors, regardless of their social status. It's easier to involve yourself when projects are carried out collectively and when there is a possibility of missing out. The possibility is always there: to benefit from an experience, from a shared experience. I think it is necessary. Just the experience of a collective effort, driven by communities that at some point take on a project together—this has effects.

In our experience, even at a small scale, there is an extremely strong expectation of the public authorities that we will be able to regain the commons and regain space. We have spaces now that are so-called public spaces, that have been in some way privatized for a single function, and we can free these up in a way and open it to those who need it more than others, observe it, redefine it, replace the rules, find modes which are modes of relation, modes which avoid establishing a relation with others only when forced and by a priori means—which at their base are not efficient for what society is looking for and for what is necessary today, if we want to move forward on questions of engagement and the commons. From the moment there were rules, they were enforced by people like us, and of course there is a set of other people who don't want to follow them because this isn't the way they can thrive. So in this way we personally have to be capable of saying at a certain moment, "These rules, maybe we can at least question them for awhile in terms of territory and in terms of time." And trust ourselves on that. And perhaps realize that it is actually a failure.

At 104, we take time to explain what effects this has, these communities who come there, and at 104 there are no rules—perhaps only one, a ban on smoking, indicated in a corner, but otherwise there are no rules. Over the years a form of self-management has been put in place. On the question of cleanliness, for example: leave a space that's clean for whoever comes after, it's simple. And we write on small stickers the effects it has on the life of the structure: "By collecting your bottles for all these years, you saved this much, in money, and this has been reinvested in the project. You've also saved this much in carbon footprint." All these daily gestures have an effect… the paradox is that in principle, by providing people with the liberty to implement and occupy the spaces in a private way, we've saved where others want to implement communal management only through economic restrictions. To end with these questions of rules and liberty, I believe that we absolutely must be capable of bringing an experiential dimension into play, in our management of spaces and in our lives.

CA'ASI,
Architecturestudio.

Venice, Italy, 2008.

The ecological crisis puts forward the collective as a regime, and no longer as an exception. The forms of governance are evolving: a static ensemble once called upon at the beginning of a project becomes dynamic, reactive, and integrated. Collective decision-making is thus permanent and supports the project over time, allowing it to adapt to unforeseen events, to change direction if necessary. This involves putting an end to the solitude of the architect as author and integrating discourse around the project into the project itself. Are the program or the plan still useful for designing within uncertainty? We need open tools, directional tools which gradually integrate the information, problems, and hazards that the project encounters on its way, and which allow it to constantly adapt.

Stimuli for Paris

Paris, France

Mitterrand's major projects in the 1980s instilled a new dynamic. Autonomous, without urban prerequisites, without coherence per se, these major projects transformed Paris, as Beaubourg had already modified the nearby neighborhood. Their worldwide resonance reinforced the image of Paris as a hotbed of culture. Like many European capitals, Paris, with its Haussmannian image, evolved into a huge preserved sector, a new museum of arts and popular traditions of which we, as inhabitants of the city, would be the visiting-visited actors, and where our cultural specificity would be found only in our sources. These major projects therefore called for a counterpart, so as not to dispossess the inhabitants of their cities. At the time, in contrast, in opposition but in synergy, with minimalism as opposed to maximalism, we proposed "a thousand small projects for a large urban project in Paris."

The stimuli approach, investing a multitude of residual plots of the urban fabric of the capital and its nearby suburbs—a minimalist prefiguration of the future Greater Paris—therefore constituted the more humble and contextual counterpart.

For a year, we visited the center of Paris in an exhaustive way, the first seven *arrondissements* and an area 200 meters wide towards the north-east suburbs, street by street, courtyard by courtyard. We were struck by the large number of empty plots located in strategic places, struck by the fact that these plots, like gaping wounds in the city, were abandoned or misused (building depots, electoral signs, parking places, billboards, landfills...), struck to discover that most of them belonged to the cities or the State, struck by the mediocrity of twentieth-century urban furniture, struck by the physical and psychological divide between Paris and its periphery, struck by the lack of information about the city, in the city. We proposed to rebuild them as hubs of network services, using urban acupuncture to revitalize the district energy circuits.

The Stimuli remain topical, with climate change and the end of the urban sprawl forcing us to find endogenous land resources to intensify the city and its uses.

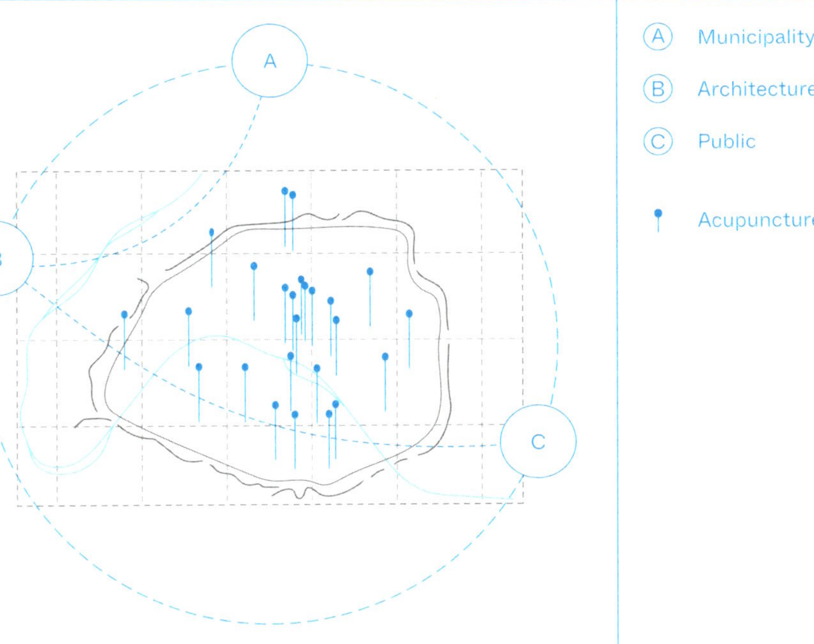

Ⓐ Municipality
Ⓑ Architecturestudio
Ⓒ Public
Acupuncture project

What does a design project propose under these conditions? Our lack of imagination is an admission of powerlessness. There is a duty, however, to leave the future open and to create fertile ground for a community to come. A common criticism of Hans Jonas' *Imperative of Responsibility* is that he summons a heuristic of fear, one that dooms political action to inhibition through the abuse of precautions. More than forty years after its publication this criticism rings tragic, so deplorable is our inability to act collectively in the face of climate challenges. We should remember that in the history of philosophy, the text by Jonas was a counterproposal to Ernst Bloch's *Principle of Hope*,[12] published at the end of the Second World War and written in praise of taking risks, experimentation, and utopia. In a word: hope.

12. Ernst Bloch, *Das Prinzip Hoffnung*, Suhrkamp Verlag, 1954, 1955, 1959.

Exhibition poster
Nel Palazzo di Cristallo,
In collaboration
with CNAP
Exhibition curators:
Pascal Beausse
and Pascale Cassagnau,
CA'ASI, 2011

Re. generate

What are the regenerative economies for our territories?

Pedro Gadanho Architect, Curator, and Writer

Jean-Baptiste Fressoz Historian

Ingrid Nappi Economist and Professor at École des Ponts ParisTech

AS Explore, moderated by Alain Bretagnolle and Romain Boursier, Partner Architects/Urban Planners, Architecturestudio

Architecturestudio interrogates the impact of the economy of transforming our territories in a context which requires integrating nature in a symbiotic relationship, one of interdependence, along with expanding our definition of the notion of the commons and rallying politics around the "good use" of resources.

With Jean-Baptiste Fressoz, Pedro Gadanho, and Ingrid Nappi, we decipher the cognitive biases of the development and real estate economy. It appears that our models of energy transition, of chains of values, and of sustainable cities are insufficient to maintain the equilibrium of the planet.

This provides an opportunity to imagine hypotheses of an economy redefined around a good management of the commons, not by individual interest but by collective interest in a "good use of resources."

We equally interrogate what knowledge must be employed to collectively define the aims of a "blue economy" in terms of teaching, practices, and creativity. In concrete terms, what actions should be prioritized in order to direct the transformation of our models towards a regenerative economy?

163. **Low Carbon**

RESTRAINT
- Frugal station | Metropolitan Area of Greater Paris, France

BIO-BASED
- A wooden living environment to support healing | Geneva, Switzerland
- A wooden landmark as a new workplace | Nice, France
- A wooden shell for expanded liturgy | Créteil, France
- Clay/wood balance for bioclimatic architecture | Saint-Laurent-du-Maroni, France

CIRCULARITY
- In-situ reuse of stone cladding | La Défense, France
- Preserved barracks, diverted windows | Nancy, France

189. **Resilience**

CAPABILITY
- Bioclimatic interstices | Mirecourt, France
- Increased habitability | Buenos Aires, Argentina

AGILITY
- Reversible street-level floor | Créteil, France
- An architectural envelope for mutable uses | Zurich, Switzerland
- Habitable rooftops | Cairo, Egypt

ANTICIPATION
- A hospital in extreme conditions | Les Abymes, France
- Hospital-oasis | Tangier, Morocco

211. **Welcoming the living**

- Observing the living | Denqing, China
- Biotope island | Palaiseau, France
- Plant-covered platform | Cergy, France

Nanterre, France.

Economy and Resources

Through its etymology, *oikonomia*, for Vitruvius, defined the good management of the household, and by extension the good management of resources. It is only recently, with the rise of capitalist doctrines in the nineteenth century, that this benevolent and helpful notion of exchange moved beyond the fields of fairness and the common good. Since then, economics has aimed for the continued optimization of the productive apparatus, with the goal of consistent profitability. The development of liberalism accelerated the process; today the financialization of real estate and the gradual commodification of buildings marks a point of no return. This neoliberal game defines a difficult productive framework, often sacrificing ecological and societal issues in the name of a project's profitability, but it is the one we are working with. If the dominant logic is that of calculation—and buildings are the operations—shouldn't the architect assert him- or herself as guarantor of the material quality of buildings?

What are the regenerative economies for our territories?

Romain Boursier

Good morning. Three teacher-researchers are with us today to discuss the economy of transformation of our territories, to question our models, our objectives and value systems, and to define our present and future priorities in terms of actions.

We will start by examining the cognitive biases that underlie our overconsumption societies. We will then review the knowledge that needs to be collectively mobilized to reconsider our value systems and lifestyles. Finally, we will discuss the avenues to be explored to bring us closer to an *oikonomia* that is circular, resilient, and symbiotic.

Alain Bretagnolle

The Greek term *oikonomia* defines a notion whose etymology literally means the proper use of home or household resources. We use it today to extend it to this common home which is the Earth.

Jean-Baptiste, your work helps us to appreciate the challenge our economic systems are facing today. You point to the issue of accumulation at the origin of the Anthropocene. Can you tell us how the Anthropocene is also an Accumulocene?

Jean-Baptiste Fressoz

The notion of crisis and that of transition are related to the same temporality. Behind the term "environmental crisis" is the idea that what we're experiencing is just a rough patch, that we'll find a solution to make the transition. With the notion of the Anthropocene, Paul Crutzen, winner of the Nobel Prize in Chemistry for his work on the ozone layer, wanted to show that what we're experiencing is much more profound than an environmental crisis. To find such powerful changes in the constitution of the planet, we have to go back in geological time. The level of CO_2 in the atmosphere has not been so high in three million years! The strength of the notion of the Anthropocene is that it places our problem in the context of the planet's lifetime.

Like that of crisis, the notion of transition euphemizes what needs to be done. It transforms a gigantic issue—removing carbon from the economy—into a simple technological transformation. It's not a question of changing society or even changing civilization, no, it's only about changing technological infrastructures...

So, Accumulocene: it started as a game around finding other names for the Anthropocene. The Anthropocene incriminates humanity as the entity collectively responsible

Frugal station

Metropolitan Area of Greater Paris, France

Architecturestudio is working on the design of several "frugal stations" as part of the Grand Paris Express project. In the different urban contexts encountered, from residential areas to mono-functional business parks, cars still dominate the use of public spaces, to the detriment of pedestrians. Green infrastructure needs to be restored, on abandoned roads, neighboring wastelands, or by planting lines of trees along major roads. New stations are often located at the junction of existing infrastructure nodes where the range of services offered need to be rethought according to new modes of transport.

How can the urban insertion of such iconic facilities of the future public transport network—as markers of the territory—be envisaged? How can the elaboration of needs and design standards be questioned? How can mitigation strategies be explored, while paying close attention to ecological continuity, to the choice of compact and low-carbon construction, as well as to the question of the reversibility of perennial structures?

To this end, the agency has developed the principle of the frugal station, by engaging in a process of sobriety and optimization, and questioning the notion of comfort recommended in relation to actual needs. This approach initially applies to the compactness of the projects, so as to maximize the surfaces where trees are planted directly into the ground, and favor cool islands. A second approach seeks to put forward open-sided and covered bioclimatic design, whose aeraulic comfort conditions are guaranteed by dynamic simulations. A third approach tends to conceive passenger spaces located above-ground and at first basement as reversible and open to future unplanned uses, with natural lighting and ample and modular dimensions.

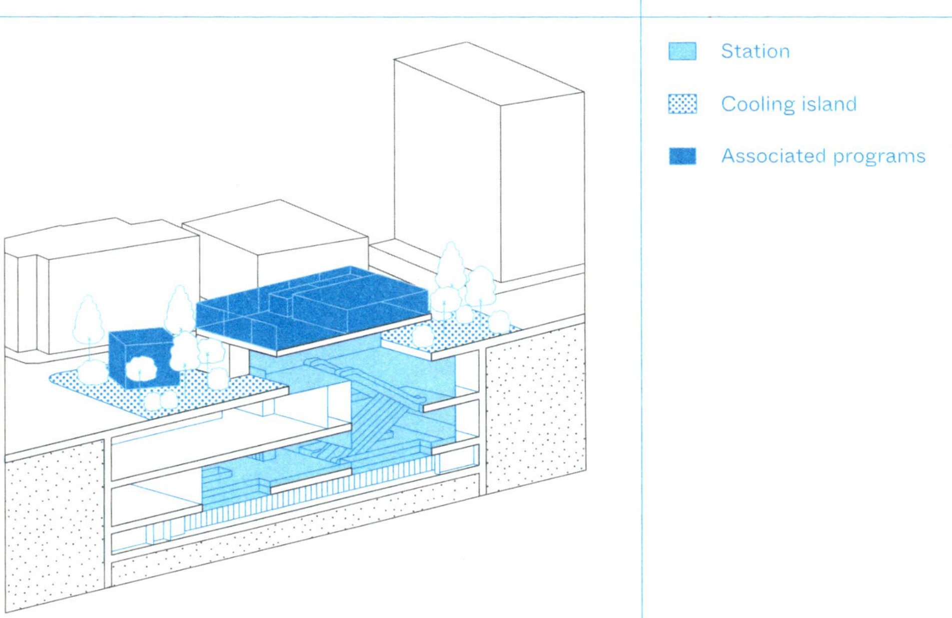

Station

Cooling island

Associated programs

Nancy, France.

Unfortunately, the average architectural production that results from this market law is generic, often mediocre, and tasteless: "In housing units, the entryway-kitchen-hallway serves as a living room. Balconies, if they are included, are shallow. Windows are narrow and in the worst cases are trimmed with PVC. Finally, the catalogue of materials used to clad the buildings is varied: brick siding, slabs of stamped concrete, lacquered wood, or colored plaster. The quality of the products covering the exterior insulation of the housing units gives little hope as to their durability."[1] Our notion of economy is confirmed today by the negation of quality and durability in these buildings. Market logic is slowing down a transition that requires a reassessment of our relationship to resources in the long term. But its influence over politics skews democratic debate and generates an ethical vacuum in the way we conceive and construct society. Ecology, as a collective ambition, calls for an alternate notion of economy.

1 See Margaux Darrieu, *Les architectures totales de la ville néolibérale*, in AOC, February 2023. Translated from the original French: "Dans les logements, l'entrée-cuisine-couloir fait office de salon. Quand il y en a, les loggias sont peu profondes. Étroites, les fenêtres sont serties de PVC dans les pires des cas. Enfin, le catalogue des matériaux qui habillent les immeubles est varié, briquettes en parement, plaquettes de béton matricé, bois lasuré ou enduit coloré. La finesse des produits emballant l'isolation extérieure des logements donne peu d'espoir quant à leur pérennité."

for the environmental crisis. However, we know very well that responsibilities vary greatly from one people to another, from one social class to another, etc. The Anthropocene basically recycles the old Malthusian narrative, in which the human species as a biological entity is caught up in a kind of battle against nature. Hence the proliferation of alternatives in which my friend Christophe Bonneuil and I have played a major part. The point of the notion of Accumulocene is to insist on this non-transitional dimension of the history of techniques, energy and matter. On a global scale, we have never substituted one energy for another. We have never consumed as much coal as we do now, as you no doubt know, but we have also never consumed as much wood. Wood is still an extremely important energy source in the modern world. In 2022 it has produced twice as much final energy as nuclear power. So we are still living with age-old energy sources. This idea of accumulation doesn't only apply to energy, it's true for all materials: our consumption of raw materials has continued to increase, raw materials are never obsolete, despite the inventiveness of chemists... Obsolescence doesn't apply to materials, the only thing that works are bans. The use of asbestos, for example, has decreased worldwide. Architects and the building industry in general have obviously played an essential role in this accumulation process. Buildings account for 40% of CO_2 emissions according to the IEA. Construction is also a major emitter, mainly because of cement and concrete. But traditional materials are not disappearing either. Bricks and wood, glass and plastic have never been used as much as they are today in construction. Concrete has not made bricks disappear, yet, a priori, these two materials are in competition with each other. The problem with transition is that it's a comfortable notion. Everyone's happy with it because it would basically allow us to just keep going, but with a clean energy system. That's just great. In my opinion, this is a form of denial of the enormity of climate change. A form of climate denial that is much more subtle than climate-skepticism, and therefore much more important to flush out.

Alain Bretagnolle
Is it in this sense that you say that the energy transition projects a past that does not exist onto a future that still remains ghostly?

Jean-Baptiste Fressoz
Yes, that's why I work on these issues. Initially, this notion of energy transition came from small groups of intellectuals from the atomic energy sector, to put it simply, who then disseminated their expertise to the public. But if you consider the history of discussions on energy from 1900 to 1970, there is never any mention of transition.

A wooden living environment to support healing

Geneva, Switzerland

The *Mikado* project for the new inpatient and outpatient buildings of Geneva's children's hospital has taken the form of welcoming, elegant, efficient and inclusive architecture, open onto the inner park as well as the city.

This architecture is designed specifically for its users: the children and their families, of course, but also the entire medical staff and other hospital employees. It is guided by a constant concern for comfort and functionality, and the practical and ergonomic nature of the layout of the various departments is constantly sought after, with specific attention paid to the relative scale of children. In this context, wood, with its symbolic association with childhood—fairytale forests, huts, toys—as well as its warm materiality, seemed to be the perfect material to meet the objectives of the project.

The building was constructed as a new articulation, thus marking the southern entrance to the hospital with simple and legible volumes. It offers continuity with the existing context while at the same time standing out from it, in a singularity that reinforces its role as a building emblematic of a hospital renewal that leaves more room for people.

Designed to connect the technical platform and emergency room to the children's inpatient building, the new hospital maximizes sunlight and views of the surrounding nature. Its facades with their refined lines interact with the landscape through a set of terraces. They increase the quality of life and the comfort of interior use. In keeping with the spirit of a warm and near-domestic environment for the care and healing of children, nature is also present in all the indoor spaces through a choice of wood-based materials. The rooms as well as the corridors and waiting and treatment areas are bright, comfortable and soothing.

Mikado has been imagined as a new unifying place at the HUG's children's hospital. It is a project that is both rational and sensitive, whose architecture is both sober and functional, and which has been designed for the long term in view of a circular and sustainable economy.

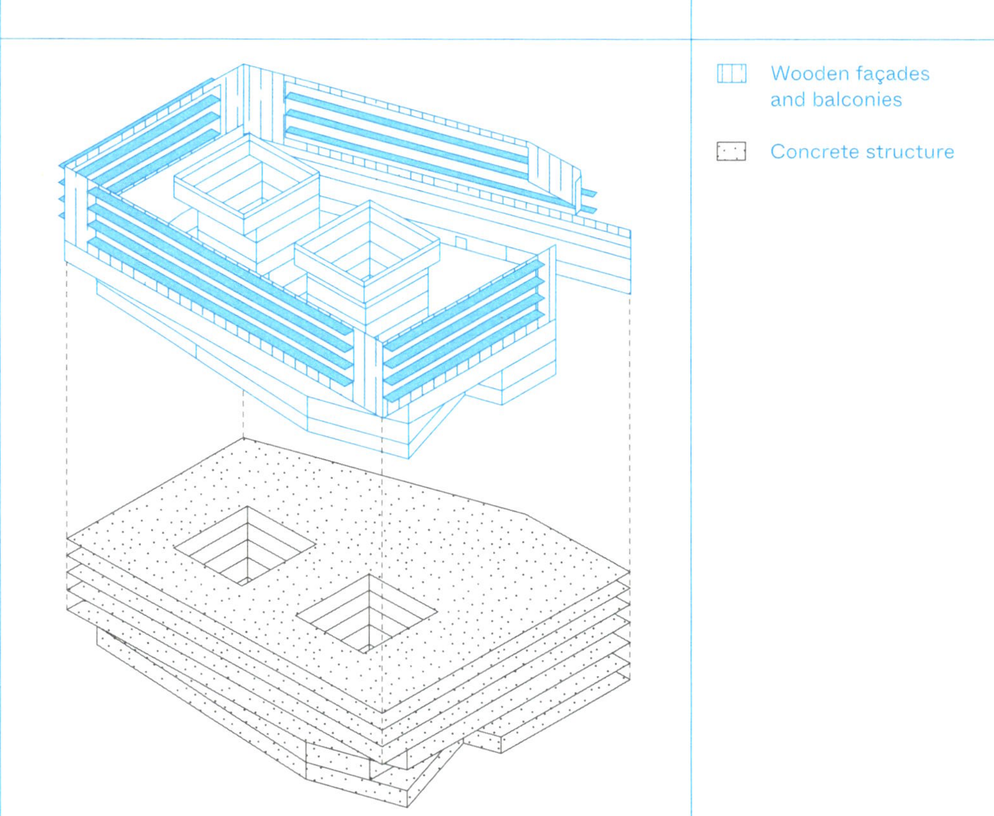

Wooden façades and balconies

Concrete structure

Palazzo Meridia, Nexity Ywood, EPA Eco-Vallée Plaine du Var, Architecturestudio.

Nice, France, 2020.

The industrial world still maintains a very concrete relationship to material resources, and exemplifies an economy of resistance. Materiality— almost the flesh—of industrial work makes it possible to read the sequencing of tasks and to understand the long time frame of projects. If the great challenge of the twenty-first century is to improve control over our resources, could the material transformation of the world—and the transmission of meaning we give it through collective work—perhaps allow us to face this challenge?

Romain Boursier

We can see that our beliefs are false, and that our consumption is increasing. How does this affect architecture in concrete terms? Ingrid Nappi, you've been speaking to a wide audience on behalf of the French Ministry of Culture, precisely to explain the real estate economy and its impact on architectural quality. How does the financialization of this real estate economy ultimately accelerate consumption? Have you identified new externalities, or an increase in the complexity of the processes that have changed the relationship with project briefs?

Ingrid Nappi

I think we need to define and distinguish things. How do we define financialization? With this terminology, we're referring both to new sources of financing for real estate—other than traditional bank loans, i.e. banking access to real estate that appeared in the 1960s—by appealing to the financial markets, and in particular via structures such as large real estate companies or investment funds, and to new market finance stakeholders that have a financial approach and definition of real estate value. Financialization appeared quite suddenly in France in the real estate sector at the end of the 1990s as a solution for managing the 1991 real estate and banking crisis, the result of an overproduction of office buildings. We mustn't forget that the real estate sector was in a proper slump, with a large number of property developers going bankrupt because they had overestimated demand. One of the ways of managing this crisis was to call on so-called "opportunistic" investment funds, defined as such because they appeared when markets could no longer regulate themselves. These opportunistic investment funds, notably Anglo-Saxon funds, precisely appeared between 1997 and 2002, and changed our view of the property market. Their particularity is that they brought a very short-term vision to the industry and real estate market, which the latter were not at all used to. Real estate was thought of as a very long term business, traditionally with a very asset-based approach over several decades. Suddenly, in the space of a few months, new economic stakeholders arrived on the French market, using new financial indicators to hold property in the short term, and favoring not the traditional rental yield, but a short-term capital yield, i.e. a prospect of capital gains. This made it possible to overcome the crisis. Let's remember that there were office real estate operations that were no longer being set up, ZACs[1] that were in financial difficulty and on the verge of bankruptcy. So, from an asset-based approach to real estate, we moved to a financial approach over the course of a few months. This process was called financialization. Subsequently, financialization became more pronounced and was fueled by

1 French urban development zone

A wooden landmark as a new workplace

Nice, France

Close to the agricultural plain of the Var river, the Palazzo Méridia is a tertiary sector project at the interface between city and nature. Its construction meets the conditions of true sustainable development through the enhancement of outdoor spaces, energy management, and low-carbon architecture.

The project relies on the local climate and the inhabitants' experience of their territory to highlight spatial innovations, which in turn become drivers of social innovation. The innovation here lies in the creation of shared outdoor spaces, which extend the indoor work spaces. These spaces merge to give rise to a genuine three-dimensional living space, open to all forms of programming, both formal and informal, and of new uses, behind the outer layer of the façade.

This large protective mesh houses spaces that may be appropriated, that shake up routine, encourage interactions, sharing and encounters thanks to large landscaped terraces surrounding the office floors. Here, in an edible garden made up of successive terraces that rise towards the sky, plantations can be consumed. The architecture here speaks of commons associated with new use values, and suggests a more open system of relationships within an attractive working environment.

The building is also in line with the age of eco-responsibility thanks to its high-rise wood frame, which allows for a dry construction site with reduced deadlines, low WW emissions, little noise, and very little waste.

The building's load-bearing elements on eight floors—except for two concrete cores to address seismic risk—are all made of wood: posts, floors and CLT (cross-laminated timber) load-bearing façades. The 900 tonnes of French wood used have helped to sustain the regional and national wood industry. At the time of its delivery, it was the tallest tertiary sector wooden building in France, far exceeding the requirements of the "*Biosourcé*" (bio-based) certification.

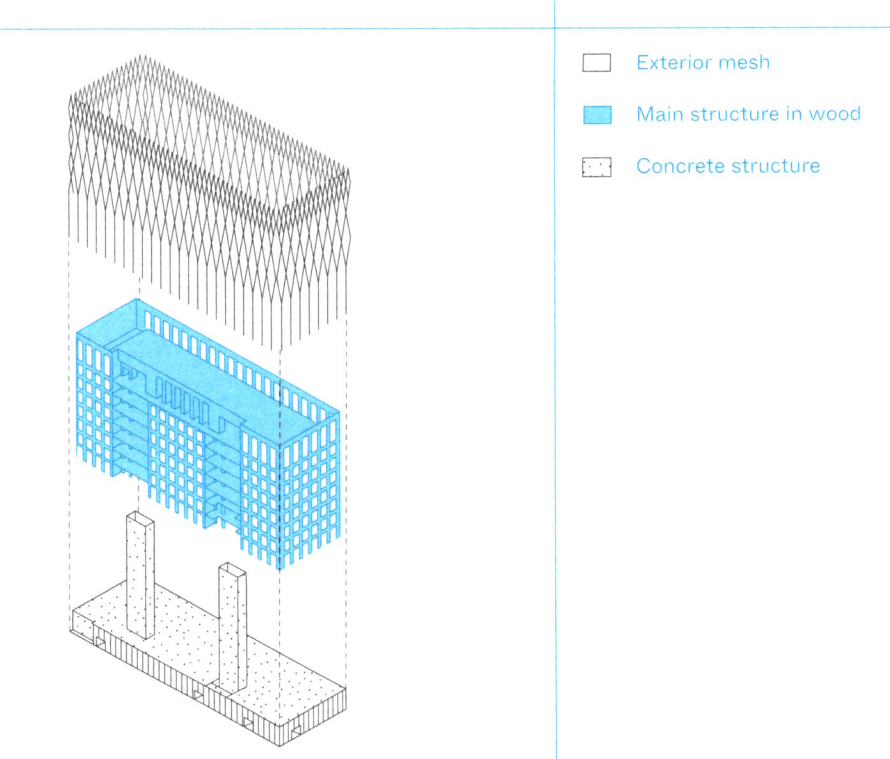

Exterior mesh

Main structure in wood

Concrete structure

Palazzo Meridia, Nexity Ywood, EPA Eco-Vallée Plaine du Var, Architecturestudio.

Nice, France, 2020.

The transition to a more resource-efficient world also involves new relationships to living things. The question is difficult, but how can we reconcile the conservation of our industries with the preservation of biodiversity? How can we not make living beings subservient to the industrial cause, but rather develop collaborative or convivial tools, in the sense intended by Ivan Illich?[2] The promotion of an economy of restraint speaks to a new pact with the non-human, one beneficial to all parties, and aimed towards the peaceful equilibrium of ecosystems. It isn't an economy of restriction, but one based on the invention of better, shared forms of living that we must establish.

2. Ivan Illich, *Tools for Conviviality*, Harper & Row, 1973.

a very particular and favorable economic context, that of an absence of inflation and an economy with very low interest rates which facilitated indebtedness. The movement concerned large investors and long term owners who divested themselves of their housing stock to concentrate on non-residential property, and above all office buildings. This quickly led to a crisis in private rental property marked by a shortage of housing, and to remedy this, private rental investment was encouraged.
And of course, everything focused on net financial profitability after tax, which is why several tax exemption measures were produced to help households invest in residential property, while institutional investors were disinvesting in offices. This is the context in which financialization took place.
In this context of financialization, and rather later, came property developers, who, with the Élan law,[2] as well as other measures, entered the housing sector, particularly social housing. This is when things started to change for architects. If they were not part of a large agency, particularly in France, they gradually lost the monitoring of construction sites because developers were well organized. There are large developers as well as many small developers, but most of the turnover of developers is still carried by large real estate groups which themselves have their own project management and construction subsidiaries. Architects who, in France at least, used to work with project managers by designing projects and adapting them based on a very holistic approach, are increasingly losing construction site management. We have been studying this with the *Observatoire de l'économie de l'architecture* (Observatory of the Economy of Architecture). We have clearly understood that the economic role of architects in this value chain has begun to change.

Romain Boursier
How has this affected the city?

Ingrid Nappi
There's been a huge change. As I mentioned, we've gone from an asset-based approach to a financial approach, and are now moving towards an environmental approach. We've realized that real estate is a major emitter of greenhouse gases, waste, etc. New constraints mean that we can't afford to lose sight of the environment. New constraints mean that we can no longer build as we used to. And above all, we have this societal approach, which is of course linked to Covid, but also to an increasingly accelerated consideration of the well-being of users. We are moving towards this use value. This is what was highlighted, particularly in residential property with the subprime crisis in 2008, when we saw the financial

2 French property law

A wooden shell for expanded liturgy

Créteil, France

The architecture of Créteil Cathedral, which was inaugurated in 1978, was a response to the liturgical and pastoral changes brought about by the Second Vatican Council in this new town in the Paris suburbs: a church that is not actually monumental, inserted as close as possible to the social system of this new diocese. Its implementation addresses the emerging issues of the twenty-first century: a cathedral that is more open, more visible, and larger.

The white architecture of Charles Gustave Stoskopf serves as a shell for the new cathedral, which is clad entirely in wood, inside and out. This uniqueness in terms of material, while allowing a clear reading of the two layers of the building, evokes traditional cathedrals, as stone vessels whose mass was cut and chiseled by light, and bears a requirement of unity and simplicity.

Natural wood, as a living, warm, humble, and noble material, outlines the curves of the building's timber framework and brings the community together in the celebration of the sacraments. The interior articulation of the two spherical shells, which meet above the altar in the outpouring of colors of Udo Zembok's magnificent stained glass window, is punctuated by the repetition of spruce arches parallel to the liturgical axis. It qualifies the density of the sacred space and its elevation sheltered by the exterior cladding of pre-weathered Douglas fir panels. This vertical deployment has made it possible to accommodate a tribune and to double the building's capacity.

During construction, a temporary cathedral was built on a neighboring plot of land using recycled scaffolding on which a waterproof canvas was stretched.

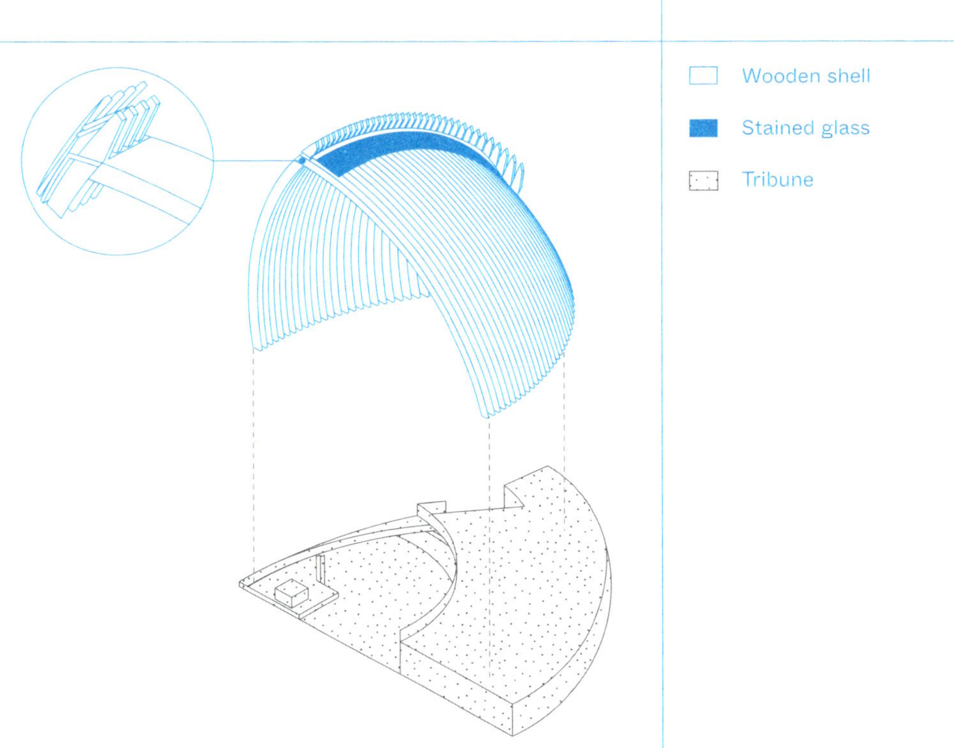

Wooden shell

Stained glass

Tribune

Cathedral of Créteil, Diocesan Association of Creteil, Chantiers du Cardinal, Architecturestudio.

Créteil, France, 2015.

value become completely disconnected from the actual value, which led to the much-talked-about financial bubbles. Since the Covid crisis, we have been investing more in the value of well-being, the value of use. Architects play an important part in this scenario. Project managers will consider surface areas, the number of square meters, based on their development appraisal. Architects, on the other hand, will think in terms of quality. We can see that the emphasis is completely different. We always talk about environmental value, but today we're mainly concerned with social issues. It is essential that the two parties communicate and understand each other.

Romain Boursier

Pedro, I saw you reacting to this. Do this financialization and these market bubbles have an impact on the very shape of our cities?

Pedro Gadanho

I'll have to answer "no" to that. I will explain myself, and also go back to the previous questions, because when we're discussing financing, I think we're discussing details related to a much larger problem. This is not the first thing I would consider regarding the paradigm shift that Ingrid mentioned. What was said about the economy in the past sounded like age-old ideas, ideas from an old world that no longer exists, even if we're not always aware of that. We've experienced great changes in the last two or three years.

First of all, I'd like to go back to the idea of the Anthropocene or the Accumulocene, or what others have called the Capitalocene. As a famous writer said, it's probably easier to end the world than to end capitalism. And that's the real problem. We are still in a capitalist system that is driven by economic models that have become very complex, and maybe we're asking the wrong question.

We could very well imagine other economic models based on well-being, rather than on economic growth, and could introduce these elements into the architecture equation.

But before that, let's talk about a resource-based economy.

We have reached a state of population overshoot today.

There are now eight billion of us since last month: the human species is now taking up so much space, that there is a risk of our presence disrupting what has been functioning for centuries and centuries according to its own economy. I'm talking about the biosphere, and the fact that we have introduced the technosphere into this perfectly balanced system. What defines the biosphere? It is a system based on solar energy, which manages to produce a true circular economy and constantly renews itself. Decompose, renew, decompose, renew. That is exactly what our system of accumulation and waste has not yet

The Blue Economy

How can we move from an economy of exploitation—motivated by supposedly infinite growth on an Earth with decidedly finite resources—to an economy of transforming environments, one which aspires to reestablish a system of balanced exchanges at the scale of the planetary ecosystem? This new economic and social model, a model for an abundant and inclusive future for all, is only conceivable following negotiation between local actors, located within territories, and external, globalized, and de-territorialized actors. We must establish a new equilibrium between resources and their mobility, considering a world that is both anchored and open to the outside, both local and connected.

Clay/wood balance for bioclimatic architecture

Saint-Laurent-du-Maroni, France

The creation of a Ministry of Justice complex in Saint-Laurent du Maroni is a symbolic and large-scale project in this town in western French Guiana, located far from the major institutional facilities, and whose history is inseparable from that of the penal colony and French colonization.

The unusual situation of French Guiana—the only European territory located in South America—creates a specific constraint for the local economy, and notably for construction projects. Materials from industrial sectors are mainly imported from Europe to meet the criteria of European standards, and to compensate for the absence of local industries. From the outset of the project, the requirement for bio-based and geo-based materials on site appeared to be essential. The nature of the soil, clay-based, and the presence of a nascent raw clay brick industry, allowed us to integrate this material as an input into the project. The use of local, exotic wood was also made possible through a growing local industry, which exploits the resources in accordance with the criteria for the preservation of the Amazonian forest. The project is an opportunity to strengthen the local economic system.

The *Cité du Ministère de la Justice* in Saint-Laurent du Maroni includes a courthouse, a set of support buildings and a prison. The courthouse faces the public space of the new district, and acts as the linchpin of the city's entrance. Its architecture is contextual and evocative of Guyanese culture. An outer layer of large openwork wooden palms shelters a volume of raw clay from the weather, which integrates all the courtrooms. In the gap between these two layers, the Salle des Pas Perdus (public lobby) is naturally ventilated, swept by the trade winds, and open onto the landscape.

The other buildings of the *Cité Judiciaire* have also been designed using this combination of raw clay walls and wooden framework, supports for the roof structure which shelter the buildings from the heat and encourage natural ventilation of the spaces. The idea of "the right material in the right place" has been a guiding principle for the project; the use of concrete has been limited to spaces accessible to the inmates, in order to meet the required safety and security criteria.

The design of the Penitentiary Center prioritizes the orientation of the buildings according to the sun and trade winds, in order to guarantee appropriate solar protection and optimal natural ventilation, and thus promote user comfort.

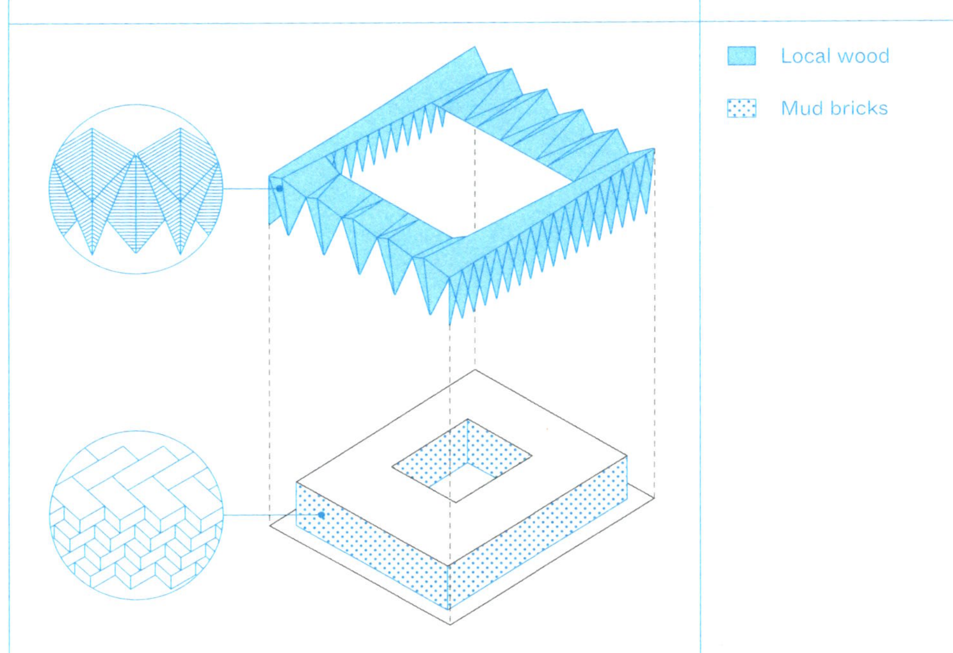

Lomé, Togo.

been able to imitate. And that is the actual economic problem today: how can we transform our technosphere into something that resembles the biosphere? How do we transform our system, which basically produces nothing but waste?
We need to change things, much like we did during the Covid crisis. One of the great positives of this crisis was—and I think Bruno Latour also mentioned this—that it proved to us that capitalism can be stopped unexpectedly from one week to the next. We effectively stopped the economic system that was moving us forward, and spent months with a system in suspension. We should have tried to design new economic models based on this situation. But unfortunately we were too eager to get back to normal, and getting back to normal has brought us back to the same issue we faced to begin with.

Romain Boursier
Jean-Baptiste, according to you, did Covid mark the end of capitalism?

Jean-Baptiste Fressoz
It's probably a bit of an exaggeration to put it like that. It marked the end of small sectors of capitalism such as air transport, and even that's not quite right, as planes were flying empty. CO_2 emissions went down by 6-7%, which is not that much. The big infrastructures continued to operate. Agriculture, fortunately, was still running somehow, but agriculture still represents a good quarter of emissions. I think Covid was an interesting thought experiment, but we shouldn't think that what we need to do is similar to what we did during the Covid crisis.

Romain Boursier
But if we look at the IPCC's guidelines, we would thus have reached the same target reductions as those resulting from the Covid crisis management.

Jean-Baptiste Fressoz
In order not to exceed the notorious 2ºC by 2100, we'd have to repeat the reduction of 6-7% each year for thirty years. But if it's easy to reduce aviation, it's more complicated to reduce fertilizer use.

Alain Bretagnolle
Pedro, there are different ways of approaching the subject, the American government has just injected hundreds of billions of dollars into the market with the Green New Deal. Does this seem like an effective solution to you? Europe, for its part, is using the regulatory approach. Jean-Baptiste mentioned this earlier. In your opinion, in the face of such urgency, what is the most appropriate solution between these two approaches?

The blue economy is a proposal put forward by the economist Gunter Pauli.[3] His program lays out a model of society that is not utopian and that to meet the basic human needs—food, shelter, energy, education, and health—starting from what is locally available. Suggesting a reversal of values, his project favors optimization over the maximization of production, equality over inequality of distribution, diversity over uniformity of co-existing ways of life, resilience over control of inhabited environments. For Pauli, it is also a question of setting nature back on its evolutionary trajectory, of restoring to the earth its qualities as a vital substrate, of rebuilding the productive mechanism of short supply chains and of supporting the emancipation of local populations.

3. Gunter Pauli, *The Blue Economy: 10 Years, 100 Innovations, 100 Million Jobs*, Paradigm Publications, 2010.

In-situ reuse of stone cladding

La Défense, France

The restructuring of the ACACIA building, designed in 1986 by the architects Gino Valle, Fernando Urquijo and Giorgio Macola, and located along the *Esplanade de la Défense* in Courbevoie, has been approached from the angle of reuse, particularly for its façade, as part of a low-carbon project. These intentions echo—on a city-wide scale—the ambitions to make Paris La Défense one of the largest low-carbon business districts in Europe.

We have been entrusted with a classic nine-story building, emblematic of the 1980s La Défense district, with its façade clad in finely dressed grey and black stone. The project therefore proposes to reclaim this cladding, to organize its removal, sorting, cleaning and physical and chemical examination. Treated on site, the stones will then be re-laid according to a careful layout to form a more thermally efficient complex.

The new facade will cover an office building with reinvented uses. The technical equipment on the roof terrace will be replaced by a vegetation-filled protected terrace for users to relax on. The roof of the company restaurant on the second floor will house an auditorium and a co-working space that will be open onto the city. Finally, the floors of the base will be redesigned so that they may be more welcoming, more comfortable and more flexible.

Project approaches have changed, everything is imagined in terms of short supply chains, and the inventory and understanding of the inherited resources are part of the initial observations: 3D surveys, fall risk management, verification of regulatory and insurance expectations, test sites, ATEx (*Appréciation Technique d'Expérimentation*, i.e. Technical Experimentation Assessment)… The planning method has also evolved, the principle of a clean slate is no longer appropriate. Taking control of the existing has become fundamental for developing new possibilities.

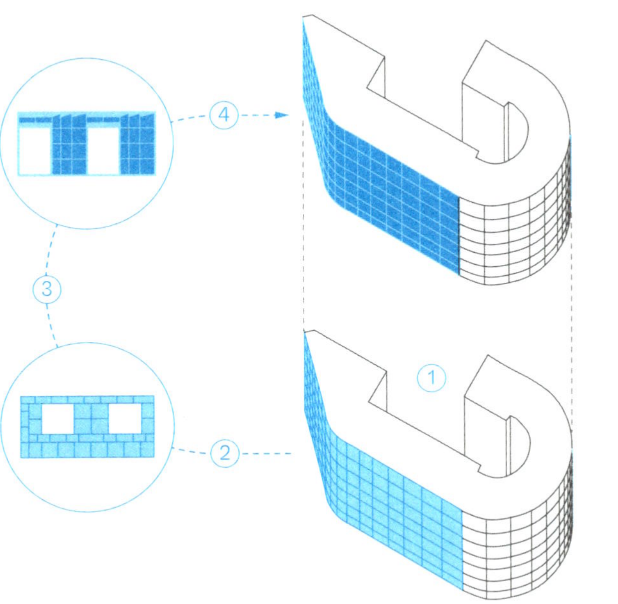

1 Existing envelope
2 Removal of stones
3 In-situ cleaning
4 Re-laid

↑ → Amman, Jordan.

The blue economy isn't restrictive; it is neither frugal nor structured upon diminution. Its project is based on an ethic of temperance and of the justifiable need to rebuild our individual and collective ways of living. It is a project of improvement, one based on another concept of wealth and consistently motivated by the notion of "more:" more freedom, more fellowship, more connections to nature, more equality between human beings. Keeping in line with our philosophic origins, the blue economy invites us to question what a good life is today.

Pedro Gadanho

I really don't know. You'd have to be a magician to figure out the right way to do things. The interesting thing about the American model is that it's based on tax incentives for people to produce things the right way. We don't know if it will work, because as we know, the American political system and its two-party system is very tough, and everything may come to a halt. But the fact is that on the other side, the European Green New Deal is focusing on the energy transition. Some scientists say that it's an illusion to think that this will improve things. In the words of Jean-Baptiste, the technological infrastructure needed for this transition project will only add energy to the system. We will deplete other resources before we reach this goal. And therefore, solve one problem by adding a bigger one. Another interesting aspect of this discussion is that recently some scientists have started to say that focusing on climate change might be a bad idea in the long run. For them, by focusing only on climate change, we're focusing only on the symptoms but not addressing the overall issue. We should be directly addressing the ecological emergency and the disruptions it has introduced in the global system—which will worsen as we consume and extract more resources. If we consider architectural activity specifically, shouldn't we avoid using new resources and just use what we already have? One way would be to reduce new constructions and focus only on recycling and reuse. This is more easily applicable in developed countries than in developing ones. Another way would be to impose a moratorium on new construction, and even start demolishing, in order to give back the space to desert and nature.

Jean-Baptiste Fressoz

The carrot is replacing the stick, which is interesting, but this incentive policy is still based on a vision of the transition as a technological substitution. Since the 1950s, there has been a lot of study of technological substitution, how technologies replace each other. The problem is that, as I mentioned in the introduction, raw materials and energy do not behave in the same way; they're not in a substitution relationship, but in symbiosis. The history of energy, the dynamics of energy and materials, has been overlaid with models of technological substitution that work very badly. So the most likely outcome is that, by heavily financing renewable energies and especially electric vehicles, we will continue to consume other materials such as aluminum, steel, cement, etc. And therefore continue to emit CO_2 galore. This is not meant to criticize renewables. Solar panels and wind turbines have a much lesser impact than batteries, cars, roads and buildings. The issue is not so much the consumption of rare earths in solar panels, which is real but small, but the rare earths that go into electronics and batteries.

Preserved barracks, diverted windows

Nancy, France

The Thiry barracks is a former military barracks built by the architect Richard Mique in 1769, in Nancy's Royal Sainte-Catherine neighborhood. It comprises three buildings framing a parade ground. The project concerns the transformation of two of the buildings into an administrative center to house government services, as well as the redevelopment of the parade ground.

These military buildings, designed to accommodate 4,000 men in large dormitories, are undergoing a major transformation: modification of the interior distribution, energy renovation, flooring replacement, and reinforcement of the foundations in order to meet programmatic challenges and provide users with a suitable working environment. The buildings, which had been unoccupied for forty years, had been partially renovated until the 1980s. The external double-glazed windows no longer meet the regulatory thermal insulation criteria.

A reuse approach has been set up in partnership with the association RéciproCité: a quantified diagnosis has been carried out in order to list all the elements that could be reused on site or on another site in Nancy: interior and exterior joinery, floor coverings, suspended ceiling tiles, switches, radiators, sanitary equipment, etc. In the context of our project, all the existing windows will be reused; once removed, they will be reinstalled with an alternative use: as interior joinery, incorporated into the separating partitions between offices and corridors. This diversion of the window frames makes it possible to install large bay windows in line with the corridors and provide abundant natural lighting in the central "active strip," while respecting programmatic and budgetary constraints.

The parade ground will be entirely renovated in a "circular" manner: the 340 parking spaces currently required will be created on stabilized ground around a central green square laid out as a rain garden. The reduction in parking requirements will make it possible to enlarge the central green space without requiring heavy roadway demolition.

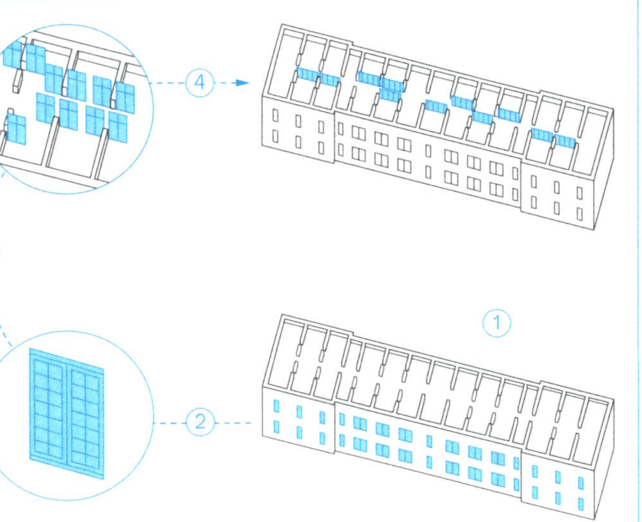

1 Existing building
2 Removal of windows
3 Sanding of windows
4 Interior joinery

The question is as central as it is serious. In her lecture on September 11th, 2012, upon receiving the Theodor W. Adorno Prize, the philosopher Judith Butler posed this question in a radical way. Starting from the observation that we have collectively built a world entirely "structured by inequality,"[4] she questioned the very meaning of action in an era that seems cruelly devoid of it. Linking moral and political questions, she establishes the recognition of life's vulnerability as a condition of living together: "I am quite sure that the answer to the question of how best to live cannot be rightly answered by destroying the subject of life."[5] Her lecture was a landmark and led to the creation of one of the most beautiful texts of contemporary ethics. Her strong words were carried by the severity of the question: how can one live a good life in a bad world?

4. Judith Butler, *Precarious Life: The Powers of Mourning and Violence*, Verso, 2004.

5. Judith Butler, "Can One Lead a Good Life in a Bad Life?", Adorno Prize Lecture, 2012.

There are technologies that we're going to need, and renewable energies are one of them. The question is, what are we going to do with all this energy? If it's only to run 1.5 billion cars as we do now, we won't have made much progress... Because these cars are made of steel, and increasingly of aluminum, which is even more energy-consuming, and if we add 600 kilos of batteries, we won't have solved anything. In countries where electricity is not too carbon intensive, such as France, the carbon footprint of mobility has been halved. Dividing by two puts the two-degree horizon back a little, but it changes absolutely nothing in the end. What really is a shame is to use good technologies, such as solar panels and windmills, to drive inefficient techniques such as private cars. That's the root of the problem. Because obviously, if we have cars, we have roads, so we have cement. The maintenance of existing roads alone consumes a lot of cement. In France, 35% of cement is used for roads, despite no new roads being built.
We really need to change our vision of things; we're in the process of transposing the conventional petrol car into the electric model, which makes absolutely no sense.

Romain Boursier
Ingrid Nappi, would you also like to say something on the subject of mobility?

Ingrid Nappi
Indeed, we can see that the system is at the end of its tether. Architects, to come back to this profession, must also integrate mobility into their projects. We mustn't only think of a building as a source of financial return, for the household or major investors, but also of a building as a source of savings: savings in terms of materials, in terms of mobility. Rethinking the city with smaller, denser blocks makes sense. We live in a global world, and we are also returning to much finer scales. The concept of saving in terms of mobility also means promoting a certain a way of life in neighborhoods and cities.

Romain Boursier
You have come back to the level of inhabitants and citizens. Pedro Gadanho, what do you think of this issue of the democratic malaise, as it also concerns our lifestyles and behavior? The French government organized a citizens' convention for climate which put forward 149 proposals to reduce the effects of climate change. It then retained only 10% of these proposals. You say that public authorities don't seem to be prepared for the consequences of climate change, whereas inhabitants are. You also say that all the problems are not being communicated by those who govern us: food shortages, population growth, etc. In the face of this democratic deficit

Bioclimatic interstices

Mirecourt, France

Mirecourt junior high school is an important building in more ways than one. Its structure and floors, made from 15,000 m^3 of Douglas fir and spruce, the majority of which being solid wood, made it the largest timber construction site in France in 2004. Its High Environmental Quality avant-garde design, with natural ventilation, a wood boiler room and passive solar heating allowing for a 50% reduction in energy consumption, has not gone unnoticed. We believe, however, that the main quality of this school does not lie in its environmental performance, which would not have made much sense without taking into account the primary objective, that of providing quality reception and work areas for the education of students.

The school was to accommodate 800 pupils and include teaching premises, a school library and information center, a covered play area, a sports ground, an astronomical observatory, an administration building, a 300-seat restaurant, and five staff accommodation units. We have expanded this project by adding a vast indoor protean space, which houses and prioritizes the various activities in different blocks, and an outdoor amphitheater. This interior space of several thousand square meters acts as a large thermal buffer, which contributes to the energy performance of the building and also offers "extra" space, available to both pupils and teachers. It has no particular allocation beyond its participation in the distribution of educational spaces, and can therefore be used for any type of activity. We have simply organized it into several scales and places, to accommodate different levels of socialization of the children. This space has partly been used by the school in an organized manner, for uses "forgotten" in its initial program, such as student lockers, but also and above all, for formal uses, including lessons and educational activities, and informal uses, in the form of games.

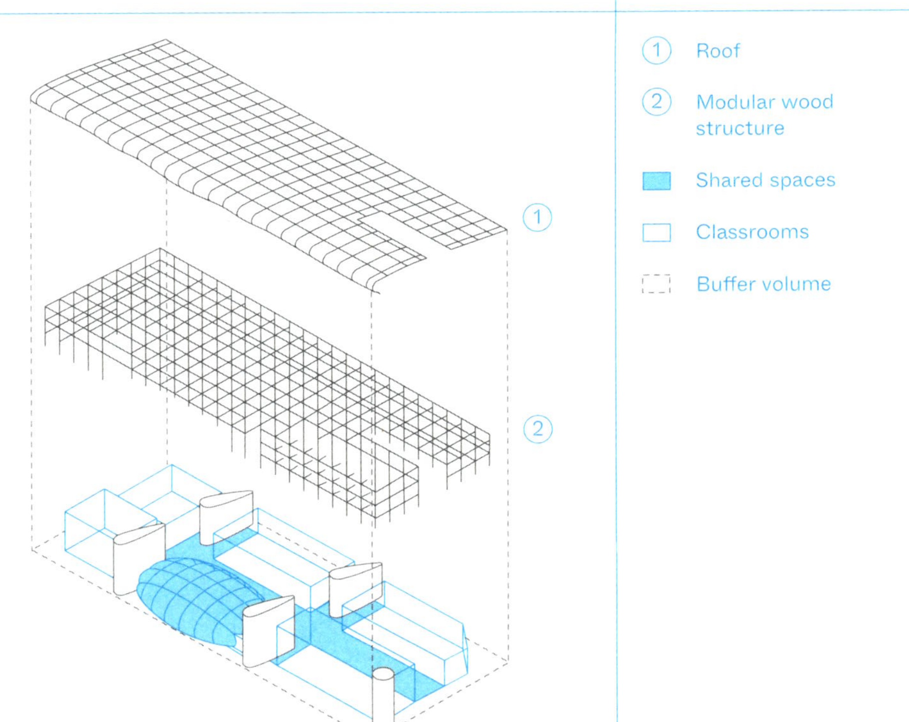

(1) Roof
(2) Modular wood structure
Shared spaces
Classrooms
Buffer volume

Towards a Systemic Approach to Transformation

Considering an economy of transformation implies a radical shift in our way of thinking. It impacts our notion of the project, shifting from a *planning* of territory to the *managing* of inhabited environments. It is in this shift that we realize that the former was reductive and prevented us from seeing things in their complexity. Today, an evolution of the project is possible: systemic in its method, the regeneration of environments is our object.

and the reluctance of our politicians, what modes of expression and citizen pressure can be envisaged?

Pedro Gadanho

This takes us back to the global issue which is that in a democracy, consensus-based change takes too long. Some thinkers talk about the possibility of the rise, very soon, of eco-fascist systems that will impose the necessary changes, because we are on the brink of catastrophe.
When we consider the scenarios we are facing according to science, things are always worse than we'd like to think. As far as the media is concerned, we shouldn't be scaring people.
But I think people, especially young people, are quite aware of these risks and do want this change. But the political system does not respond to these demands. Often for electoral reasons.
This is one of the main obstacles that needs to be overcome.
It would affect people's quality of life. So nothing gets done.
This is obvious in France. For me, the fact that the yellow vests movement was complaining about the rising cost of fossil fuels was very telling. But what we're facing is too big to be taken lightly, and our relationship to comfort has to change in the next few years. We are left with no choice.

Romain Boursier

We need to look further ahead.

Pedro Gadanho

Yes, but of course hope lies in the fact that this may lead us to experiments regarding commons and more collaborative and participatory economic models. I also think we need to show how this can work so that people's view of some of the comforts that they take for granted today may change. If we understand that we can really have a more balanced quality of life, more in harmony with nature. We haven't talked much about nature, but it is the issue at stake here: how, in fact, we can think of architecture as part of the natural processes taking place within the global system. Once we have made this paradigm shift in terms of thinking, we can start to think about an architecture that really integrates notions of decomposition, recycling, renewal, and therefore really move towards a circular economy model.

Alain Bretagnolle

Thank you, Pedro. Gunter Pauli, in a book called The Blue Economy, develops exactly this type of statement. In particular, he made an international inventory of local initiatives in communities that were in a state of disarray. He shows that there are paradigm shifts to be made culturally, but, for him, solutions exist. And the question associated with this is:

Increased habitability

Buenos Aires, Argentina

The Summers building is the result of a series of fortunate coincidences that led to an encounter between Architecturestudio, Zas-Lavarello Arquitectos, and Jack Green, two young developers with the ambition to exceed real estate standards in the city of Buenos Aires. Located on an ordinary and cramped plot of land bordered by two blind party walls of different heights, it contributes to the renewal of the Palermo district, which is undergoing major transformation, by offering innovative spaces and tertiary uses.

As Buenos Aires is nearly on the 35th parallel, it is possible to work out-of-doors throughout most of the year. That is why we gave future users the possibility of extending their activity onto the building's balconies. The latter are protected by a glazed layer made of mobile silk-screened glass slats, which wrap the built volumes in a set of curves tangential to the facades of the adjoining buildings.

A mapping of solar gains and a parametric study allowed a 78% reduction in direct solar gains. The external layer was developed based on a combination of five types of glass slats. The screen printing on these slats was designed using force fields to play with light reflections with a random dimension. The interior facade, consisting of sliding glass doors, allows for many uses, including the total opening of the building and the reception of a maximum amount of solar gain in winter, which makes it possible to work in the in-between space with a laptop computer in all seasons.

In this deep building, lit by only two facades, the vertical core acts as a light periscope. It offers wide perspectives onto the city while bringing natural light into the heart of the building. In order to offer other informal uses in outdoor spaces and to further enhance the experience of moving through the building, this periscope opens onto a landscaped terrace which thus becomes a meeting point, an event space and a relaxation area for the staff. Below, the terrace and gardens on the ground floor allow rainwater—the weather being increasingly stormy in the Argentinean capital—to infiltrate.

Summers was awarded the AFEX (*Architectes Français à l'Export*) Grand Prix in 2020.

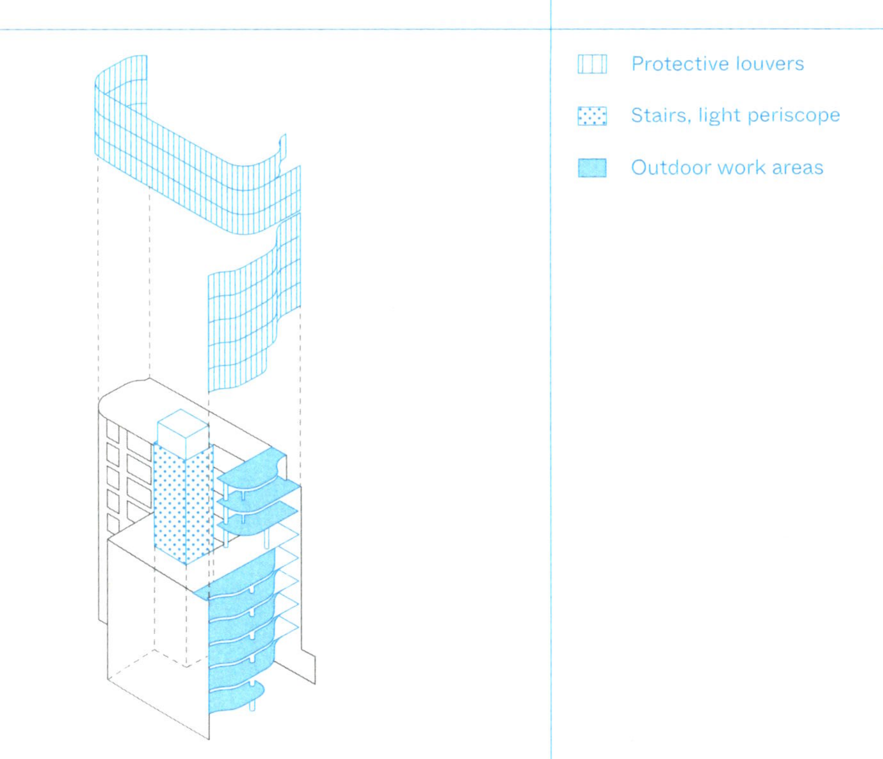

Protective louvers

Stairs, light periscope

Outdoor work areas

SUMMERS

Summers Office Building,
Jack Green,
Architecturestudio,
Zas-lavarello Arquitectos.

Buenos Aires, Argentina,
2019.

what is the right scale for initiating this change in ecological civilization? Is it the local scale?

Pedro Gadanho

Naturally, if we want to move towards a model in which we use natural resources in a balanced way, that model has to be local. But of course we can also benefit from the technological acquisitions we have made in recent years, especially in terms of sharing experience and knowledge. The fact that we already have technology and knowledge that have given high-precision agriculture, for example, means this could be applied directly elsewhere without having to go through all the mistakes we've made in the past. The change has to be local, but it has to be connected and make the most of our sharing abilities. In the field of architecture, this is quite relevant, and already happening. Collaborations are taking place between people from India or Africa studying in Europe and creating models and innovations related to the local needs of the places they come from, and that's really important. I think it's also a mission for architects to cultivate these exchanges, while also exploring their local situation in terms of resources, economic cycles, and community participation.

Alain Bretagnolle

Jean-Baptiste Fressoz, you have studied material flows through customs management. In this debate between local and global, some people talk about bioregions and short supply chains. Is the flow logic that must be taken into account in the response to climate change located at the right level with these bioregions?

Jean-Baptiste Fressoz

First of all, when we study international trade and the flow of materials between countries or groups of countries, we understand that the system is stifled by inertia. In other words, the end of globalization is not in sight. The biggest shocks in history, i.e. the First World War followed by the Spanish flu, reduced trade, but only temporarily. In terms of CO_2 emissions, these shocks represent small notches in a continuously rising curve. Similarly, the 1930s crisis reduced international trade, but not that much in the end. So to imagine that globalization will stop because of Covid, because of tensions between China and the United States, etc., seems to me to be a mistake.

Secondly, the circular economy is a bit like the energy transition: everyone is in favor of it. You have to know that a circular economy is already very much in practice in a specific field, which is steel: we recycle 90% of the steel used, and this works very well. This does not prevent us from producing 1.7

From an epistemological point of view, the ecological sciences—which are based on the recognition of interactions between living organisms and their environment—call for the consideration of relationships. By raising awareness of the deadly character of dissociative logic and by encouraging us to think about what binds us together as living beings, ecology affirms a comprehensive, ecosystemic world. A project, therefore, only makes sense if it is systemic in dimension. As the result of collective hypotheses, it supports the synergistic transformation of environments.

Reversible street-level floor

Créteil, France

Near the Henri Mondor Hospital and the *Grand Paris Express* station, the *Triangle de l'Echat* development project transforms a former motorway junction into a future peaceful and mixed-use neighborhood. Architecturestudio is building a 90-unit housing project there. In an environment marked by a diversity of buildings, the project meets the urban intentions of creating a layered city. It offers three types of collective dwellings: the base on which the operation rests vertically, the body which develops duplex-loggia dwellings, and the villas which carve out volumes in the background, multiplying the outdoor spaces and the pleasures of living above ground.

In this context of ambitious transformation of public spaces, how can we design a building that embodies this new polarity and amplifies the objective of pacifying public spaces, while developing the use of bicycles, and encouraging inclusive social interactions? How can the closed figure of quiet environments be opened up onto the central landscaped garden? How can we rethink the way addresses are distributed in public spaces? How can we anticipate the changing needs and functions of street-level building floors near a hospital and future transport hub?

To do so, the agency worked on the design of a street-level floor, based on the qualities of a pedestrian city that may guarantee the qualities of the '15-minute city', through the pleasure of walking, the services that can be found along the way, and the evolution of the uses that it houses, and that bring it to life. This street-level floor is opened up by a large 5.5-meter plinth which frees up passages leading to the heart of the planted blocks, and gives access to the entrance halls of the blocks of flats. This space is diversified by the projects that have been established there. A shop marks the corner, and the lobbies and bicycle rooms have been made visible to encourage their daily use. The street-level floor is also reversible due to the fact that *Atelier-Logements* (units for artist to work and live in) are located on the pedestrian walkways, which benefit from large double-height volumes. The creation of addresses is thus implemented in the public domain, at the heart of the block, or both, in the event of a division of use. Such indeterminacy of use seems to us to be all the more important if one projects oneself in the future, near a hospital, with the development of freelance health-related activities for example, or even local co-working services.

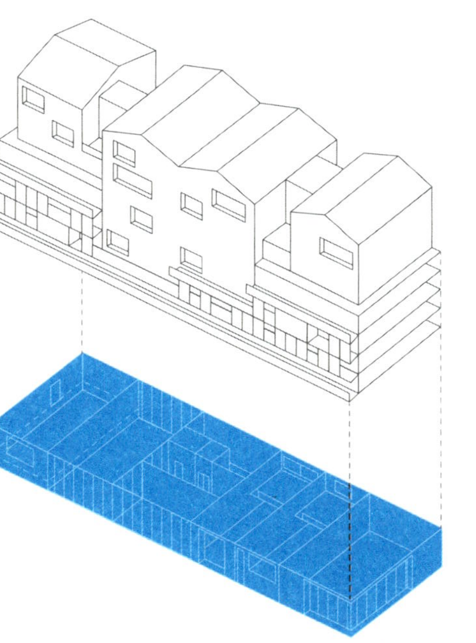

Body of the building

Reversible street-level floor

Inhabited environments are threatened: we see phenomena everywhere of segregation between human establishments and natural environments, and internal divisions within socio-cultural environments. This critical state is the result of a legacy of urbanization founded on principles of the division, rationalization, and segmentation of space. It is the product of a way of manufacturing the urban aboveground, giving precedence to economic imperatives over social, cultural, and environmental realities. The effects are numerous: the depletion and weakening of ecosystems, phenomena of isolation and fragmentation of the city that question the commons, and the rupture between urban and biological rhythms.

gigatonnes of steel on the side. And recycling steel means using electric arc furnaces which consume a lot of energy.

This idea of closing material cycles first emerged in the 1800s among small groups of intellectuals and industrial chemists in Paris. At a time when everyone was complaining about pollution in Paris, their response was: "We're going to create a circular economy, industry X is going to recover waste from Y and all this is going to be perfectly well organized. This institution, called the Conseil d'Hygiène et de Salubrité de Paris (Hygiene and Health Council of Paris), was created in 1802. Its aim was to organize the proper circulation of materials at the level of a city, in order to create an urban circular economy.

As far as bioregions are concerned, this seems logical, but many countries rely on international trade and import agricultural goods to live. This became clear with the war in Ukraine: blocking grain exports at the port of Odessa has had absolutely catastrophic repercussions for a large number of African countries. Interdependencies must therefore be taken into account.

Bioregions, in France at least, appeared in the wake of neo-Malthusianism, of this idea that soon there will be no more oil, and therefore no more transport, and so we'll have to feed ourselves with what we produce locally. The problem is that the climate crisis is not a Malthusian issue at all. The problem is that we have far too many resources, not too few. We have far too much coal, far too much gas, far too much oil.

And climatologists tell us that we are likely to burn up the planet before we run out of these resources. The idea of bioregions comes from an ecological school of thought that goes back to the 1970s, the decade of the oil crises. When Naomi Klein writes *This Changes Everything*, we have to take it literally and it tells us that we also need to profoundly change our environmental thinking process. All these patterns of thinking around the idea that "we're going to run out of something" don't apply to the present climate emergency.

Pedro Gadanho

I'd like to qualify this idea of the impact of circular economy on architecture. There are a couple of ways in which things are starting to develop. One of them, of course, is material recycling: for example, concrete from demolitions can be turned into carbon storage and used to make new pavements, and so on. The recycling of materials has improved considerably, which is very interesting for our line of work. We are also starting to plan circularity starting with the design of buildings, so that they may be dismantled, and materials be traced and reused. There is a need for an economy to be organized. And there are also technical innovations involved. Many of these initiatives are still in their infancy. They are therefore not at a

An architectural envelope for mutable uses

Zurich, Switzerland

The Pergamin I and II building complex is located where the former industrial site of the Manegg paper mills used to be, in the immediate vicinity of the rail and motorway network, and marks the entrance to Zurich's *Greencity* eco-neighborhood. The first building houses offices on an active base of shops, showrooms, conference rooms, and restaurants. In the second building, on the edge of Sihlwald nature park, offices have been converted into a nursing school by the purchaser, increasing the attractiveness of this new urban polarity, which brings with it numerous housing developments. Together with the neighboring buildings by Gigon&Guyer and JSWD Architects, the two buildings are intended to form not only a new service center, but also a connected, dynamic city fragment integrated into the landscape of Zurich's Sihl Valley.

The guiding principle of the project is the creation of an "architectural valley" protected from the motorway and its pollution, a space of amenity and informal interaction, to which all architectural elements contribute. The facades of the buildings facing this valley are designed as rock monoliths that direct the view in different directions from the main axis, towards the interior landscapes and the surrounding mountain ranges. The angular geometry of the valley is softened by the presence of circular spaces where people can meet, which combine benches and vegetation.

Pergamin II, which is marked by two vertical fault lines, includes panoramic terraces overlooking the valley and offering views towards Zurich city center. Pergamin I, located at the prow of Greencity, has a smooth and transparent double-skin façade, the grid of which is randomly decorated with bronze elements to create a luminous weaving effect. This monolith responds to the monumental scale of the road infrastructure below, and offers optimal working conditions with modular and flexible floor plans as well as abundant natural light.

Both buildings have obtained LEED Platinum Core & Shell and Greenproperty Gold certifications with high objectives for quality and sustainability: geothermal heating, low energy consumption, high insulation, and daylight control.

The "architectural valley" shows the regeneration of a former industrial site into a new urban habitat, which integrates the natural environment and is open to evolution.

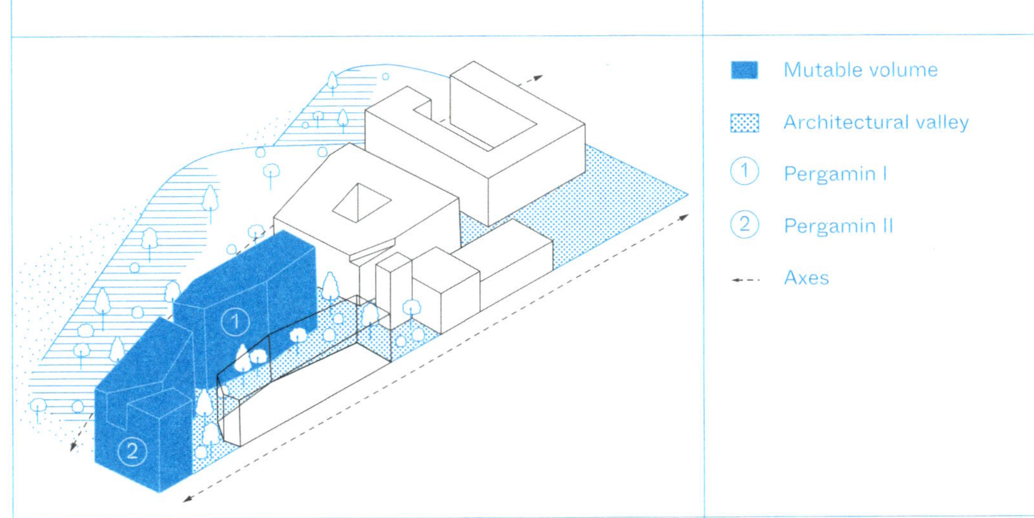

Mutable volume
Architectural valley
1 Pergamin I
2 Pergamin II
Axes

Pergamin I et II,
Losinger Marazzi
AG, CSL immobilier,
Architecturestudio.

Zurich, Switzerland, 2021.

stage in which they may be used on a large scale yet, and might simply come too late to effectively address urgent needs.

Jean-Baptiste Fressoz
It's interesting to discuss this with architects, because your materials precisely do not seem to be making much progress. As much as solar panels have progressed, cement has not. Consider works from the 1920s: cement then was made more or less as it is now, in large rotating furnaces. There's been some progress in terms of efficiency, but fundamentally, not much has changed. A lot of gas is getting burnt in cement plants in Europe. But 90% of cement is still produced using coal. It's the same thing for steel, and 40% of steel is used in construction. You have to realize that things are not going well in your fields.

Romain Boursier
With regard to the reduction of our energy consumption, thermal renovation for example, what role do architects play? How do they fit into the value chain?

Ingrid Nappi
In this group of different stakeholders, most of them think in the short term. This is the case when developers are setting up projects. Financiers also think in the very short term. The only ones who have a long-term vision of the real estate object are architects, since they are the link between the past, the history of the site (the building must fit into a context), the present (what the needs are), and the future—they must anticipate, for example, the reversibility of the building. Moreover, the value that architects can have is that they are at the junction between the contracting authority and the project management authority, and that they may defend this time factor.
The problem, particularly in France, and as a generality for new constructions as well as for renovation projects, is that architects are not often consulted... And here, I think that we can note the difference with Germany, for example, Belgium, Spain or of course, a leading country in these matters, Switzerland. The value of architects is also a question of regulations.

Romain Boursier
Absolutely. And precisely, are you suggesting a new way of intervening regarding this notion of value?

Ingrid Nappi
I'd like to come back to the Observatory of the Economy of Architecture. The idea is to recognize the economic value of architects in the production chain. Because if we want

One of the first reasons for the dissociation of territories is the separation of scales, at the levels of both representation and action. Scales are specific frameworks, distinct from one another. Their articulation is useful for understanding the transitions which support inhabited environments and unfold *through* **them. An architecture of environments is thus necessarily** *trans-scalar* **and seeks to interrelate local, regional, and global issues. A resource economy is unthinkable without this back and forth. It is a question of understanding, in the same system, the earth as soil and the Earth as a planet.**

Habitable rooftops

Cairo, Egypt

In New Cairo, near the American University, and about a twenty-minute drive from the New Capital, lies the future mixed-use district called "Urban Walk" which, as its name suggests, is dedicated to pedestrians, offering them access to everything (from housing to offices, shops, culture, leisure, care, park, education) within a quarter of an hour's walk.

The blueprint for this mixed-use neighborhood was drawn up by Solidere, the company that rebuilt the historic heart of Beirut, designed at the time of the French Mandate based on an orientalised Haussmannian model, while making it essentially pedestrian-friendly and conducive to walking, window-shopping and to outdoor drinking and dining. Before Beirut fell into a new dark period, its city center had become a model for several countries in the area, which discovered the virtues of balanced density, shaded streets, public space favoring inclusive interactions, and urban architecture within which each building and the urban ensemble of which it is a part, define each other. New neighborhoods with the urban form and lifestyle of European cities that the world loves so much have thus begun to flourish in many Middle Eastern cities that spread in the twentieth century as cars became the main means of transport.

With along one side, one of the main arteries of New Cairo, and on the other, the central park of the Urban Walk, the Urban Business Lane business district is structured around a pedestrian shopping street punctuated by squares and plazas whose outdoor drinking areas open onto the central park.

We designed the architecture and public spaces of this neighborhood, defined its urban and architectural identity, and took up the challenge of doing so based on modular office buildings (due to marketing imperatives) while successfully achieving the sequencing and diversity in terms of typological unity, both being necessary to build the character of the district. The landscaped roofs of the project are visually and sometimes physically connected and open onto the park and the horizon. They will be hosting multiple activities by day and night.

Thanks to the well-defined relationship between solids and voids, but also to screens acting as solar protection for the facades, merging one into another in a series of parametric sequences, which may vary according to the needs of the work spaces and the contextual singularities of each facade: solar exposure, façades facing another building or, on the contrary, open views, location in the neighborhood: facing the park, the avenue or the inner promenade, etc. A sequencing process at the pace of pedestrians, stimulating their walk between the public spaces and shops, cafés and restaurants, all the way to the converted roofs connected by narrow footbridges.

Footbridges

Inhabitable rooftops

Pedestrian shopping street

Another essential transversality is found in today's fields of knowledge. Architectural culture, which is condensed in the design approach and is inherently transdisciplinary, plays thoroughly with this capacity for displacement and transposition, in and towards extraneous knowledge. The ecological issues of our time are an invitation to further expand our interdisciplinary relationships. Deciphering, designing, or planning environments means exercising and practicing this skill, by collectively mobilizing distinct but complementary knowledge.

to implement a circular economy and establish recognition of environmental value, we must recognize the transversal approach of architects. We must understand their added value to the real estate product. This is an opportunity to change the way we look at architects in France, beyond the aesthetic value, and possibly the philosophical value that they embody.
In France especially, architects are considered above all as artists. If they want to play a role in these new production sectors, particularly in renovation and in the circular economy, they must become aware of their actual economic value, of the positive externalities that they generate. This necessarily requires an understanding of other economic stakeholders and their economic reasoning. What is the economic reasoning of users, property developers? What is their economic calculation? What are the possible sources of funding? What is the economic calculation of investors? How can financial profitability be improved in the short or long term? How can my building be reversible? How can bio-based materials add value to my building in the long term? We don't measure all this, but it's essential.
We must also consider the economic value of what the building can bring to the neighborhood, to the city. This is important. We have to be aware of the economics of the system and how other economic stakeholders think.

Pedro Gadanho
That's very interesting. I think you're absolutely right, and that there is a historic opportunity for architects to assert their role within this value chain. This is one of the arguments presented in my book *Climax Change!* We need to change the impulses that drive us to produce architecture. The opportunity is similar to that of the first modern movement involving the globalization of building materials. We could become key stakeholders because we're the ones who prescribe the materials that will be used and the solutions that will be adopted. And this role, more than the artistic one, will be much more important in the years to come, in directing markets and building systems towards better and more sustainable solutions. Architects have to become aware of their potential, and not stop at this idea that they may be the masters of formalization, of creating beautiful objects.

Alain Bretagnolle
The same idea applies to education. Are "starchitects" doomed to disappear?

Pedro Gadanho
I think they're long gone. After 2008, we were already reading articles saying that the party was over. Even Macron is telling

A hospital in extreme conditions

Les Abymes, France

Hospitals are meant to "mend the living," to quote the title of a fine book by Maylis de Kerangal. However, they also and above all address human beings in all their complexity, culture, anxieties, and hopes. This dialectic between efficiency, flow, and technology on the one hand, and sense of welcome, spatial quality, and caring for others on the other, is the guiding principle of the design of the Guadeloupe CHU (University Hospital).

Volumes that make people feel welcome and find their way easily, a structuring sense of geometry, natural light, and a relationship to the outside world that qualify the itineraries, colors that personalize the atmosphere, attention paid to the smallest constructional detail, all these elements bear architectural witness to the consideration given to hospital inpatients. This architecture of care borrows a spatial archetype from Guadeloupean society by bringing together the various specialized centers and technical or administrative functions around "Rue Caraïbe," a welcoming and reassuring backbone, a place for socializing, sharing and living that stands apart from the medical lexicon.

The building follows the gentle slope of the surrounding land and underlines the topography with a delicate conception of the vegetal landscape and water cycle. Both the protection provided by the roofs and facades, and the solar energy and energy recovery processes contribute to the environmental performance of the project, which has been certified High Environmental Quality.

At the same time, the West Indies are being subjected to a rare concentration of climatic factors, particularly tectonic ones, which present significant risks. We therefore had to provide solid answers to these issues, which are in conflict with the objectives of care. The University Hospital of Guadeloupe will be able to accommodate a massive inflow of patients in the event of a pandemic, natural disasters, or traumatic events. A disaster zone, an isolation unit, numerous adaptive beds, and prioritized flows make it a benchmark hospital in terms of response to pandemic crises. A highly advanced earthquake- and cyclone-resistant design will also allow medical acts to be carried out in the most extreme climatic conditions.

This new building complex, which is adapted to the climate, to environmental risks, and to the island lifestyle, presents a symbiosis between medical technical performance, the attention paid to the person being cared for and to the medical staff, and the Caribbean spatial and cultural universe.

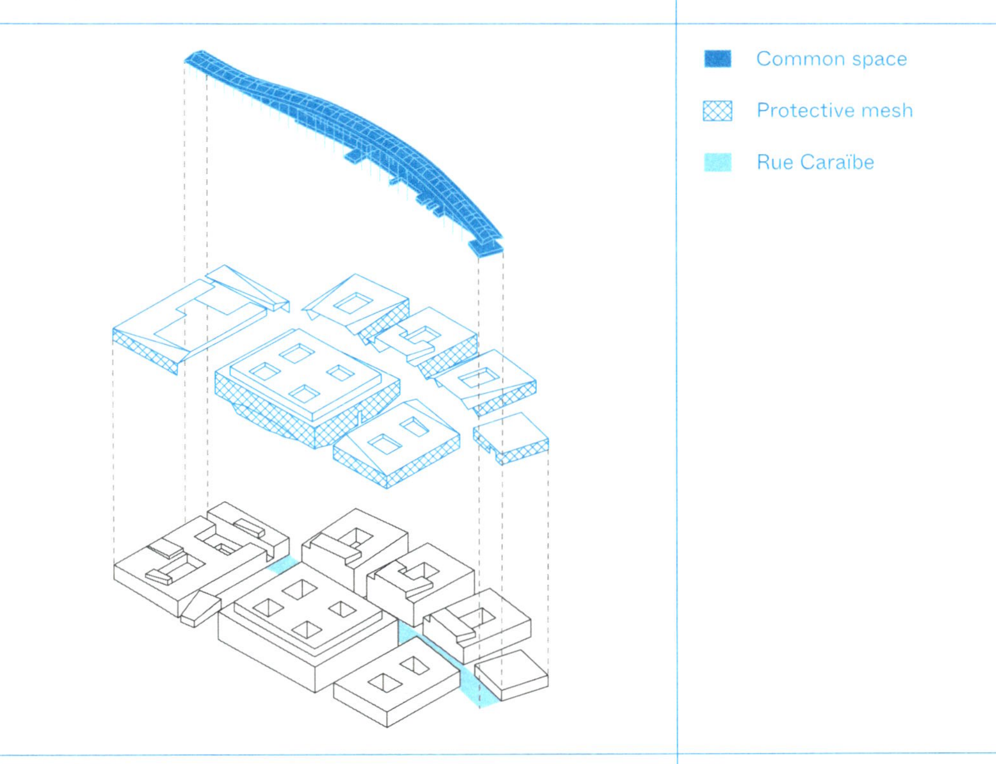

Common space
Protective mesh
Rue Caraïbe

"Al Nahr" mixed-use tower, Al Nahr construction, development and realization, Architecturestudio.

Beirut, Libanon, 2023.

This synergistic thinking centers on interactions and the processes at play. A notion of the project as a search for synergies thus implies a variation of the systemic approach on all levels, from co-design to co-habitat. Nonetheless, this logic of cooperation between actors, whether human or non-human, is at times insufficient for restoring the ecological balances of inhabited environments and is a necessary, complementary, and regenerative approach.

us that the age of abundance is over. The star architects themselves have moved in other directions. Look at Norman Foster. He is now one of the champions of a more ecological approach to architecture, and even if his way of doing things may be dubious, he seems genuinely committed to this role.

Alain Bretagnolle
We can indeed see that the latest Pritzker awards highlight other values for architecture and the recognition of architects' work.

Pedro Gadanho
Yes, people like Lacaton, Vassal and others are working with ideas that already indicate that the direction is shifting.

Alain Bretagnolle
There is a lot of talk today about taking care of the environments that we share with other living beings. In your opinion, Pedro, will this transform our practices and design methods, by taking into account this dimension of nature or living beings?

Pedro Gadanho
I think it's something that's starting to happen in small circles, and will hopefully influence more and more people. I'm talking about things such as interspecies design, which has moved from the art field to the architectural field in the last two or three years. Architects are starting to consider the needs of natural stakeholders. We are at the very beginning of this kind of experimentation, while simultaneously going back to something that already existed in the history of architecture: biomorphic or organic design that is inspired by the principles of nature, in terms of structure or adaptation to the environment, etc.

Alain Bretagnolle
Jean-Baptiste, you're an environmental historian. This is a relatively new discipline. Do you see your discipline, its research objects, and the public's appetite for it evolving?

Jean-Baptiste Fressoz
You know, the history of the environment is increasingly becoming the history of everything: the history of techniques, the history of matter, the history of the economy. What's interesting is that in the 1980s and 1990s, what was fashionable was cultural history, that sort of thing, with philosophical approaches. The point of environmental history is that it has pushed history towards more materialist fields.

Hospital-oasis

Tangier, Morocco

Designing a new hospital, especially when the project is a large one—800 beds in this case—can easily lead to focusing on the technical objective only: a building intended to receive equipment gathered on a technical platform where doctors will have all the tools necessary to treat their patients at their disposal, and where flows will be clearly prioritized and kept under control. A hospital is much more than that. To provide proper care, technology is not enough. Hospitals must also offer a sensitive setting where patients, staff and doctors can work, treat and be treated in a calm and pleasant environment, but also develop human relations and maintain a sense of the outside world.

In Tangier, we initially built a transitional space with urban qualities, which signals the presence of the hospital in the city and creates a link with the latter. The entrance area and technical platform are entirely protected by a horizontal sunshade that covers the entire hospital access area, over 150 meters long. This monumental canopy, eleven meters above ground, with the play of light and shadows of its extensive protection, provides a gentle welcome for patients and their families, and creates the conditions for a social life to take place around the hospital. The architectural element extends into the building complex and covers the inner courtyards—which thus remain temperate throughout the year—and gives it a sense of unity and tectonic coherence. As an expression of Moroccan lifestyle, an Andalusian-inspired garden was created at the entrance to the site to provide coolness and shade, and as a transition between the hospital and the city.

The white architecture of the hospital reflects the tradition of Moroccan architecture, without being a pastiche. To limit the use of air conditioning, different architectural elements of passive solar protection were used: the consultation departments are located around small planted patios, the façades of the base floor are protected by large horizontal surfaces of white concrete, and the façades of the rooms located above the canopy are clad with a pre-façade made of white fiber cement panels, designed in the style of a mashrabiya to protect the interior spaces from sunlight. Beyond the implementation of technical devices, the environmental dimension is approached through the architecture and envisaged, above all, as an element that enriches the perceived experience of the spaces.

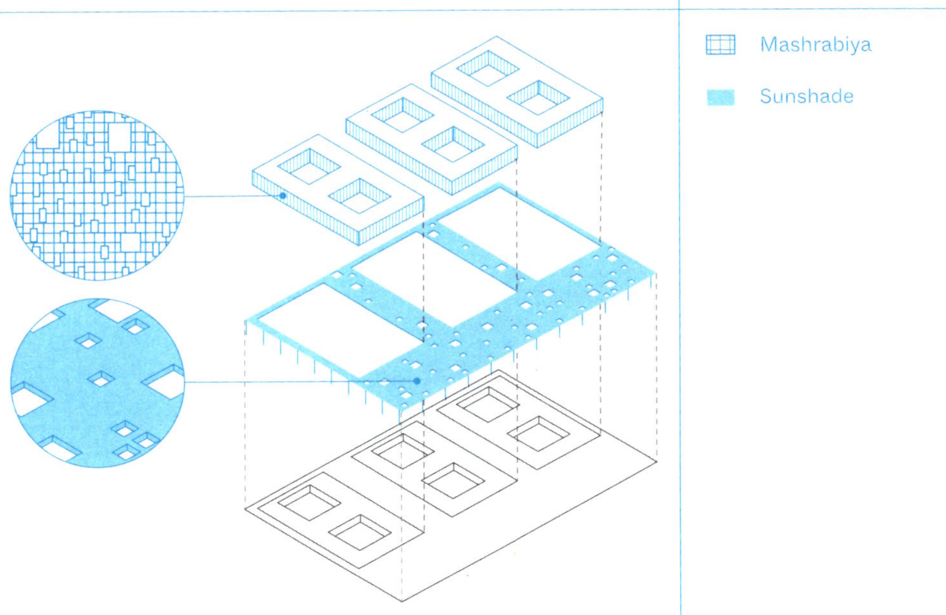

University Hospital in Tangier,
Ministry of Health,
Kingdom of Morocco,
Hajji & Elouali,
Architecturestudio.

Tangier, Morocco, 2021.

The general decline of inhabited environments, either natural or constructed, invites the design project to develop a logic of support and repair, driven by an ethics of care. It seems necessary today to consider and compose with metabolic dynamics and the resilience of environments. Their regeneration problematizes our capacity for action, and can also nurture, at times, a preference for inaction. In calling into question our capacity to act, in a world where each gesture has an impact, the regeneration of these environments equally questions our ability to undo—doubling the logic of isolating its object by a logic of withdrawal, or even the erasure of all traces of anthropization.

Pedro Gadanho

From an academic point of view, the curriculum shouldn't only include environmental history, but also ecological sciences, which should be part of an architect's curriculum. We are all aware of the different phenomena that occur on a daily basis, from droughts or floods to sea level rise to species extinction, but we still see these phenomena as separate from each other and isolated. We experience these issues, but rarely do we put them all together in the same picture. If we don't integrate this kind of logic, a holistic logic of understanding complexity, into the making of architecture and cities, then we're really missing the point.

Jean-Baptiste Fressoz

Since you asked me a historiographical question, I must say that architects who have written history books on cities or even buildings have played an important role in environmental history, because they have shown interest in subjects on which historians had not focused much. One book, for example, that influenced me a lot was *Nature's Metropolis* by William Cronon. It's a materialist history of Chicago. It doesn't focus on the successive innovations that made the city, but on its history as a metabolism.

Romain Boursier

As you can see, we have moved into the field of the knowledge economy. I have a question for Ingrid Nappi. How does teaching economics in architecture schools contribute to such an opening?

Ingrid Nappi

Once again, I think that France stands apart from other countries, because when we consider the curriculums of the Écoles Nationales Supérieures d'Architecture, we can see that economics is not taught there. It is implicitly and too often associated with finance and often opposed to culture. Understanding economics starts by understanding where value comes from, and the system of economic stakeholders involved in the value chain of the production of the built environment. For architects, it involves understanding the economic reasoning of other stakeholders in the production chain, so that they may find their place and be paid fairly. Today in France, architects are above all considered to be a burden because they are paid a percentage of construction costs. That's unbelievable! We're talking about the frugality of materials, cost reductions... this shows a discrepancy. How can architects be remunerated fairly if their value is based solely on construction and on an economy linked to mass production? This rationale is outdated, it dates back to when we had endless resources, and didn't

Observing the living

Denqing, China

As the site of an initial "Magic Valley" exhibition in autumn 2019, the Xia Zhu Lake Garden pavilions achieve the ambition of the city of Dengqing to develop ecotourism through occasional cultural and educational events. Dengqing, which is famous for its mountains and seaside resort, its rice, bamboo and tea cultivation, its fishing and silk production, takes its name from an ancient Chinese saying: "Righteous people are like crystal clear waters."

In the heart of Zhejiang province, the project follows an international consultation aimed at highlighting rural culture and promoting the richness of a lifestyle that is close to nature. This site, which will be used for display and experimentation purposes during the exhibition, offers a flexible space that can be converted into an ecotourism facility (hotel, restaurant, conference center). The ultimate needs of the project and its development will thus be taken into account during and after the exhibition in terms of functional division, the organization of flows and architectural design in order to initiate a sustainable development structured around environmental, social and economic issues.

Based on the concepts of harmony and symbiosis with their natural environment, the four Xiazhu Lake Garden exhibition pavilions have been built on the mountainside. They promote a lifestyle that combines modernity and ecology in a place where sports activities and cultural exhibitions meet. The wooden slats along the facades as well as the green roofs accentuate the lines of the landscape, while the folds of the roofs merge with the silhouette of the mountains. The architecture, by framing this majestic panorama, thus creates a dialogue with the tea plantations and the mountains in the background. The park welcomes the full diversity of the fauna and flora of this rich ecosystem, thus offering a closer relationship with the latter through educational tours and events.

With its powerful relationship with nature, the project aims to become an ecological and cultural platform of national importance, by offering a unique experience between art and landscape.

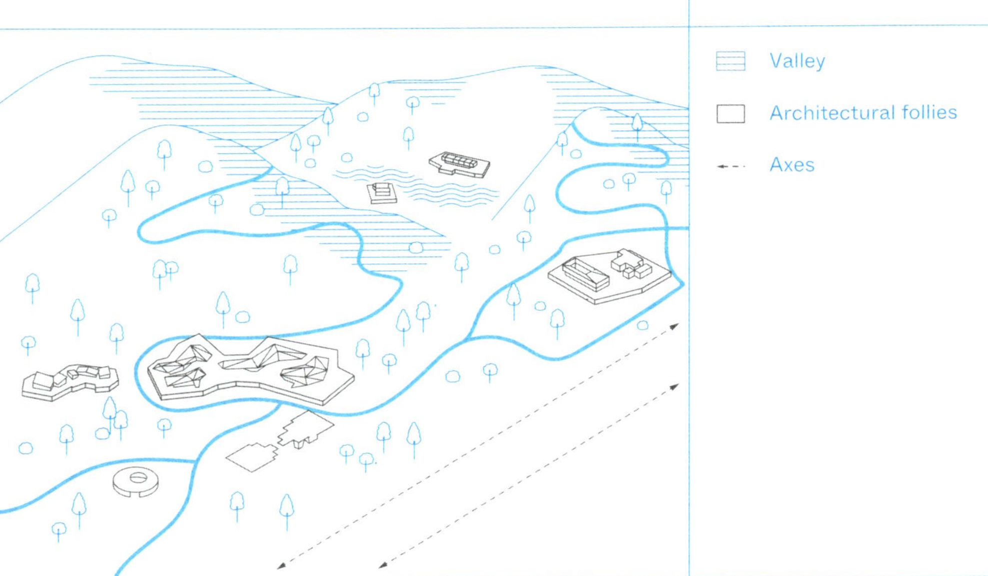

Valley

Architectural follies

Axes

Exhibition pavilions
Xiazhu Lake Garden,
Zhejiang Dechen Tourism
Development Co. Ltd,
Architecturestudio.

Denqing, China, 2020.

While it can transform our ways of dwelling and living, sustainability is also a lucrative business, one serving ecological solutionism. This green economy at times generates bigger problems than the ones it claims to address. The issue of energy is an example. Wind and solar power, even if they consume materials and produce CO_2, are still good technologies. But replacing all combustion engine vehicles with electric vehicles, served by these power sources, is nonsensical.[6]

6 Jean-Baptiste Fressoz, As Explore, "What are the regenerative economies for our territories?", January 25, 2023.

need to think about decarbonization and ecological value. Yet architects have multiple values: cultural, social, societal, technical values, and so on...
Economics is also about understanding how prices are set. Of course, the economics of construction, learning how to calculate the cost of construction, that exists, but that's not what I'm talking about. I'm talking about understanding the economic microcosm. In France, that is not taught. It's associated with finance, which is taboo, with the financialization of real estate, etc., which is not the case in other countries.
The situation is different in major engineering schools where the teaching of economics is a historical reality. I see this at the École des Ponts, where I've been teaching a real estate economics course for over twenty years in the SEGF department (economics, management, and finance). I meet students from the Civil Engineering department and other departments, from other engineering schools, engineering students who already have this culture of economics. Architects should really acquire this culture of economics, especially today, with the multiple crises we're going through. We need stakeholders with a multi-dimensional approach. And that doesn't exist, because everything works in isolation. We can observe this in the production chain, particularly in the project management sector: all the new regulatory standards that are making production more complex and more expensive mean that design studios operate separately, whereas there is a need for cross-disciplinary approaches, in order to make savings.

Alain Bretagnolle
Pedro, what did you tell your students, especially at Harvard, when you were doing the research work that led to your book *Climax Change!* so as to integrate all these constraints and stimulate responses?

Pedro Gadanho
Firstly, that we need creativity, innovation. But that we should reward innovation in the context of reuse, reconstruction and renovation, rather than rewarding creativity in the production of new objects. I think this is important. These changes in what we value within the discipline, within the profession, are really important. In other disciplines we see a lot of highly innovative solutions, regarding issues related to decarbonization, integrating nature, using biomaterials, etc. Tech start-ups that have started to develop these ideas are rapidly entering the market. In the field of architecture, it's a pity that ideas should often remain good ideas that just go nowhere. We have to find ways to integrate these ideas into economic

Biotope island

Palaiseau, France

The Danone teams had told us that their business was to offer food based on natural products produced by natural processes. We worked with this paradigm in mind by designing a form of architecture that works closely with nature, and even leads to food production.

The building, which houses research and development halls, laboratories and offices for the Danone group's Research, Development and Quality Assurance departments on three levels, is located in the heart of a future neighborhood dedicated to university excellence, research and cutting-edge industries. This pioneering project is integrated into a contemporary environment where nature largely dominates, and contributes to the creation of a sustainable and ecological urban system.

The landscape of the Saclay plateau, interspersed with agricultural land and wooded areas, inserts itself into the buildings through two vegetation gaps, thus creating an organic vibration within the premises. The variations of the vegetation throughout the seasons make the building's articulation evolve and offer its façades natural protection: leafy in summer to protect from solar gain, and leafless in winter to let in free heat. We chose to start with hops, which grow very quickly, so that a beautiful vine may develop on the façade wires over time. Harvesting has become a ritual activity for the occupants of the research center, who are thus fed by an architectural device.

The project has replaced monocultural practices and recreated plant and animal biodiversity by developing a local food-producing wetland. This quality was rewarded by the 2007 Essonne environment awards for the quality of the biodiversity recovered on the site.

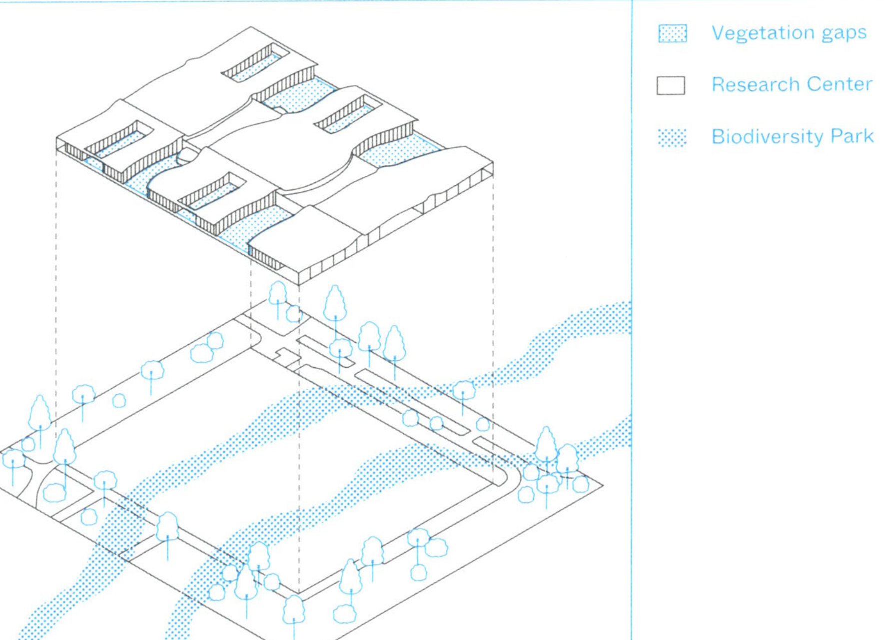

Vegetation gaps

Research Center

Biodiversity Park

This race for performance displaces the problems more than it resolves them, and continues to deepen social inequalities through contradictory actions while at the same time valuing individualism and preventing any political vision. This short-term approach to ecology is a delusion. We need new narratives, new projections, new horizons. We need to once again imagine the long term, collectively. And for this, we need to move away from a purely economic, utilitarian argumentation.

Starting from a critique of utilitarianism to define an economy may be surprising, since the notion coincides with the idea of economy as formulated by Adam Smith.[7] The doctrine is also virtuous: utilitarianism is an ethics of action guided by the improvement of collective well-being.

7. Alain Strowel, "À la recherche de l'intérêt en économie. De l'utilitarisme à la science économique néo-classique," in *Droit et intérêt - Vol. 1 : Approche interdisciplinaire*, Brussels, Presses de l'Université Saint-Louis, 1990.

systems. Because if that doesn't happen, then we're wasting our creativity. And again, it's all about interdisciplinarity. About taking a step aside towards this slightly different knowledge, in order to integrate alternative economic cycles.

Alain Bretagnolle

This leads to a question, perhaps a little simplistic, but that is driving the profession. Are the solutions to be promoted rather high-tech, low-tech, or both?

Pedro Gadanho

Both. Only yesterday there was talk of new forms of cement made from food waste. And it's a fantastic idea, but it has to be mass-produced to have a significant impact. We need to move in that direction and use this type of scientific innovation. But at the same time, we also have to go back to traditional, or pre-modern, ideas, I'd say, in which the built environment was much more in tune with local climatic conditions. Simple solutions existed, and we tend to forget about them. It's kind of a waste.

Romain Boursier

On this subject, Jean-Baptiste, you have looked at the work of the IPCC, particularly Group III, which has put forward a number of solutions. What is your view of these innovations?

Jean-Baptiste Fressoz

IPCC experts, like everyone else, are obsessed with innovation. What is striking about Group III of the IPCC is that they completely accept the idea of the energy transition. No questioning. For example, the 2ºC targets, and even more so the 1.5ºC targets, are becoming so unattainable that we are forced to integrate negative emissions into the models, a great number of negative emissions, 200 gigatonnes of CO_2 to be stored by 2100. 2100 is plenty of time, but it means several gigatonnes of carbon per year that we have to recover from the atmosphere and store elsewhere. There is a 2008 report on CCS, the Carbon Capture Service, which explains, for example, that we're going to recover CO_2, liquefy it and then store it in the oceans, where there is so much pressure and where it is cold enough for the CO_2 to remain liquid. So we would be creating large lakes of carbonic acid 6,000 meters below sea level. That sort of thing...

This Group III of the IPCC also includes another very important research group, created in 1972, which was called the IIASA, for International Institute for Applied Systems Analysis. Atomic scientists work in that group, and I think that the cultural, sociological, and historical trajectory of people who think about energy on a global scale plays a role. These are people

Plant-covered platform

Cergy, France

The Engie tower, built by the architect Renzo Moro in the late 1970s, is one of the symbols of the foundation of the new town of Cergy. It is located in the heart of the agglomeration, next to the Prefecture building, in the immediate vicinity of the eponymous RER[1] station. On the slab characteristic of 1970s urban planning, this urban totem stands out with an architectural style that elegantly raised an office tower on a hill pass, on top of a brutalist-style concrete base. A technical volume crowns it all, proudly bearing the mark of the industrial era, and thus consecrating the optimism of on-going technical progress. The high-rise building, which has been vacant for several years, is to be decommissioned and its use changed. The new project will combine student accommodation in the tower, with a co-working facility in the active base; the car parks at street level and the station esplanade will become shops, gyms, and restaurants to provide a new, lively urban façade.

The demolition of the upper floors of the tower would lead to the rupture of the pre-stressed slab on which the building rests. It must therefore be loaded progressively as deconstruction proceeds. The solution adopted is to create a natural park at the top of the tower for residents. A change of era, a change of frame of reference, the symbol of limitless technical progress is thus replaced by a panoramic hanging garden, which hosts relaxation areas, beekeeping activities and agricultural production. A new environmental microcosm will thus be created, and reinforce the biodiversity of this urban site.

The architecture of this plant-covered totem was designed as a symbol of the paradigm shift in our society: in its relationship with resources through the reuse of an existing structure that it was unthinkable to demolish in view of the carbon footprint involved, in the urban and social revitalization that the project engages, in the welcoming and revitalization of a new biodiversity with which we share our living environments.

1. Suburban Express Railway in the Paris area

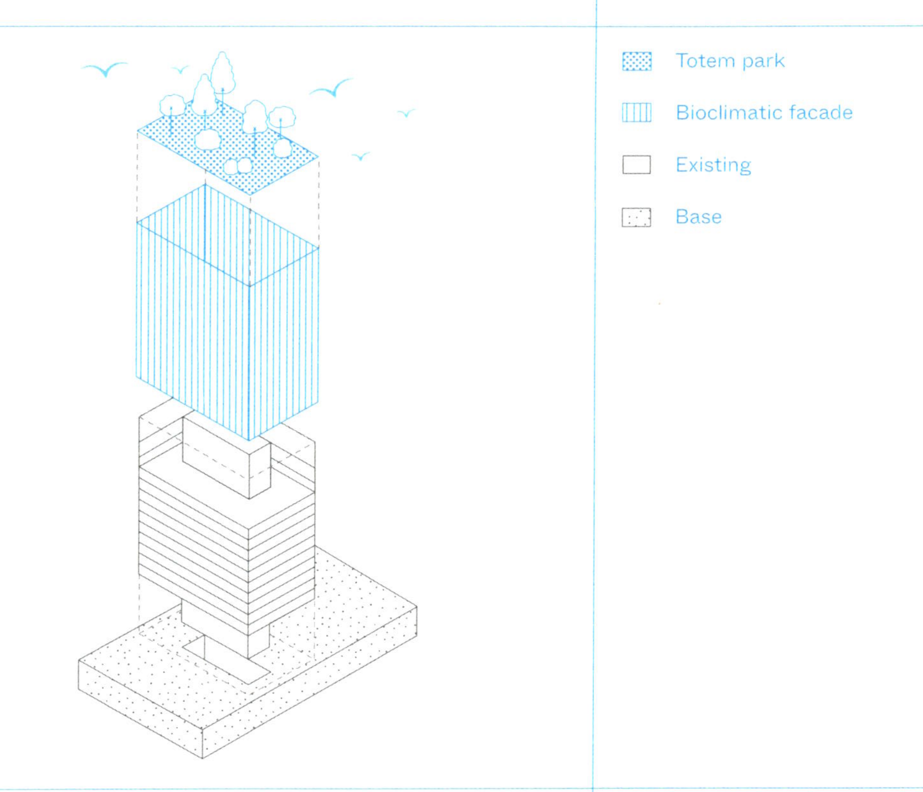

It values what is useful to society. But what needs to be challenged belongs to a different order. First, the consequentialism on which utilitarianism is based (which justifies all action according to a prediction of results) is now incompatible with the general uncertainty that characterizes our time. The very idea of the project must change: we are waiting for an ethics open to the unexpected. Finally, utilitarianism is still the tool of a dominant economic model devoid of values, symbols, or ideals. An economy of transforming environments is, on the contrary, a political and symbolic reclaiming. It is an economy of the common good, of the disinterested, repairing inequalities and restoring collective values.

who have a certain vision of things. And this plays a role in the current proposals.

To come back to architecture, the key thing is to move architects from production work to renovation work, to put it simply. It's pretty incredible, when you think about it, how the construction industry overall has managed to escape the vindictiveness against climate criminals. The oil industry suffers from a much worse reputation, even though it's equivalent in terms of emissions.

Pedro Gadanho

I mentioned this in my book: ecocide has now been recognized by international courts. Soon architects will be looking at how they contributed to crimes against Nature by pushing forward the use of concrete, glass and steel. At the rate cancel culture is growing, I think we could be facing these kinds of questions pretty soon.

Romain Boursier

This is a good way to introduce the final part of this discussion. Although we intervene more on existing buildings, the work of architects is more complex than just improving the thermal renovation of buildings...

Alain Bretagnolle

From this point of view, the housing production chain requires the reorganization of skills. All economists say that the cost of environmental inaction generates more expenditure than dealing with the issues in time. Today, we're no longer talking about mitigation, but adaptation to climate change. Wouldn't one of the solutions be to recognize the economic value of natural resources, which modernism has considered to be free and available? And even to evaluate ecosystem services as part of a new economic equation?

Jean-Baptiste Fressoz

We should be careful on this point, when we say "economists have shown that;" it depends. It's a debatable point.

William Nordhaus, who recently won the Nobel Prize in Economics for his work on climate change, said that it's better to do nothing because the optimal temperature, which will allow us to optimize the GNP, is +3.5°C. So some economists have played a role in ideologically encouraging the disaster. And then there are others, Stern in particular, who produced a report that said: "All of this is based on a very important discount rate, if you set a very low discount rate, or even zero, all of a sudden it becomes profitable to make major efforts right away." There are debates within the economic world, but generally speaking, the Nordhaus model is the one that the economy has adopted today.

As far as valuing nature is concerned, actually putting a price on nature was considered from the beginning of industrialization. During the eighteenth century, people were concerned about the environment. They were concerned about the environment, especially since, at the time, the environment was what determined the health of populations. In the absence of a bacteriological paradigm, when people fell ill, it was because of an environmental change. Fumes, pollution, were perceived as extremely dangerous. And those who dealt with that were the police. In Paris, there were twenty police districts with a police commissioner in each of them, and they disciplined craftsmen who emitted too much smoke or who let disgusting things flow onto the street. When the activity was obviously too harmful, they removed it from the urban area. For industrialists, this was a major risk. At the beginning of the nineteenth century, they explained: "We cannot invest in activities that we know are going to be polluting, if we run the risk of losing our rights to maintain them by decision of a simple police magistrate." This sentence was written by Chaptal, who was a chemist, an industrialist, a polluter and who became French Minister of the Interior. Hence the transformation of the regulation by 1810 decree, which established the regime under which we still operate today: industrialists are the ones who must request authorization. This sounds green enough, but in fact it's the opposite. Because once you have the administrative authorization, you're safe. Once the Minister of the Interior and the Council of State have told you that you can produce this in such and such a place, the neighbors can do nothing else. Or they can go to the civil courts. And the only thing these courts can do is to award damages for pollution. And so throughout the nineteenth century until today, most of the regulation of pollution has been based on the cost of pollution. This corresponds to the civil code law: you suffer damage, you receive compensation. You see, giving nature a cost was the system that industrialists wanted. In 1810, this is what they were already saying. They can afford to pay, what they want is legal stability. That way of regulating seems optimal, but it isn't new; it has accompanied capitalism for two centuries and it hasn't solved the pollution issue. It has contributed to it. Industrialists make efforts because sometimes pollution costs them a lot, but in the end it doesn't change much.

Pedro Gadanho

Let's also note that it may be time to consider a change in the way we measure carbon impacts. Today, we rely on a system of carbon offsets that leads to greenwashing. The EU is currently looking into how to limit such greenwashing. Carbon offsets are magical thinking, and they present a distorted vision of reality. The only question, the big question in terms of economics,

Danone Research Center, Danone Vitapole, Architecturestudio.

Palaiseau, France, 2002.

By considering the short term while architecture is an art of the long term, utilitarianism leads us, today, straight into a wall. The concept may be reassuring; it is a principle of "appeasement," as Georges Bataille ironically claimed. But reducing architecture to its utilitarian concerns means considerably limiting the field of action. It means forgetting that architecture constitutes capital of non-quantifiable, non-calculable, and non-monetizable values.

is how we can instead implement a carbon tax that is global and that everybody pays to regulate the amount of emissions they're responsible for.

This would of course have implications for architecture, because if you have a carbon tax to pay when designing a building, it will act as an incentive to reduce its impact and even go beyond carbon neutrality. We should be designing carbon-negative buildings, buildings that will eventually provide more energy, store carbon, etc. And as soon as such incentives emerge, I'm sure our creativity will respond and we'll start innovating in terms of architectural forms, so that they may incorporate such systems. I really think that the big change that is still being resisted is actually imminent. We just need to move from carbon offsetting to a real carbon tax that would produce a new economic paradigm.

Romain Boursier

And if it were applied on a global scale, it would make it possible to finance more virtuous technology transfers in developing countries too. Ingrid Nappi?

Ingrid Nappi

It's true that today, what we ask of architects is first and foremost to produce surfaces, square meters, and that this real estate project should be financially profitable. This is what architects are paid for by project managers as a solution to their economic equation. We should think about other indicators, such as volume, carbon footprint, etc. The value of architects is to be the guarantors of the long term and to contribute to exchanges between disciplines. This added value must be invested in the circular economy, the economy of resources.

Alain Bretagnolle

We're going to move from quantity to quality.

Jean-Baptiste Fressoz

If I may say just one small thing regarding the carbon tax. The carbon tax was what the Europeans were suggesting for the Kyoto Protocol, and in the end tradable energy quotas were adopted. This solution was especially favored by the Americans, who then withdrew from the Kyoto Protocol. So we end up with a system that we did not really decide on. You should know that the carbon tax is currently supported by oil companies. Exxon, for example, is financing a think-tank on the carbon tax. Recently, an Exxon official was tricked. In a conversation recorded without his knowledge, he was asked: "But how come you support the carbon tax?" And he replies: "That's easy actually, it'll never pass. No government, no American president, will ever pass a carbon tax on their people. So it's perfect. We

Danone Research Center,
Danone Vitapole,
Architecturestudio.

Palaiseau, France, 2002.

say we're in favor of the carbon tax, which allows us to keep extracting oil." What they're really afraid of is that we might ban the gasoline-powered car, this is what it's about.

Bahrain National Theater,
Ministry of Culture,
Kingdom of Bahrain,
Architecturestudio.

Al Manama, Bahrain,
2012.

8. Georges Bataille, *The Accursed Share: An Essay on General Economy*, Zone Books, 1988.

In his famous essay, *The Accursed Share*,[8] Bataille drew on the theory of gift/counter-gift developed by Marcel Mauss in the 1920s to write his essay on "general economy," a radical counter-proposal to the market economy. He highlighted the fact that the principle of gift/counter-gift established a social contract, one which mutually engaged both giver and receiver in a relationship in which the stakes went beyond the purely utilitarian dimension to engage the symbolic representativity of the protagonists. Not long afterwards, Karl Polanyi drew on this same principle of reciprocity to make it a possible foundation of the economy.

Xie Zhiliu & Chen Peiqiu
Art Museum,
Shanghai Pudong
Development
Construction Engineering
Management Co. Ltd,
Architecturestudio.

Shanghai, China, 2015.

Polanyi's main critique of the market economy is that it assumes a prioritization of the economic over the social. For Polanyi, the logic of social incentive—which renders the counter-gift a free yet obligatory act—sets social ties above financial gain. This leads him to assert that the market economy is a construction of economic liberalists and not a natural human trait. The economy thus defines the symbolic value of exchanges that connect us to one another. It is a science of relationships and their value system. Polanyi's theories and his definition of a humanist economy could be extended to the non-human. The evaluation of nature as complex processes of exchange, and the recognition of living beings as a community of ecosystem services,[9] inter- and trans-specific,[10] are today interesting avenues through which to consider an economy/ecology of inhabited environments.

9. We have been trying to assign value to biodiversity since the 1970s, either economic or at times commercial. The idea of ecosystem services implements the evaluation of environments according to their usefulness to humans. The researcher Virginie Maris recently returned to this idea by critiquing its utilitarian and thus anthropocentric approach, and by opening it up to the rest of living beings. See Virginie Maris, *Nature à vendre: les limites des services écosystèmiques*, Editions QUAE GIE, 2014.

10. The philosopher Emanuele Coccia also takes collaborations between species as the basis for a reflection on the living. See Emanuele Coccia, *The Life of Plants: A Metaphysics of Mixture*, Polity, 2018.

From *O Peixe* (The Fish)
Jonathas de Andrade, 2016

This short film by the Brazilian artist was shot in 2016 in a fishing village in north-east Brazil. We see a man embracing a fish he has just caught, in ritualized gestures simultaneously gentle and violent. Jonathan de Andrade highlights the relationships between humans and nature, between human and non-human, specific to animism. The film questions violence disguised as benevolence within a system of domination where humans reign supreme.

Inhabiting the world **differently**

Which representations can support our relations with living beings and with processes of care for inhabited environments?

Lyes Hammadouche Artist, Researcher, and teacher at the Central Academy of Fine Arts, China

Catherine Larrère Philosopher Professor Emeritus of Philosophy at Paris I – Panthéon Sorbonne

Albena Yaneva Sociologist Professor of Architectural Theory and Director of the Manchester Research Group (MARG) at the Manchester Urban Institute

AS Explore, moderated by Alain Bretagnolle and Romain Boursier, Partner Architects/Urban Planners, Architecturestudio

If the climate emergency calls for a redefinition of our relationship to the world, it also calls into question our way of designing and representing our habitat in the long term—in a concept of time that is cyclical and no longer linear. It equally calls into question imaginaries associated with this concept. It is in the relationship that each cultural community establishes with its environment that we discover the articulation of the social and the environmental. Catherine Larrère lays out new forms of partnership with nature, a symbiotic co-habitation with living things and an eco-mimesis, in order to revisit technical action to the benefit of more humble environmental action. For her part, Albena Yaneva—contesting the inadequacy of the static representation of buildings in a reductive Euclidean space—calls for "representing a building as a navigation through a landscape of contested data," or for a new mode of representation to complete the long and complex process of intentional choices that reflect the material dimensions of architecture and that, in essence, translate different desires for inhabiting the world. Artists such as Lyes Hammadouche, also a researcher, question our awareness of the world and propose renewed representations of the living by showing, at the interface with environmental science, that which is before our eyes but still invisible to our intelligence.

231. **A Heuristic Approach**
Grégory Quenet

235. **Designing Differently**

RE.SITUATING THROUGH THE PROJECT
RE.DEFINING THE COMMONS
NEW PARADIGMS
MEASURING WITH TIME

243. **Orienting Oneself**

RESOURCES
GOVERNANCE
BLUE ECONOMY

Living In and Building Time

In her discussions with Bruno Latour, Professor Albena Yaneva takes up the story of Marey's chronophotographic gun to reverse its perspective. To recall: Étienne-Jules Marey was a physiologist. He was interested in photography, with the aim of better understanding how living organisms function. In 1882, he combined a gun with a circular chamber in which there was a plate able to take twelve consecutive images in a second. A flying seagull therefore appears twelve times on the same plate, thus opening up a way of studying the morphological function of animals and humans through the breakdown of stages of movement. For Yaneva, this principle must be reversed.

Which representations can support our relations with living beings and with processes of care for inhabited environments?

Romain Boursier

Today we are going to address the issue of the representations of our inhabited environments. During our previous round table discussions, we focused on the relationship to resources and the mobilization of stakeholders in response to these challenges. Today, we are considering the question of the representations of our environments from the point of view of our dependence on living things and the finiteness of our earthly resources.

First of all, we will be asking our guests about the limits of anthropocentric methods of representation. We will question the obsolescence of our dualistic conception of nature and culture, and the insufficiency of our Euclidean notions of space. Secondly, we will consider the extent of our impacts on inhabited environments. How does evaluation stimulate creativity in architectural and urban responses? In what way do the sciences of observation of living things suggest different representations of the world? Finally, we will be asking our guests about the symbiotic or even restorative dimensions of the project. From this perspective, what role can be played by the digital modeling of nature? Which philosophical and artistic directions can prevent us from succumbing to the alarmist temptations of our time?

Alain Bretagnolle

We will start with Albena Yaneva. You wrote *Latour for Architects*, in which you refer to his actor-network theory, amongst other things. Could you tell us a little bit about this theory? And since your book is addressed to architects, what is the message that Bruno Latour wanted to convey to the profession, from your point of view?

Albena Yaneva

The book is entitled *Latour For Architects* and was published with Routledge in 2022. It is an introduction to the social theory of the French philosopher Bruno Latour. This small book presents the methodology of actor-network theory for architects and researchers in the field of architecture and urban research.

Latour's pragmatic approach is presented as an alternative to the critical approach that continues to dominate architectural discourse and theory. This book presents some of the concepts of Latour's philosophy, translated for architecture.

Grégory Quenet

A Heuristic Approach

How is it that our time has become so disoriented? After having believed so strongly in a unidirectional arrow of time during the *trente glorieuses*, and even more so through nostalgia for that imagined period of prosperity: belief in an arrow pointing towards a homogenous future without limits. Having believed ourselves outside of history, outside of its consistencies and its tensions, its bifurcations, each present thus became its own norm, detached from the past and the future. Isn't it strange to see buildings less than twenty years old that must now be completely rehabilitated because they have become outdated, brutally rejected in a twentieth century that wasn't concerned with climate, living beings, or the earth? Architecture must rediscover its framework—that is, duration—which is quite different than accounting, with its balancing of numbers without concern for processes. What is a sustainable solution that isn't made to last? This is what happens when sustainable development is conceived as a calculable relationship between present needs and future needs, without considering what connects these two points: the trajectories of those who inhabit the Earth, and who thus find themselves without commonalities.

An arrow is something quite different than a compass, or rather it is a compass gone wrong, as no matter path we want to take the direction to get there doesn't change. This is how I see the compasses presented here: a strong gesture that breaks with unidirectional extension due to the objects that we might take in hand and use to orient ourselves according to the gradients of the *Tracé Bleu*. Of course, these compasses are more complex than the compasses of conquering explorers with their single needle, as here the multiplicity of factors needed to re.source must be taken into account (water, soils, space, time), to then make choices on how to re.act in this repopulated world (by matter, by all living things, by humans), and finally to work towards re.generating (depolluting, restoring, cultivating and preserving, co-benefiting). But in the end, it is a return to the sources—as etymologically, a resource is from *resourd*, to look to Old French, or *resurgere* in Latin, indicating that which reappears and regenerates. In a tour de force that has succeeded beyond all expectations, neoclassical economics has created the imaginary of a great underground storehouse which needs only to be found in order to draw from it without limits. To instill this illusion of resources as inexhaustible, it was necessary to cut the links that embed beings in time and space, which in turn calls into question quite profoundly the trajectory of architecture itself in this modernity and, as such, the new directions to be taken. Is a building constructed to be delivered at a certain moment, or to last? Is a new building an extension of human territory or a form of commons between all living beings?

These very simple questions interrogate the new narratives of architecture, those we must invent to respond to the numerous issues rousing the profession today. What is a narrative? It is an ethical and heuristic compass that allows us to orient ourselves, as the environmental historian William Cronon has masterfully explained starting from Aristotle's *Poetics*. A narrative has a beginning and an end, and thus provides moral direction. It consists of redistributing elements in time, assuming causal links between them and, in this way, it is a tool of knowledge. It divides up the world by including some beings while excluding others, those who are not in the narrative; recounting a narrative thus consists of making choices. In the end, we always recount history *to* someone, which allows us to create links and solidarities. But each of these elements can be twisted because, as stated by Aristote, history serves just as well to narrate the truth as untruths. Compasses are thus imperative, required to be as proven and as refined as possible, because everything has changed with the Anthropocene: on an Earth that is no longer stable, as was the magnetic field of the initial model, we must learn to orient ourselves in a world in motion—and therefore with multiple compasses.

New Compasses

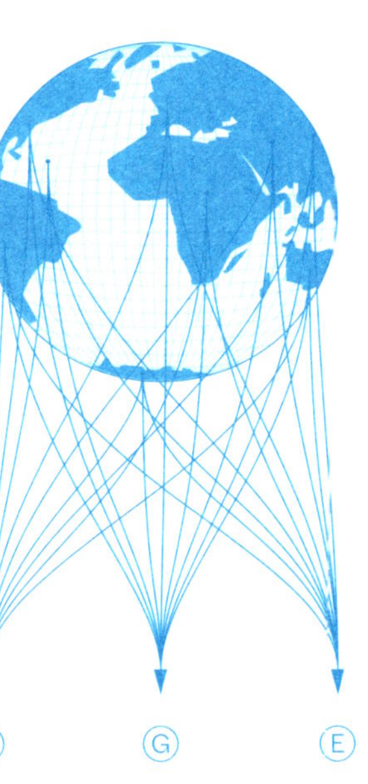

(R) Resources
(G) Governance
(E) Blue Economy

This translation is all the more important now, in our current climate regime, in order to address the problem of the cohabitation between humans and non-humans. The pragmatic approach focuses on understanding the architects' practices, and not just their ideologies and theories. You could say that it is a theory that broaches architecture "in the making," and that's why I wanted to show you this image which represents this duality, the image of static architectural objects on the one hand, "Ready Made Architecture," and on the other hand, architecture in the making through the practices of architects, "Architecture in the making" [image 1]. The Latourian approach consists in following the actors and enables us to treat humans and non-humans in a symmetrical way. Latour's sociological

Image 1

approach is especially relevant for architects, because we are increasingly aware of the social nature of architects' practices, and also of the fact that the products of architectural design contribute to the creation of the social fabric. In addition, we are now questioning traditional notions of architectural knowledge, innovation and creativity, and this approach helps us to re-evaluate and re-imagine the field of architecture.
Finally, we tend to recognize the active role of objects, materials and technologies in our practice nowadays. For example, the models and software we use every day are active objects in architectural production. They are important "mediators," as Latour would say.
The second image I wanted to share is an image that represents this duality, with nature on one side and society on the other [Image 2]. Following Latour, you might say that society cannot explain architecture. You have to follow the actors in order to understand architecture, you have to follow the actors in order to understand the climate situation or this new "climate regime."
Latour uses the term "social" to refer to society. For him, the social does not designate a domain of reality, but rather a movement, a transformation, an association between different entities, regardless of their nature. Since the social is

We don't need static representations of movement, but rather moving representations of what appears to us as immobile: architecture. Because "everybody knows [...] that a building is not a static object but a moving *project*, and that even once it is has been built, it ages, it is transformed by its users, modified by all of what happens inside and outside."[1] Architecture is, for her, a "contested territory" or a "controversial space," caught in a perpetual movement of successive iterations—from its initial program, from the context in which it is born, itself changing, from its rules of construction, and from its multiple conceptual adjustments of its uses, always evolving in time.

1. "'Give Me a Gun and I Will Make All Buildings Move:' An ANT's View of Architecture," Bruno Latour and Albena Yaneva in Geiser, Reto (ed.), *Explorations in Architecture: Teaching, Design, Research*, Birkhäuser, 2008, pp. 80-89.

Image 2

a movement, the idea is to follow the actors (both human and non-human) in order to understand it, to trace it.
The Latourian approach invites us to go beyond the traditional dichotomy between nature and society, nature and culture, nature and architecture. Architects can play a very important role in overcoming these divisions, these dualisms. This role consists in rethinking, re-imagining and re-conceptualizing the cohabitation between humans and non-humans. It has taken on an even greater importance in the context of the new climate regime. This is the most important message we can draw from Bruno Latour's sociological approach.

Romain Boursier

Thank you Albena for this contextualization. This duality between nature and society is very present in our Western culture and I would like to ask Catherine Larrère this question. In your book, *Thinking and Acting with Nature*, you note this opposition, which distances these two worlds, whilst simultaneously protecting them from each other. Can you explain this paradox?

Catherine Larrère

It is difficult to explain the origin of a dualism which separates what has to do with nature and what has to do with society (or culture). Elements of this dualism can be found as far back as antiquity, in the work of Plato, Aristotle, and certain Greek philosophers. But it really began to take hold in the modernity of the seventeenth and eighteenth centuries, and it was very much linked to scientific developments. Modernity was characterized by the emergence of a uniform science, from Galileo to Descartes and Newton, a sort of great synthesis that made it meaningful to talk about Science at that time. Naming a science of nature meant transforming nature into an object, as opposed to humans, who have subjectivity. This dualism effectively resulted in the development of a science which found applications from the nineteenth century onwards and enabled

Cité des Arts,
Montpellier Méditerranée Métropole, SA3M, Architecturestudio, MDR Architectes.

Montpellier, France, 2021.

The present era is that of time. Uncertain. A reflection on contemporary life might start this way. We are living in uncertainty; how can we adapt habitats to what we cannot foresee? The climate crisis calls for redefining our relationship to the world with reference to new ecological, social, and economic paradigms. It also questions how we might design our homes within flexible and cyclical time—time that is no longer linear. The search for a temporal representation is essential today for considering an architecture of time, and the project of its continued transformation.

an unprecedented mastery of natural phenomena. But people also discovered its limitations.
For Latour, it was by no means self-evident to distinguish between the order of nature on the one hand and the order of freedom and human spirituality on the other. There is the issue of animals, for example: which side do we put them on? Considering them as machines is absurd, of course, but at the same time it corresponds to certain ways of treating animals, particularly in factory farming, to the point of being intolerable. It is equally absurd to consider humans as a species with free will that can decree what it wants when it wants, without depending on natural necessities and this "new climate regime." In truth, we are simultaneously very powerful and powerless. There is no discontinuity, from the most natural to the most cultural: nature is not only a physical mechanism, there are living things, and living things introduce contingency into nature. To present humans as kinds of gods, masters of themselves and of the universe, is therefore absurd.
Rather than a clear-cut separation between nature and culture, humans and non-humans, we need to consider a kind of continuum, in which the relationships are not so much hierarchical as symmetrical or reciprocal.

Romain Boursier

The concept of nature is changing, and so are our actions. Does the concept of "wilderness", which you use, contribute to this idea of empowering nature?

Catherine Larrère

Essentially, this separation put nature on one side and humans on the other. Nature was resources, what was given to us to do what we wanted with. In the United States, the settlers didn't take the time to cut down the trees in their rush to the West, they cut them in half and waited for the wind to break what was left. Which shows what a violent attack it was.
In this relationship between nature and humanity, nature had to be given an importance again. So the Americans placed the spaces that had not yet been destroyed beyond the reach of human action. This is what was called the wilderness.
This term, borrowed from the English translation of the Bible in the seventeenth century, corresponds to what was called the "desert" in French during the same period. It is a place from which man is absent, and that has been enhanced by the creation of parks: Yosemite, Yellowstone and many others, and with the Wilderness Act (1962), which is the legislative act that regulates the protection of nature in the United States. The wilderness is presented as spaces where natural processes are not hindered and where humans are only temporary visitors. Assuming that such protection makes sense in the United

Re.situating through the project

Inhabiting the world differently not only requires that we be aware of the paradigm shifts underway on the planet, but also that we strive to act accordingly, each at our own level of ability. This is the work undertaken by Architecturestudio around the *Tracé Bleu*—in the fields of architecture and urbanism that it specializes in—which takes on an operational dimension with the creation of three methodological compasses. They have been designed to guide us in a novel way, by taking into account all the existing and future agents for developing common projects. These compasses are instruments for steering the preservation of inhabited environments. They echo the three previous chapters of the *Tracé Bleu*, i.e. Re.sourcing, Re.acting and Re.generating, and allow the stakeholders of a territory to be guided in the development of a blue strategy specific to each project. They thus formalize the way in which our societies must address the issue of ecosystems and their underlying resources, support them and regenerate them. This commitment must include all interacting ecological agents, as well as models of a regenerative economy for our inhabited environments.

Whether as project owners, project managers, inhabitants, or citizens, we all operate in unstable and always provisional contexts. As a matter of principle, the question that everyone should ask themselves at the beginning of any project is: what am I going to receive, and what am I going to offer the community, the ecosystems, and future generations?

This renewed approach requires a new exploratory narrative, which can be divided into three phases:

From "what is already there" to planned commons

Recognizing an existing situation through the capacity of its stakeholders to conceive new and collectively established commons, in accordance with the conditions of life on earth.

From planned commons to the definition of their governance

Expressing, through collaborative governance, the way in which we define the proper transformation of our environments while respecting the interests of all present or future ecological stakeholders and agents, whose interests are taken into consideration.

From the governance of commons to their implementation and evaluation over time

Implementing not only solutions that are beneficial to all and allow the regeneration of all living things, but also evaluating them over predefined periods, and measuring the co-benefits of this new blue economy.

This representation of time within (or through) the project is a major field of research. First, the necessary circularity of design processes requires a constant renewal of attention to the built object, its uses, and its relationship to living things. Post-occupation evaluation, while already a widely developed process in the countries of northern Europe, is a first step towards this goal as it identifies—through evaluation and objectivizing—the value added to architecture and planning with specific criteria for each context and each operation. This methodology anticipates issues of a building's flexibility and scalability, up until the moment of its destruction and the reuse of its components in the framework of a circular economy. This consideration in cyclical terms, of the project as a continuous process, involves taking into account both the past and the future of each decision.

States, the same is not true for the rest of the world. For example, it would condemn Asian forests where people and forests have coexisted for centuries. Besides, how were Yosemite and Yellowstone created? By driving out the Native Americans who were there before the settlers arrived, either by chasing them away completely or by turning them into park rangers. It is believed that 90% of the populations present when the European settlers arrived in North America disappeared in the century that followed, mainly as a result of the diseases brought by the settlers. These spaces that were discovered were not virgin spaces, but spaces that were once inhabited and are now deserted.

Romain Boursier

In your book, you talk about the interrelationships that humans, in their diversity, have with these living things. How can we imagine a society in which culture and nature would support each other?

Catherine Larrère

There are now protected natural areas almost everywhere, but this is not enough to curb what is known as the erosion of biodiversity or the sixth extinction. The concept of biodiversity is based on the expression of biological diversity, which was introduced in the 1980s. Biodiversity is often understood to mean the diversity of species, but it includes all levels of life: genetic diversity, the diversity of populations, species, ecosystems, etc. This concept also has the merit of not being dualistic, in the sense that biodiversity is not linked to the presence or absence of humans. Two telling examples: the Norman bocage was co-created by humans and nature. The layout of fields or meadows surrounded by hedges, which are themselves maintained, is both a natural and a human process, and biodiversity in the Norman bocage reached its peak in the nineteenth century. Here we have a human presence that does not destroy nature but, on the contrary, maintains biodiversity. The other example, which is even more telling, is the Amazonian rainforest. Although we spontaneously think of the Amazonian rainforest as a wilderness, historical ecological research has shown that, there too, there is a co-action between local populations and nature. We observe a different distribution of species where humans have intervened, so there too we have an example of a co-evolution between humans and the forest, which is why when we destroy the Amazonian rainforest, we are not only destroying natural environments, we are destroying living environments for living beings, including humans.

Re.defining the commons

Moving from a world of common goods to the commons of the terrestrial world requires that we question our relationships to resources, as well as the consequences of actor-network interactions and the systemic effects of our economies.

The ongoing project of transforming what is already there departs from the modern linear process, towards a "mode of exploration between different processes that engages multiple existing entities throughout the world," to follow Bruno Latour.

To do so, we have chosen to extrapolate the conventional use of the compass, which allows us to explore the world with an unambiguous orientation, in favor of several compasses (...) that will allow us to navigate this more complex and uncertain world. This was done by integrating new cyclical, processual, and holistic dimensions. These compasses are not exhaustive and can be supplemented and articulated with those of other disciplines, as well as adapted to each context.

Three compasses thus allow us to find our way, but also to introduce new visions into the project:

Resource Regeneration | Resource Compass

Investing in regenerative circular models, or dynamic spirals, as an alternative to the planned depletion of fossil fuels, which underlines the impasse which our linear growth models have reached.

The Inclusion of Actor-Networks | Governance Compass

Valuing co-evolutionary relationships between actor-networks, while redefining them via hybridization processes, as an alternative to environmental and socio-economic impact assessments based on set representations.

The Co-Benefits of a Symbiotic Economy | Blue Economy Compass

Cross-referencing the different economies of an environment that preserves living things, by adapting territories that have entered a learning process, and reducing our needs for the benefit of a blue economy—as an alternative to mono-criteria objectives assessed at a given moment, that repeat cognitive biases.

These dynamic compasses, by evaluating the transformation processes at work, will help us to manage this new complexity in a more systemic way, and to find new directions according to curves of growth, of inclusion, and of related outcomes.

Resource Compass

Governance Compass

Blue Economy Compass

Digital technology now facilitates this evaluative archaeology, first through the power of the archive, then through the constitution and management of databases. Post-preoccupation evaluation is an open book, one which retrospectively recounts the life of a building. A building's digital footprint thus makes its past legible while also opening up a possible future. A connected building, through the analysis of collected data, is a building that anticipates its own maintenance, adaptation, transformation, conversion, and even its own reuse. Next to the obsolete building, the digital creates an operational double, both model—a virtual model of all scenarios—and real potential of a new creation.

Alain Bretagnolle

There is talk nowadays about a new climate regime that concerns the whole planet. Lyes, you work and teach in Beijing. We are all familiar with traditional Chinese painting, in which man is represented as a tiny figure in a natural universe that exceeds him. It seems to me that the cultural revolution had an effect on this… the adoption of the market economy has perhaps transformed the Taoist vision of Chinese cosmology… So what is the relationship between contemporary Chinese culture and living things?

Lyes Hammadouche

These theories are quite recent, you know, they are being studied in the academic world. I'm thinking, for example, of Hans-Georg Moeller, who published a study on the representation of the self in China. The stereotypical image is the Chinese landscape with a tiny human being at the bottom and a gigantic waterfall. If you ask Europeans "what do you see in this picture? Describe this picture to me," a European will say "there is a tiger, it looks fierce, it's dangerous." Someone from China will first describe the waterfall, the landscape, the background, and then be able to reference the tiger that is there. Hans-Georg Moeller's research explains that in China, the relationship to the self is different from that of Europeans, because there is no objectification of the other, and therefore no distinction. On the other hand, for a long time there was the idea of the reproduction of the same, of an equivalence. This does not build the same frames of reference.

Alain Bretagnolle

Other systems of representation integrate time. Albena, you challenge our usual methods of representation of architecture or habitats, in general, insofar as these representations are static and do not cover the temporal process of the project, from design to use. You have devoted part of your work to the search for a more conceptual representation of architecture, which integrates a longer time frame and which also takes into account its social, political and ecological dimensions.

Albena Yaneva

The predominant interpretations in architecture always operate by means of separations. And these separations have always paralyzed architectural theory and methods of representation. They imply a very static vision of the building, a very static vision of the object in architecture. In my research, I have tried to abandon this static view of buildings in order to grasp them as a flow of transformations. The project is the sum total of all the series of transformations of a creative idea. If we follow this series of transformations, we end up with a very different

New paradigms

With its content and temporal dynamics, each compass makes it possible to compare, simply by virtue of what it represents, the evolution of our still "modern" era with a more "earthly" future, to use Latourian categories. The conceptual deployment is clear:

Synchronous Inversion | Resource Compass

This compass conceptualizes two opposed dynamics in a temporal circle: a synchronized shift from a system based on the cumulative exploitation of our fossil fuels, to the regeneration of existing and new resources. While the process is currently far from reality, due to the acceleration and accumulation of resource consumption, this compass represents a medium- and long-term objective, to be taken into consideration in all our present decisions when conceiving conditions of post-carbon resource abundance.

Transformation Ethics | Governance Compass

This compass shows two complementary processes around the ethical circle of the agents of this transformation. One of them is centripetal, and identifies the relationships between actor-networks during the transformation processes of existing entities via the project, based on what already exists. The other one is centrifugal, and deploys opposed dynamics of growth and regeneration which anticipate the needs of future generations, in time and space, for living humans and non-humans. An inclusion curve is thus defined on the outer edge of the figure, between existing and future entities.

Holistic Approach | Blue Economy Compass

Technological solutions to ecological problems exist, but their sector-specific and uncoordinated applications partly account for the rebound effects, known to cause imbalances. The Blue Economy compass proposes a holistic approach based on the deployment of the four economies of low-carbon and circularity, knowledge, resilience, and regeneration. Their correlation, the relevance and reliability of the solutions used, measured throughout their deployment, generate co-benefits and equilibrium.

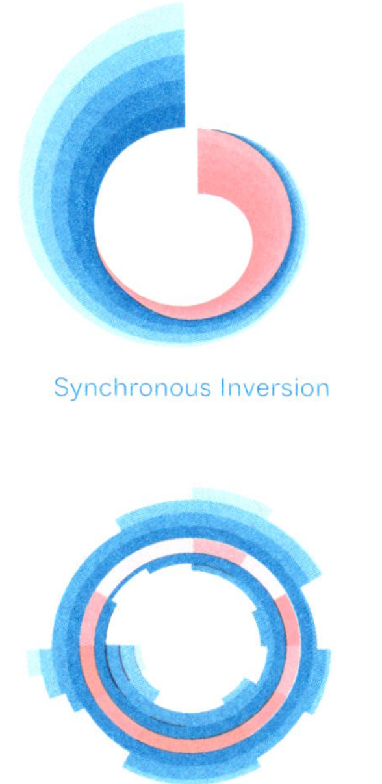

Synchronous Inversion

Transformation Ethics

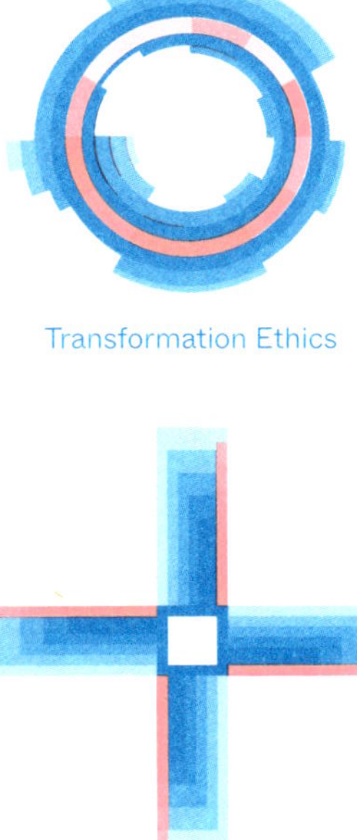

Holistic Approach

image compared to what architecture usually is. As we know, architectural projects do not follow a linear, progressive course, but rather proceed by derivations, by different detours, by controversies, by obstacles, mobilizing new actors at each stage of their development. How can we represent this?
An object that moves forward, by different detours, mobilizing ever different actors? How can we visualize the "flight" of the project, this bifurcating trajectory? That was my question. How can we define architecture, not as a static object, but as a very complex ecology? How can we follow it, represent it, visualize it?
To represent a building as an ecology, as a multiple entity, you have to develop alternative visualizations and that's what I tried to do [image 3]. In this image, there is a visualization of the controversy surrounding the Olympic stadium in London, for the 2012 Olympic Games. We followed the debates around this project on the basis of articles published in the British press, which allowed us to follow all the controversies surrounding this project, and we tried to represent these controversies. In the end, you don't see the stadium, you don't see the static object, but you see this very complex ecology and this mapping enables us to follow the evolution of the project over time and to identify all the actors involved. The advantage of this method is that we can introduce the different human requirements and the different interests of the actors involved in the production of the project into the representation. This method of visualization

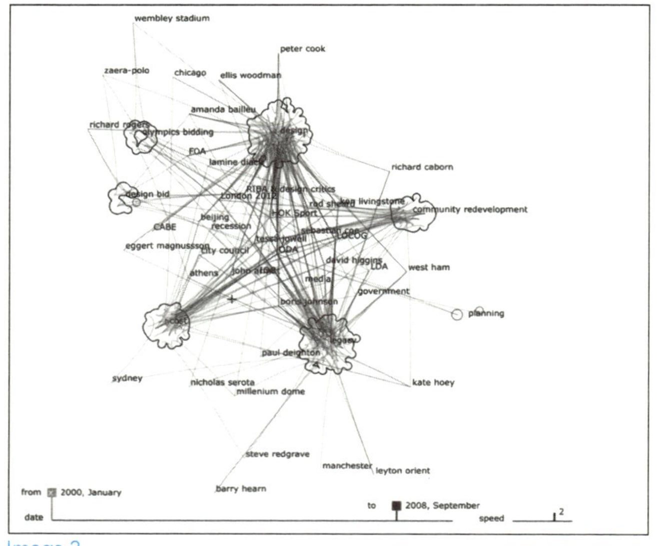

Image 3

This *digital turn* undeniably has a very concrete impact on our profession. The virtuous cycle of an architectural resource itself is getting closer; the digital allows us to manage a complex new system. But how can the data generated by these new models be used to respond to ecological issues? How can they be structured, represented, shared? How can scientific expertise from the past help us to imagine new futures?

Measuring with time

As a matter of principle, a compass refers to the need for common measurement in order to share location data and use it for each exploration. By taking up the question, "What am I going to receive, and what am I going to offer the community, the ecosystems, and future generations?" we propose, by means of a common measurement framework, to apply these questions to the notions of resources and of the roles of actors and economies, respectively.

Each compass is divided from its center, along the horizontal and vertical axes, into four quarters belonging to the physical (or carbon), knowledge, resilience, and regeneration worlds.

The three compasses share these four measures of the terrestrial environment, which they calibrate based on a temporal measurement system, inclusion- or deployment-based, to allow for the redefinition of priority actions to be shared with the project's stakeholders with a view to:

→ reducing our consumption, by addressing the question of needs and materials, based on an overall circular approach;
→ learning from the rupture of our linear models, through a heuristic dimension of exploratory processes, prior to changing our approaches and solutions;
→ adapting our existing and future territories and spaces, whether they are to be transformed or redesigned, towards a state of open resilience;
→ preserving the environment by considering living things in a new light.

With every project, with each compass, we will need to link these four dimensions in order to restore the benefits of the present and future dynamic processes at work.

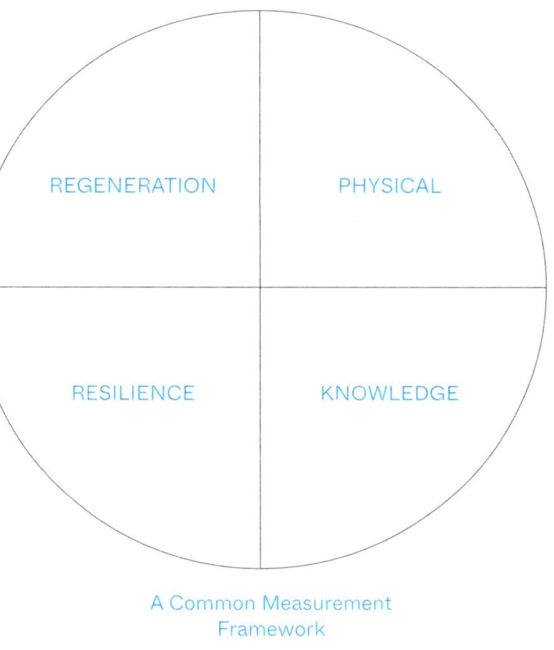

A Common Measurement Framework

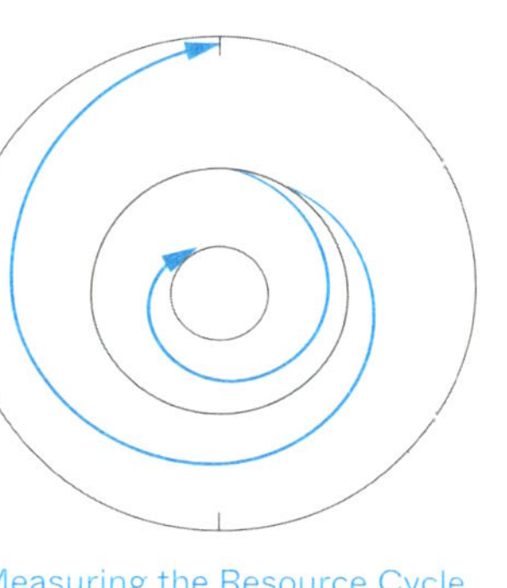

Measuring the Resource Cycle

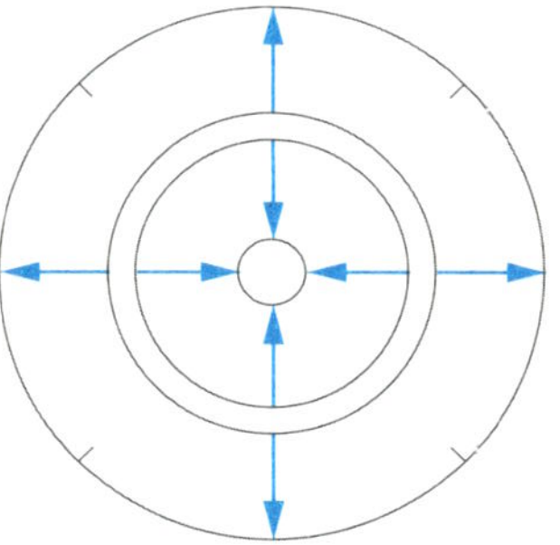

Measuring the Projection of Actors

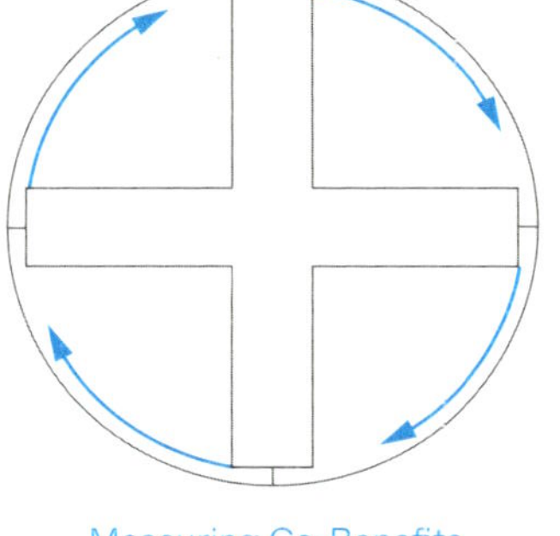

Measuring Co-Benefits

shows the building as an accumulation of different and even contradictory demands, of social, political, and ecological demands at the same time.

Alain Bretagnolle
Albena, does this mean that we can include interactions with living things in these methods of representation? This is one of the difficulties of our geometric system of representation, which is devoid of any temporal dimension.

Albena Yaneva
Yes, you can incorporate many more interests than just the interests of the human actors you would normally represent. Political actors or actors who have the power to manage a project are normally the voices that are heard, especially in complex projects on this scale, such as a stadium or an airport expansion. There are many ecological organizations that are mobilized, many communities of villages or towns that are affected by these projects, but we never see their participation, we never hear the voices of these minority communities and "the voices" of the affected species, animals, or plants. To show how the ecological balance risks being destroyed by the expansion of an airport, or by the construction of a stadium in London, we need to be able to visualize the non-humans who will be affected by these projects and incorporate their demands.

Catherine Larrère
If I could chime in here—we are talking about an architecture that takes the diversity of living things into account. I remember taking part in a round table discussion about green cities, about the greening of cities or the construction of buildings involving as much green as concrete, and this was defended as an action for the well-being of the inhabitants, for the fight against global warming, etc. And then someone in the audience asked, "What do you do with the animals?" and the architects replied, "We hadn't thought about it."
And yet obviously, putting in green means putting in insects and all the animals that go with it, and that wasn't integrated. I was very struck by this question about animals.

Romain Boursier
In your book, you mention the fact that we are experiencing the end of nature as a balance. Do you share the same need as Albena Yaneva to restore and represent this endangered nature in the complex processes of the project?

Catherine Larrère
I believe that this implies that we have another vision of architecture and of technical action in general. That we don't

The fact that the building is no longer considered as an end goal but as a part, a moment, of a continual process has direct implications for the architectural project. The first is that the project extends out in time: the architecture continues to supervise the produced work well beyond its delivery. The second is that the project stays open, available and at the service of economic, cultural, social, or ecological opportunities. This extension of the notion of "project" thus claims two new spheres of action for the architectural profession: the objective of circularity for both the productive apparatus and the economy of construction, and the overcoming of utilitarian ecological aims to open up to general interest.

Resources

We have highlighted the way in which the Resource compass simultaneously moves in two opposite directions on a fifty-year clock, with the decline in fossil fuels and the rise in renewable resources. It includes the main fields and categories of investigation, which each project can prioritize and specify according to its needs and objectives, with the external clock indicating the time scale within which the effect is expected to occur.

This first compass guides the project by defining the milestones of a blue strategy, deployed through the use and creation of renewable or low-carbon resources, and by clearly displaying its objectives so that the results may be measured over time.

The red downward spiral refers to the reduction in the long term exploitation of resources, whether fossil fuel extraction, carbon-based energy consumption for buildings, resource operation or mobility.

The blue upward spiral highlights, in an inverted and synchronous manner, the objective equivalence that could be obtained if the substitution of renewable energy sources sufficed. As this projection is problematic in the short term, it is necessary to deploy complementary urban and architectural solutions, by investing in new resources for the regeneration of existing ones. This research aims in particular to highlight the value of the water cycle, to restore biodiversity and its capacity to contribute to the balance of ecosystems, to revive more local forms of agriculture, and to associate the landscape with its food-producing and productive value. It also highlights the need to reexamine the forms of inherited territories by opening up our infrastructures and mono-functional areas to new uses, investing in our brownfield sites, using land frugally, designing reversible spaces and allowing for a chronotopia of the places we inhabit.

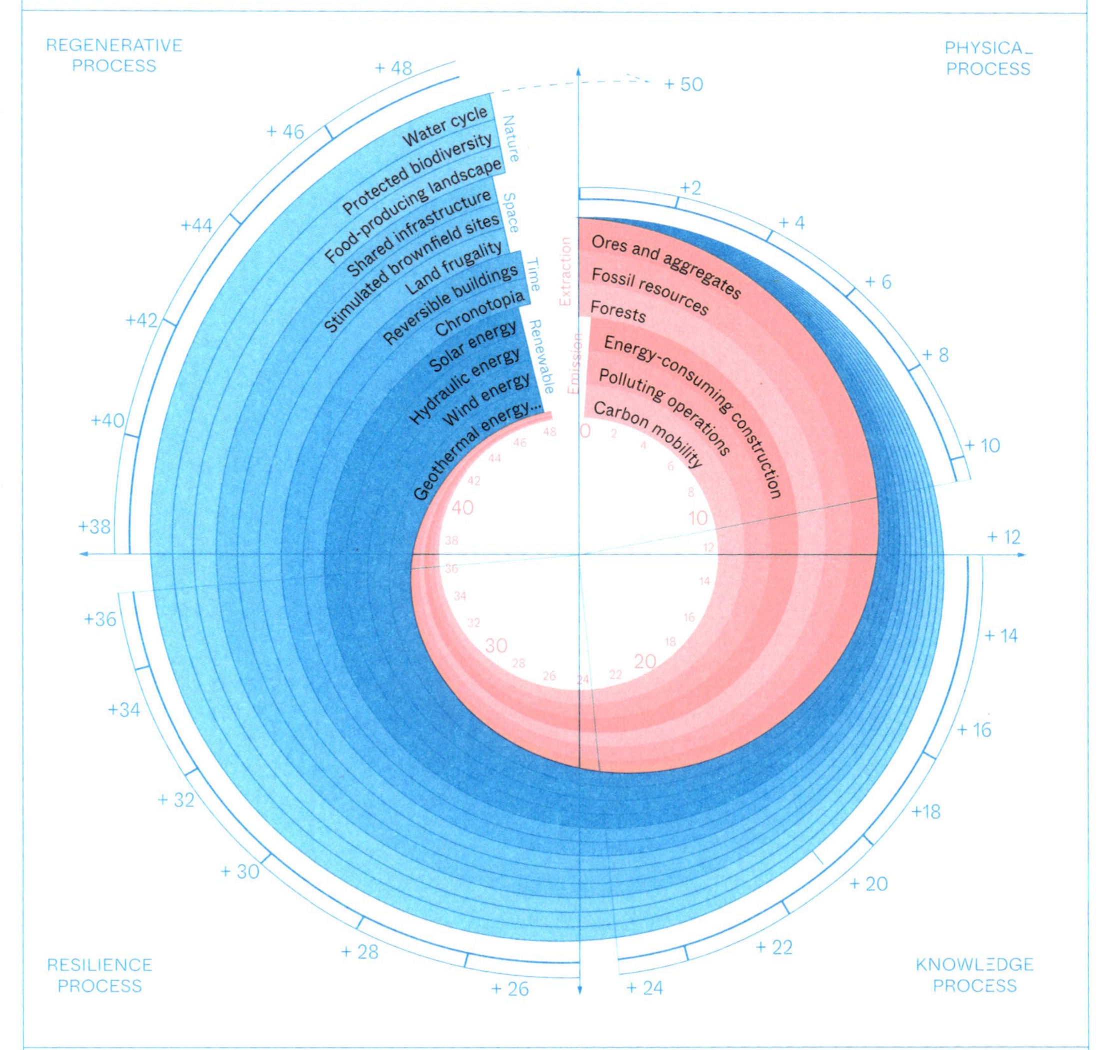

see it as a production, but as a reciprocal process. I would quote the German philosopher Martin Heidegger, who distinguished between building and dwelling. This distinction is not typically Heideggerian, it has been taken up by others, such as the anthropologist Tim Ingold, for example. We have this idea that building means building with bricks, building a technical object. But what Heidegger says is that we can only build if we dwell. That is, if we situate ourselves in an environment. This definition raises questions that we wouldn't normally ask ourselves, such as "do nomads inhabit?" Generally speaking, dwelling has been equated with a stable location, but if we take into account the myriad different ways of situating oneself in an environment, nomads do dwell. Do animals dwell? This leads us to see things differently, and this is what we criticize in our book *Thinking and Acting with Nature*: the dominant technical representation is that of production, of the imposition of a form on a material. To recall the image that Marx uses in *Das Kapital*, the difference between a bee and an architect is that the bee builds its hive spontaneously, whereas the architect always makes a plan in advance, in his head. I think that everything that is being discussed at the moment calls this idea into question. Alongside production, we introduce what we call steering, an action which takes into account the environment, which it does not produce, just as a ship's pilot does not produce his route: if it is a sailing boat, he plays on the winds, and so he invents his route by cooperating with the natural elements and making opportunistic use of them. I believe that if we want to conceive of the architectural act as more than a static act, we have to go beyond the usual models of production.

Albena Yaneva

That also means completely rethinking the notion of context. When we build, the context appears as a link that connects the architectural project to many other elements that are there, and that also interfere with the production of the project. All these elements that bombard the project from the outset: the client's demands, the clichés engraved in the minds of certain users, the customs rooted in the zoning—if you're working in New York, for example—the typologies taught in art school, the architects' preconceptions about nature, as you said, Catherine, their sensitivity in considering the ecological balances that are destroyed by the project... To go back to Catherine's example, the fact that the architects didn't think about the animals when they developed the project reveals the fact that we don't really think about this reconfiguration of what we call context, society and culture, that we don't think about the act of building as being an act of reconfiguring all the relationships to living things. We have to start over from scratch, starting from the building, from the architectural project.

The continuous project is thus a different concept of the building in its full continuity. From its design to its construction and delivery—but also its maintenance, evaluation, adaptation, improvement, and transformation up until its conversion, demolition, and recycling—this notion of the project brings architecture into an engagement with time (past, present, and future): beyond its technical purpose, it combines heritage and imagination, care and invention.

Governance

The Governance compass takes the form of concentric circles. It places Existing Entities at the center, the Agents of Transformation involved in co-decision processes in the intermediate red circle, and in the opposite direction, Future Entities in an outward expansion.

The role of stakeholders is represented by their relative importance in colored dials, the idea being to highlight, in the outer circles illustrating the governance dynamics of the project, what is not recognized and valued in the inner circles.

The second compass thus guides the project's stakeholders towards the recognition of new ecological and climatic agents, which had been missing from the process until now, and towards the consideration of their own needs, as well as those of the inhabitants and citizens concerned with the transformation of their living environments as actors fully-involved in the project process. It also confirms, through knowledge-based agents, the transdisciplinarity needed for the treatment of the systemic complexity of the projects, and the restitution of their interventions in the long run.

The perimeter for the inclusion and interdependence of the actor-networks considered is defined by the outline of the colored dials, each project being able to specify the different processes which take place among agents, and to evaluate their dynamics over time. It reflects the level of consideration of the entities either directly or indirectly involved in the project, with the Agents of Transformation thus including all the stakeholders.

GOVERNANCE COMPASS

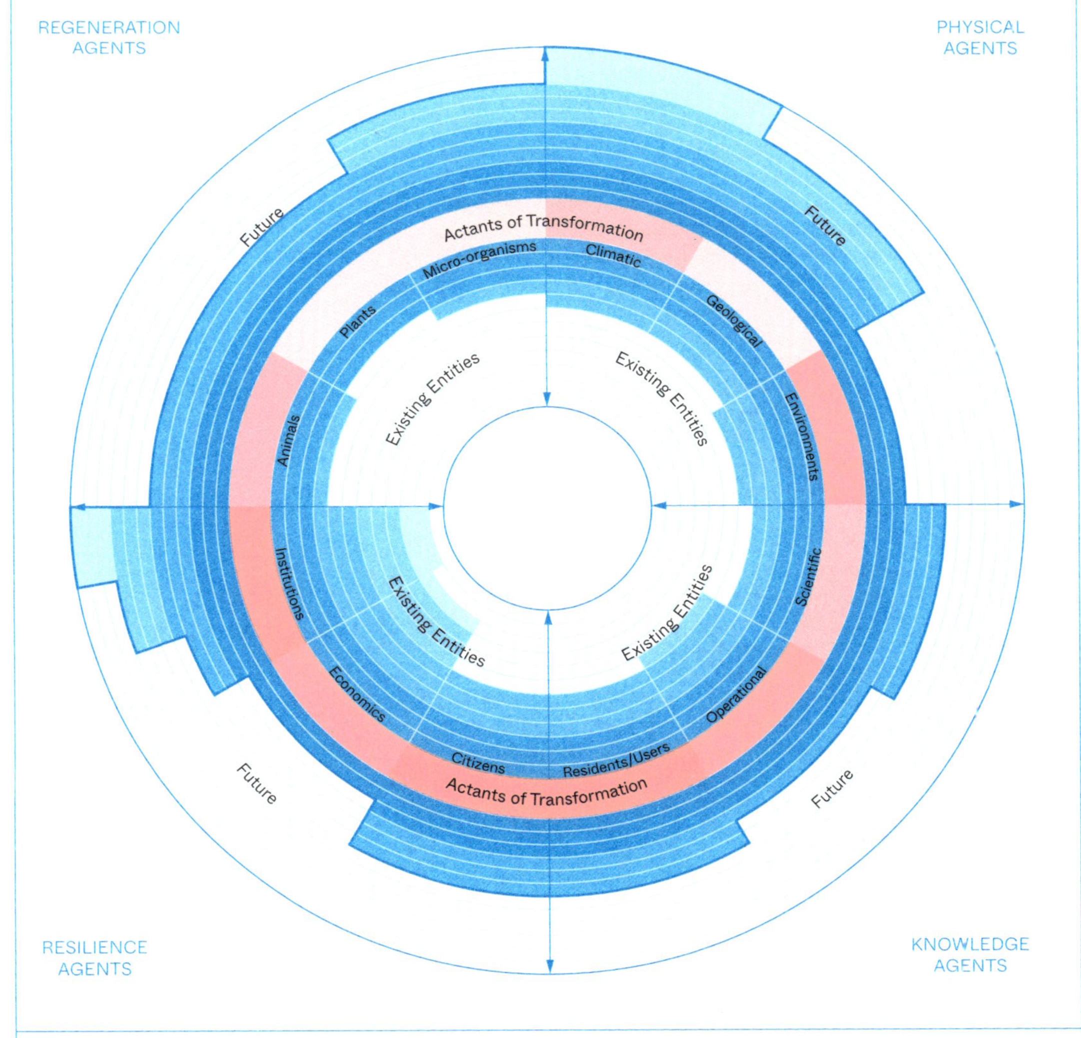

Taking Care

Tracé Bleu **is for us a framework, a new orientation of our practice as architects which involves an ethics and economy but also, and above all, another way of inhabiting the world. Today's world is a damaged, depleted, and threatened world, one which we can only inhabit by recognizing its finiteness as much as its fragility. The singularity of the Earth has always left humanity with existential questions. The Anthropocene points to another level of this awareness, perhaps late but concrete: the planet is degrading and we don't have a plan B. This is our legacy, heavy with responsibility: to ensure, by maintaining our habitat, that humans can continue to be.**

Alain Bretagnolle

When we talk about methods of representation, in our cultural context, we imagine the monofocal perspective of the Renaissance, in which there is a distinction between the observing subject and the observed object. Lyes, you have done a lot of work on the consciousness of the self and the world, and you have pointed out a number of paradoxes. On the one hand, we have a modern approach that is completely materialistic, reducing consciousness to a certain number of physical and chemical processes, even though the most advanced sciences in the field challenge this interpretation. On the other hand, we can now see that artificial intelligence, with applications such as ChatGPT or Dall-E for example, is beginning to occupy the field of subjectivity, which had been the preserve of humans up until now. So there is an anthropomorphic projection onto technology, reminiscent of Spike Jonze's "Her" or Alex Garland's "Ex Machina," which challenges our identity by means of a mirror image. Could you share your thoughts on these subjects? And perhaps also go back over what Walter Benjamin pre-empted in his work on the status of the work of art in the age of mechanical reproduction?

Lyes Hammadouche

These are subjects I am passionate about. We can start with the question of style. For me, the notion of style emerged in the history of art when the technology of mechanical reproduction and photography were being perfected. Painting lost its reproductive value, and in order to sell paintings, of such and such a wealthy family, of such and such a large and beautiful house, artists had to give their work an added value, which was that of style, the interpretation of reality, subjectivity. This explains the whole history of contemporary art, right up to the present day, in which in order to understand certain works of art, it is absolutely necessary to be aware of the artist's experience, otherwise you have no access to what is being shown.
This question of representation fascinates me because I get the feeling that we getting to the end of it. And we are getting to the end of it by means of the current questions of hard science and aesthetic questions... which ultimately converge.
I am following the work of an American researcher called Michael Levin very closely. He does a very simple experiment with worms whose heads grow back when you cut them off. He conditions these worms, he makes them go towards the light. In their natural state, they tend to go towards the darkness, but he makes them go towards the light and then cuts off their heads. The heads grow back and the worms return to the light. He observes "if I cut off the head, the supposed place of memory of this worm, this worm should not go towards the light, it should go towards the darkness." This raises

Blue Economy

The Blue Economy compass is a four-pointed figure, in the shape of a grappling anchor, which allows for the in-depth establishment of an economy. It is read as a “plus” sign, adding up the four economies that contribute to the Blue Economy—is the desired outcome—which symbolically occupies the center or axis of the compass.

Rotating clockwise from the top of the vertical axis, the criteria of a low-carbon circular economy, a knowledge economy, a resilience economy, and a regenerative economy are successively established for their relevance to the project.

Each economy is therefore driven by different measurable criteria:

→ The low-carbon and circular economy notably records objectives of non-artificialization, non-demolition, low-carbon and re-use solutions.

→ The knowledge economy records in particular the skills mobilized, the experiments implemented, their analysis and dissemination, the links to research and post-occupancy evaluations.

→ The resilience economy notably records the design of reserve spaces (capacity to integrate uncertainty), flexible and reversible spaces, and the analysis of and responses to identified hazards.

→ The regenerative economy records in particular the values of decontaminated spaces, restored environments (including the accounting management of living things), and maintenance criteria, as well as the co-benefits brought to the ecosystem.

Their deployment is measured by a circular movement, which fans out each criterion on the corresponding dial. The comparison with the initial state is measured in red. Each project will thus be able to specify the different levels of ambition achieved in relation to the current state.

This third compass guides the project towards an alternative and associative economy, which is the basis for an in-depth symbiotic approach.

BLUE ECONOMY COMPASS

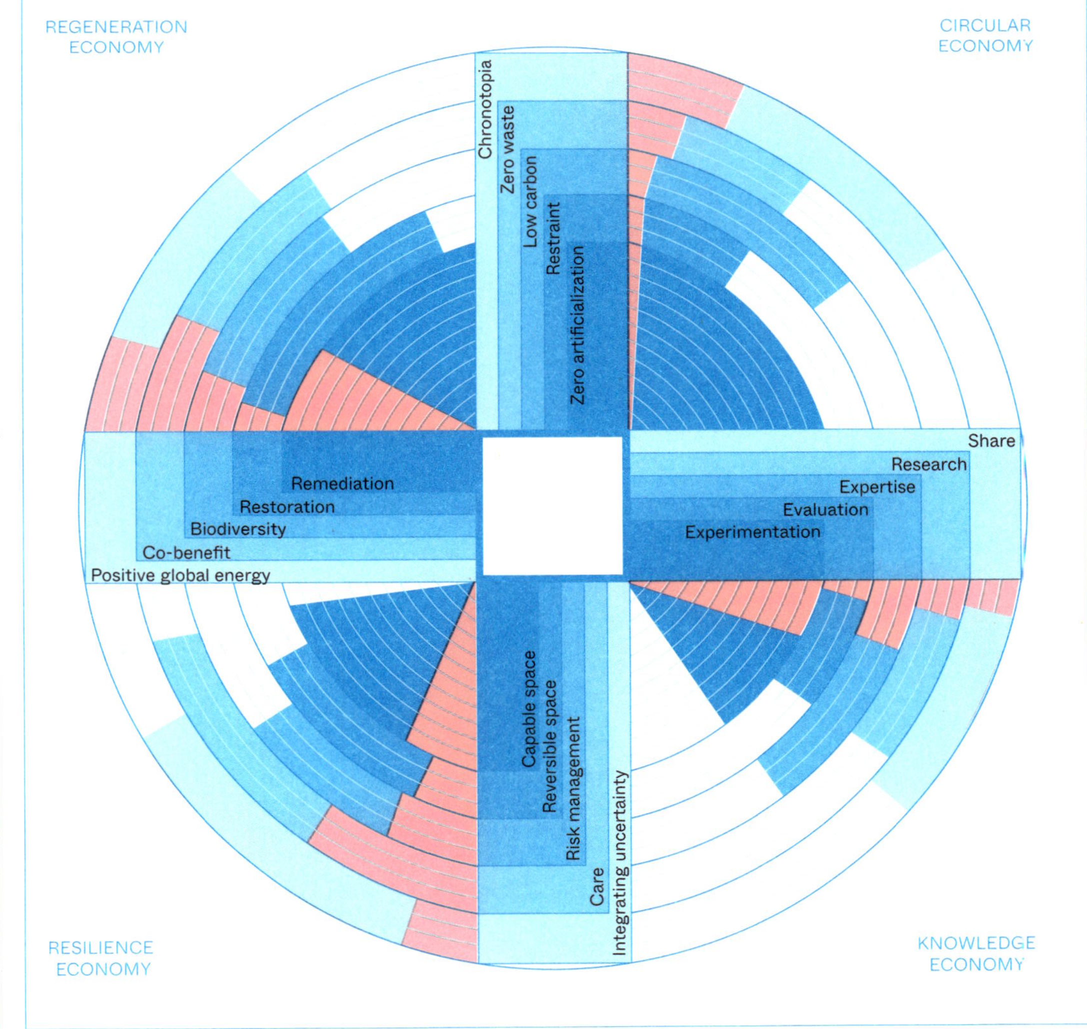

ESTP-ESEO Metropolitan Campus,
SPLAAD,
Architecturestudio.

Dijon, France, 2021.

the question of the localization of information. Possibly, the localization of consciousness. And he puts forward two theories. The first theory is that consciousness exists in the entire neural network of a body, of this worm for example, and the other theory, which is more interesting in my opinion, is that consciousness falls within the purview of sacredness or of a form of ontology, an otherwhere which would be the locality of this consciousness.

When I carried out my research with the cognitive science laboratory at the ENS, the whole demonstration they were trying to make was a reductionist, materialist demonstration, affirming that consciousness is a set of physical and chemical reactions produced by the brain, but the sum of their experiments demonstrated just the opposite. For this, they used a rather formidable tool: hypnosis. Therapeutic hypnosis tells you that you are ill from the moment that your understanding of reality is not in line with what reality is. The hypnotherapist will therefore reprogram you, to bring you back in line with reality. As an artist, I tell myself that I am completely reconfigurable: am I not a machine?

This calls the reproducibility of style into question, and this is a very relevant subject nowadays with the issue of artificial intelligence. Last week, one of my students said to me "Professor, I just fed an artificial intelligence with images of Eames (the designer) and I asked it to make an elephant chair. What do you think of the renderings?" When I was his age, I was trying to make photorealistic 3D renderings, and he's feeding a machine with a database so that it can decide, by itself, how to compose a photorealistic image of a chair, but he's not concerned with ray tracing, he's not concerned with light, he's not concerned with optics, he's not concerned with positioning, rendering, rendering times, he doesn't care about any of that. For him, it's a question of parameters, of data.

There is a discipline that is emerging, in relation to this, which also interests me from the point of view of philosophy, because it takes us back to Gilbert Simondon. And it defines a parametric vision of reality. What interests me is that this is probably the future of humanity. At the moment, you have all the GAFAMs telling you, "No, don't worry, we are making AIs that are hyper-aligned, we are making alignments," which is to say, "Don't worry, when we develop artificial intelligences they don't become neo-Nazis," like the one Microsoft made five years ago. It was a drama on social media, because these intelligences are only reflections of society, on the internet anyway. They are made according to what they have been fed. And what's great nowadays is that the debate is moving towards sacred questions, ontological questions, questions about the post-secularization of art, moral and ethical questions, etc.

This philosophy of care comes from the philosopher François Guery, who wrote, responding to Heidegger: "Since the world is already there, since its being does not await our existence, we inherit it before we can even think about it, weighing the pros and cons, and it is this heavy immediacy of the inheritance, this "pre-occupation" of the terrain of existence, that gives us over to the care for being and the diffuse understanding, the senseless sense, that being exists."[2]

2. François Guéry, "Precaution as Care," *Revue de métaphysique et de morale* 2012/4 (no. 76), p. 611-621.

For Heidegger, being in the world is *the* constant concern of what it is to be. Although concerned, the worrying being is nevertheless a being acting to absorb this anxiety, acting to take charge of the inherited world they must transmit. In his famous lecture *Building Dwelling Thinking*, Heidegger explained the semantic convergences and the common roots of the verbs dwell and build (*bauen*) and called on architects, after the war, to rebuild by offering people a form of housing that is not only comfortable and practical, but that might allow them to realize their mode of being. In a word: a dwelling. For Heidegger, we can exist only by *dwelling*. And by dwelling carefully: worry is to being what caring is to dwelling.

Catherine Larrère
All of this is absolutely fascinating and it's true that it opens up questions where none existed before, but I'm still sceptical. It seems to me that this debate about artificial intelligence confines the debate to the relationship between humans and their technical objects and leaves out what might be called an environment or nature, which remains external, even though it is the one that encompasses everything. After the 2011 tsunami in Japan, I was struck by an article by Stéphane Foucart, who presented it as the revenge of technology on humans. But the tsunami was not created by humans… This way of confining the debate to the relationship between humans and their technical objects is a way to make the world anthropocentric again, as far as I can see. It's a bit of simplistic, but you have to go beyond the purely human question.

Alain Bretagnolle
This raises several questions. Until now, history had a meaning, it was oriented by the march of progress, there was also an end to history. Nowadays, the well-being of humanity is no longer associated with technical progress. The second thing is that you often refer to Aldo Léopold, a forest ecologist in the United States, who was one of the pioneers of environmental protection…

Catherine Larrère
In the first half of the twentieth century.

Alain Bretagnolle
Thank you for specifying that. Léopold thought that obligation, that is, imposition by law, was not sufficient in this area because it required a prior social awareness of nature, and so we come back to the question of subjectivity.

Catherine Larrère
I'm also a bit skeptical about this idea of framing the question in terms of subjectivity. For me, that still presupposes an opposition between the object and the subject, and I think we need to challenge the idea of a subjectivity that would be separate from objects…

Lyes Hammadouche
This is also the idea of science at the moment. That's what it's questioning and that's what it tends to demonstrate, through the study of biology, but also the study of theoretical physics. Everything is intersecting…

Urban and landscape development in Lusail, Qatari Diar, Architecturestudio, Michel Desvignes.

Lusail, Qatar, 2016.

Like the old home we care about and maintain, dwelling is, jointly, to live and to take care of. Taking care of the world, of one's home-Earth, so that dwelling can take place. "Taking care in architecture [...] means a sudden jolt to the ways of existing in the world, ways which are more caring, supporting, and empathetic."[3] Inhabiting the world differently is thus, at the end of nihilism, to work for the living and for life.

3 Chris Younès, Céline Bodart, David Marcillon, "Prendre soin par l'architecture, la ville, le paysage," conference on Architecture and Philosophy, RST PHILAU, ENSA Clermont-Ferrand, December 9-10 2021.

Catherine Larrère

Everything is intersecting, yes, we can no longer put subjects on one side and objects on the other. Merleau-Ponty said that there were no human subjects separated from the rest, but subject bodies, which is to say that we are subjects through our bodies. I feel this calls a certain number of clear-cut separations into question. For Aldo Léopold, there was no point in taking care of nature if you didn't also improve yourself. There is a link there too. If so-called ecological awareness does not reflect back on oneself, it is useless. I think he was right.

Alain Bretagnolle

Let's move on to another chapter, the measure of the evaluation of our impacts...

Romain Boursier

Exactly. We talked about the emergence of a new concept, the concept of biodiversity, and its interactions with society. In 1992, Catherine Larrère, you spoke of a shift, at the time of the Earth Summit, which led to the Rio Convention and which aimed to ensure the conservation of biological diversity, by recognizing this biodiversity as a genetic resource to be preserved. Thirty years later, how has the concept of biodiversity evolved? How do we assess the positive and negative impacts on biodiversity nowadays?

Catherine Larrère

Our relationship to nature has changed in two ways. The first is that biodiversity is not considered as a nature separate from humans, on the contrary, since we recognize the co-action, the co-evolution of humans and the environment as being very favorable to biodiversity. Secondly, we note that this interest in biodiversity coincided with the appearance of a new ecology, which was no longer the ecology of the Odum brothers in the *Fundamentals of Ecology*, which informed ecology from the 1950s to the 1980s. It is a so-called disturbance ecology, which considers that imbalances are the rule. There are favorable and unfavorable disturbances, sometimes both at the same time. If you take fire, for example, it destroys plants and allows other plants to grow at the same time. It's not so much a question of waiting for the balance to be established, but of distinguishing between good disturbances and bad disturbances and intervening so that the good disturbances prevail over the bad ones. It's a much more difficult form of ecology.

Romain Boursier

That's interesting because it also relates to the notions of temporality that Albena Yaneva mentioned. This idea of reintegrating the regeneration of nature into the project.

Caisse d'Epargne
Aquitaine Poitou
Charentes headquarters,
Bouygues Immobilier,
Architecturestudio.

Bordeaux, France, 2017.

Over the past twenty years, societal debates—including those concerning housing—have witnessed a resurgence of themes around care. The import of Anglo-Saxon theories of care in our continental context has, so to speak, increased our attention to otherness. Coming from a more pragmatic tradition,[4] the Anglo-Saxon notion of care is both an attitude and a principle of action.

4 A notion that appeared in the United States in the 1970s and that, starting from the framework of feminist studies, confronts societal and environmental questions. See Carol Gilligan, *In a Different Voice: Psychological Theory and Women's Development*, Harvard University Press, 1982.

Doesn't the polysemy of this concept of biodiversity refer to a form of ethics or a standard of action that could define the political project?

Catherine Larrère
Let's say that it destroys static projects, by introducing the idea of accompanying environments. This is something that we can see very clearly with the new climate regime, to use Latour's words. With climate disruption, many animal and plant species and many populations will no longer be able to live where they do. You only have to go for a walk in France in summer to see that many trees are suffering. There are also birds that no longer make their annual migration, and in their case the question is not, as we used to think, to protect them in spaces, but to accompany their migration. We will also have to accompany the migration of humans who will leave their regions for climatic reasons. All of this converges.

Romain Boursier
We frequently operate in these interstitial environments, and at the agency we are conducting research into the application of "zero net artificialization" to very strongly reduce this logic of extension in favor of territories of great ecosystemic value. We can see the extent to which our representation of territories is subject to the logic of regulatory zoning, which maps out the space. In your book, you talk about Gilles Clément's notion of a third landscape. What options does it suggest, in your opinion? How does it relate to what you call the fourth nature?

Catherine Larrère
Gilles Clément shows that the three types of nature, the one that is left wild, the one that is cultivated and the one that is almost destroyed by urbanization, are all controlled by humans. Protected areas are fenced off, which is a way of controlling them. Then we impose on the land what we want it to produce for agriculture, and then we make it artificial in order to build on it. In spite of this, there is always another nature that escapes us, what might be called "autonomous nature" or "recalcitrant nature." It is the truest form of nature, the one that we will never come to terms with and that we cannot dominate, and therefore that we cannot include in spaces.

Alain Bretagnolle
In his book *The Blue Economy*, Gunter Pauli states that we must give nature back its capacity to evolve and that we have an interface role to play in this system. Albena, to develop this articulation between the built environment and living things, we could evoke something that is already very structured in the countries of Northern Europe, but which doesn't really

Onassis Cultural Center,
Alexander S. Onassis
Foundation, Ariona S.A,
Architecturestudio.

Athens, Greece, 2011.

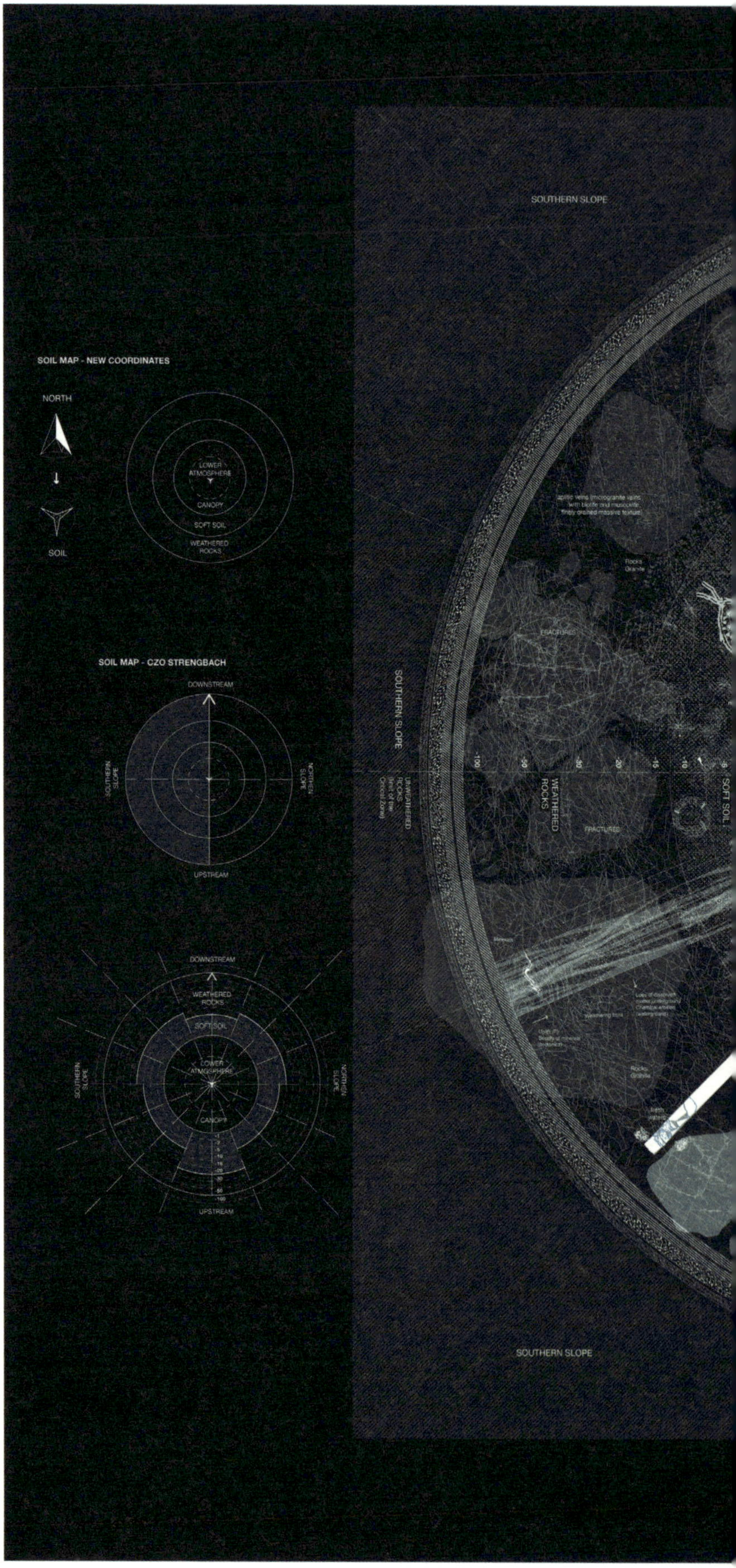

Image 4
"Sol," a map from the observatory in the critical zone of Strengbach, Vosges, France. Presented as part of the "Critical Zone Observatory Space" installation by SOC (Societé d'objets cartographiques) for the exhibition Critical Zones: Observatories for Earthly Politics at the ZKM Center for Art and Media, Karlsruhe, Germany (2020-2022). Produced as part of Alexandra Arènes' doctoral thesis in Architecture at the University of Mancherster.

DOWNSTREAM
NORTHEN SLOPE
NORTHEN SLOPE
UPSTREAM
CANOPY
LOWER ATMOSPHERE
Riverlab
Weather station
geoseismic profile
Rocky Granite
minerals
fossils
Carboniferous coal basin
THE INSTRUMENTS OF THE CRITICAL ZONE OBSERVATORY
SOIL MAP OF THE STRENGBACH CRITICAL ZONE OBSERVATORY
WEATHERED ROCKS
Rocks Granite
Fractures
Waterlogged porous sandy soils
Bacteria
Minerals
Fossils
Carboniferous coal basin
SOFT SOIL / LITTER
Diatoms
Dead trees
Sediments
Roots Mychoriza
Bacteria
Compost
Microorganisms
Soils under microscope
Sulphur
CANOPY / LOWER ATMOSPHERE
Clearcutting
Forest cover
Rain / snow
Healthy beech trees
Damaged spruces
Acid rain (Sulphur)

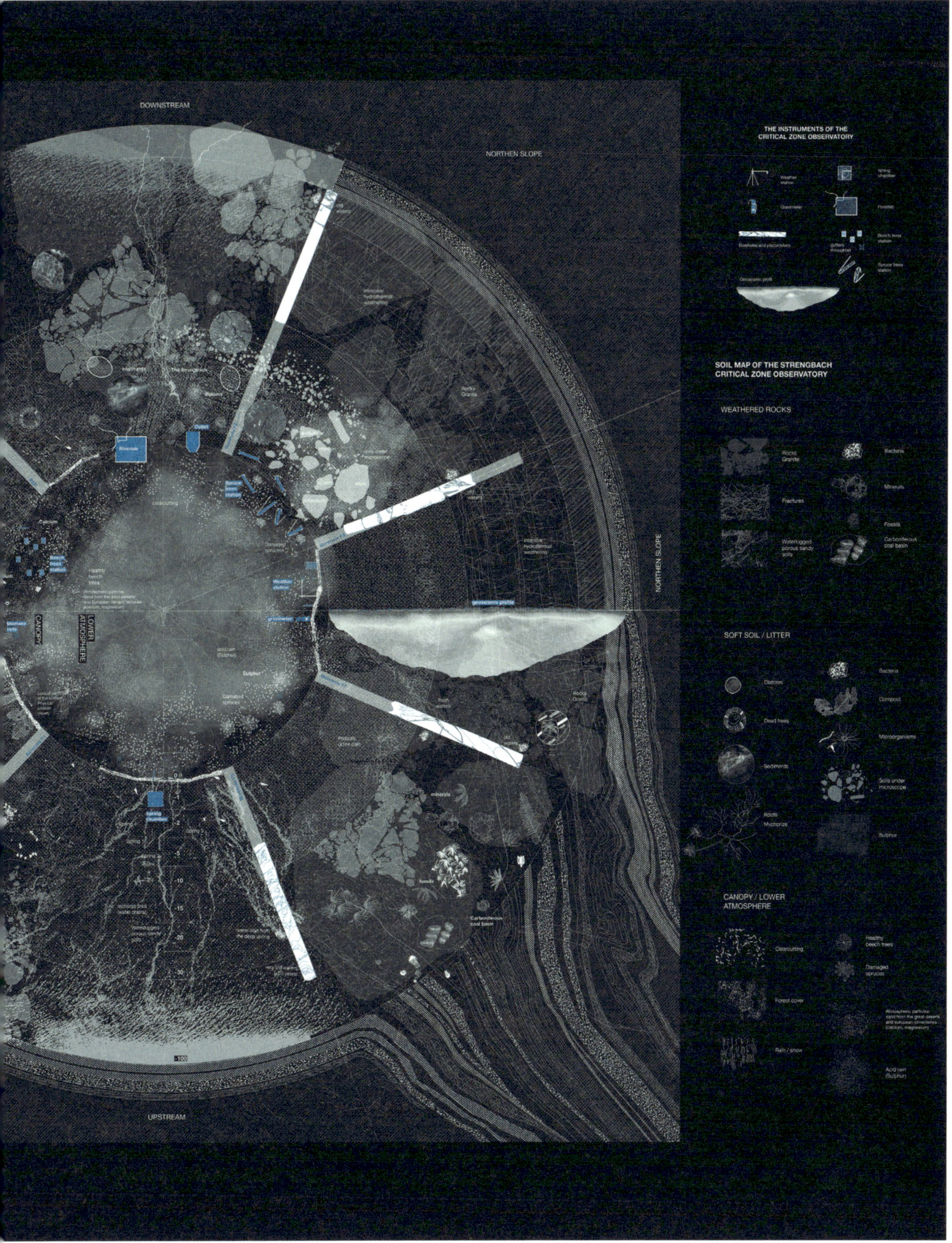

259

exist yet in France, which is what we call post-occupation evaluation. This is a multi-criteria assessment process of the life of a building after its completion. This evaluation concerns questions of use: does the building, as it has been designed and constructed, meet the needs of the owners and users, and to what extent does it also impact its environment? That is, both the human community and the natural ecosystems.
I believe that you are interested in this intersection, which could be a way of objectifying the environmental relevance of environmental and architectural projects over time.

Albena Yaneva

Yes, I took an interest in methods of mapping these exchanges between the human dimension and the ecological and environmental aspects of the building.
The repertoire used to visualize ecological and living problems, particularly in the post-occupation evaluation regime, is so rigid that it didn't really allow us to understand the real problem, we couldn't really imagine the complexity of these problems. Very often, simplistic images are used, or cybernetic images and scientific representations, and these kinds of very abstract visualizations and representations, of buildings on the one hand and nature on the other, create problems of understanding. These visualization problems have led to a misunderstanding of the ecological crisis, and it is all the more important for us now to re-evaluate this kind of representation, to rethink this kind of representation, with the help of artists in particular, in order to change the techniques of representation and the current understanding of nature.
I would like to show two examples of images or visual experiments proposed by architects. The first is a cartography by Alexandra Arènes, who is a French architect, who did her PhD in Manchester under my supervision. She proposes a distortion of the image of the Earth, a kind of metamorphosis of the traditional image of the Earth. She produced this image using a database which was built up over the course of an ethnographic study in which she followed scientists to different observatories in the Critical Zone. She proposed this visualization [image 4], where you can see the atmosphere which is now placed inside the circle, you can see the atmosphere, and around it you can see the ground and the rocks, so it's a total inversion of the traditional representation of the Earth. This representation highlights the fact that we are really in the atmosphere, that we cannot escape the pollution of the atmosphere, that it is there, that it envelops and encloses us, we are *inside of it*, we are totally imprisoned by this ozone layer. It's an example that shows how important it is to use cartography and visual art to understand the seriousness of ecological problems in the new climate regime.

Image 5
Design Earth,
Cosmorama, 2018.

I would like to show another example which comes from a Franco-American architectural collective. It's a collective called "Design Earth," and the two architects who contributed to this project. Rania Ghosn and El Hadi Jazairy, used very innovative cartographic techniques to represent the areas of the Earth affected by climate issues. They call these visualizations "geostories" [image 5], which is also the title of their book. These visualizations take us to the middle of the Earth; we are not contemplating a nature that is at a distance, but rather we are part of this environment, we are really *inside*, we are placed in the middle of the ocean and in a way, they make us witnesses to an oil extraction campaign, we can see icebergs melting, how this affects the life of the animals in the ocean, etc. It is really a cartography of climate processes, but from within. We can see that everything is connected, we can see the different arrangements being made, this reorganization of the cosmos that we follow through these geostories. We can therefore see the extent to which these innovative visualizations produced by architects allow us to understand the scale and gravity of the ecological crisis.

Alain Bretagnolle

This is what is known as a battle of the imaginations...
During a previous round table discussion, we were lucky enough to welcome Grégory Quenet, who is one of the pioneers of environmental history and who was the scientific advisor for an exhibition by the artist Laurent Grasso at the Collège des Bernardins. Grasso revisited this relationship to the cosmos by using Lidar scanner technology to perceive things from the inside. I think that Lyes must have something to say on the subject, since there are many artists who are working on this principle.

Lyes Hammadouche

The last two images are really fascinating. They remind me of an expression that is very present in Chinese philosophy, that of "Tian Yuan Di Fang," which means the sky is round and the Earth is square. The sky is round because it is perfect, it is absolute, it is transcendent, and the Earth is square because it is rational, reasoned and quantifiable. Which is also the mathematical question of squaring the circle. We can see that there are choices of parameters in these aesthetic choices. Here it is the atmosphere. The second image shows a kind of engraving, a lithography, which uses lines, and therefore geological strata, depth. This reflects a form of complementarity between the subject and the object.
To come back to my idea of style. It's not self-evident.
But for example, if I have an artificial intelligence, I can say, "To create this image, you're going to be inspired by sixteenth

Image 6
Design Earth, After Oil, Das Island, 2016.

century lithographs and engravings, and you're going to take Dalí's Surrealist style and add a perspective in the style of Brunelleschi," and I'll have this image as a possible answer. What this image gives is a point of view. What this image gives is an oriented reflection on a given problem, which will influence its understanding. We return to a cybernetic understanding of the message. My message is an intention. This is the question I ask myself as an artist.

We come up against epistemological problems in the observation of reality because our methods of observation are biased. I believe that these methods of representation of reality will really influence the directions that humanity will take in the short term.

Catherine Larrère

I'm not entirely sure. What strikes me in what you're saying, this detour by way of artificial intelligence, by way of cybernetic reasoning, I think in the end that it doesn't make much difference. What we accept nowadays, which is a major difference compared to the seventeenth, eighteenth, and nineteenth centuries, is the idea that there is no absolute point of view. If we take the famous representation of the blue planet, the Earth seen from outside, it often features on the covers of environmental ethics books because it's fragile, it's blue, it's pretty, we have this unique Earth, we have compassion. You also have to see that this image is the result of the Apollo mission, a project for the conquest of space. After the American conquest of the West, this was another project to master nature, which was anything but neutral. It's all very well to be compassionate, but it reflects a form of paternalism in relation to the domination we exert ourselves.

We are always included in what we are studying: this is as true for an ethnologist who does surveys as it is for quantum physics, we are part of what we are investigating. We are always caught up in a relationship and that's why I said that there is not the subject on one side and the object on the other. There are a variety of ways of living together. Where I do agree with you is in terms of renouncing the idea that we can have absolute control.

Romain Boursier

Is there not an echo, in what we see on the screen, of the practice of the Land Art artists in the 1970s, who mobilized technical and scientific knowledge such as the seismographic transcriptions of the earth or the recording of the pulsations of different natural cycles? Might this not be a path towards a scientific way of thinking that would reconfigure this question of representation?

The philosopher Joan Tronto defines this as the combination of acting and of virtue.[5] Virtuous action, according to Tronto, is based on an intelligence of situations and proposes appropriate responses, taking into account the vulnerability, needs, and concerns of the context in question. Virtuous action consists of five principles: caring about, caring for, care giving, care receiving, and caring with.[6] When applied to architecture, these principles are quite enlightening.

5 Joan Tronto, *Moral Boundaries: A Political Argument for an Ethic of Care*, Routledge, 1993.

6 Joan Tronto "Caring Architecture," in *Critical Care: Architecture and Urbanism for a Broken Planet*, Angelika Fitz and Elke Krasny (eds.), MIT Press, 2020.

Le Fort d'Issy,
City of Issy-les-Moulineaux,
Architecturestudio.

Issy-les-Moulineaux,
France, 2013.

There are thus two notions of care, coming from different traditions, which allow us on the one hand—essentialist—to define architecture as the act of caring for inhabited environments, and on the other—pragmatic—to steer the project towards an approach of transformation. This double definition is more than a contemporary notion. Attention to others, to the world, to living beings, is a quality of architects. This quality is not contemplative. It is in movement, transposition, projection. It is an ethics and action. There is a word that refers to this capacity to put oneself in the place of another, or to live *oneself as another*,[7] to use the philosopher Paul Ricoeur's eloquent phrase. It's about empathy.

7 Paul Ricœur, *Soi-même comme un autre*, Seuil, 1990.

Catherine Larrère
In Land Art, well, there are different forms of Land Art, but if we're talking about Nils Udo, Richard Long, Andy Goldsworthy, Penone, these were people who had the ambition to move from representation to presentation. Representation, as defined in the Quattrocento by Brunnelleschi and others, opens a window on the world, based on the human gaze, and in which the human is the master of what he sees. Whereas the stated ambition of Land Art, as Andy Goldsworthy said, was "to show what is already there." So it's not about representing, it's about presenting. Richard Long walking, making a trace on the grass. Land Art is presence, we go and see it on site, *in situ*. As for the scientific approach, from the moment it accepts to be part of what it studies, that opens up a whole new set of possibilities.

Romain Boursier
Let's move on to the third part of our discussion, which is about our capacity to act in a symbiotic way. There is a new term that appeared in the dictionary in 2020, sentience. It refers to the capacity of a living being to feel emotions, pain, well-being, and to subjectively perceive its environment. Does this kind of notion enable us to be more accurate in our representations?

Catherine Larrère
The debate about animal consciousness... there is very strong resistance... I'm not even talking about earthworms, but just about cows, horses, sheep, or fish. There are a certain number of scientists, specialists in neuroscience or cognitive psychology, who refuse to use the same word for humans and animals. For them, sentience, the new word that has recently appeared, is a way of making a distinction: sentience is for non-human living beings, but we humans have a conscience. I am therefore a little hesitant. On the other hand, what I find very interesting are the debates between the scientific discourse and the strong non-scientific, cultural resistances that they generate. This seems to me to be extremely important on all levels, particularly with regard to animal welfare. For farm animals, there has been a tendency to give objective definitions of animal welfare, whereas some ethologists have shown that animals have emotions and even speak of subjectivity. There is a form of animal subjectivity, and if we don't take it into account, we can't understand anything about what makes animals happy, unhappy or sick.

Romain Boursier
In this respect, you have argued that we should not leave the human world to go to other worlds, such as the animal world, but rather to become aware that our human world is in relation with non-humans, and that we are engaged in this system.

Creative empathy, Rimbaud's *I is another*, and political empathy are an act of the Deleuzian *becoming*. In the act of creation, attention is inseparable from intention; that is, from taking a position, from making a commitment. Deleuze writes: "Writing is inseparable from becoming: in writing, one becomes-woman, becomes-animal or -vegetable [...]."[8] Writing is always writing for someone else, or for something else, that is beyond us, that is beyond our cause. The transition to evident. Architecture operates through the same empathetic principle as becoming.

Taking care is to live like and to build for another. Taking care, through architecture, is to become aware of the *other* and to cultivate the desire for and the future of a new world.

8 Deleuze, Gilles. *Essays Critical and Clinical*. Minneapolis: University of Minnesota Press, 1997.

Catherine Larrère

All human societies have always included animals. And not necessarily domestic animals. Look at Philippe Descola, when he worked on the Achuar. The Achuar don't have domestic animals, they hunt them. But they also have protected animals, sorts of cuddly toys that they take with them, as an excuse for what they do to others. They don't kill them. Sometimes they exchange them between themselves, because one community would like to get rid of an animal, but to avoid killing it, they pass it on to another one. All human societies have always included animals, we have always had relationships with animals and our fault as moderns is that we have not taken this into account. This is what Descola shows very well. In other cultures, such as the Achuar, whom he has studied, there is no linguistic distinction between animals and humans. And we have something to learn from that, because language is thought.

Romain Boursier

Could this fuel a form of environmental action?

Catherine Larrère

We mentioned Latour, and I will borrow an idea from him, which I would summarize as follows: with non-humans, we must progress from the language of causality to the language of sociability. That is, we must stop considering that we must have a causal action on beings other than ourselves, and the economic vocabulary shows the extent to which we transfer this causal action onto humans, when we say, for example, "We have the tools to act." It's a way of speaking, but it's a mechanistic vocabulary, which proves that we address others, not as people with whom we exchange, but as people on whom we act. We must abandon this and move on to the language of sociability. That is, we must tell ourselves that we have reciprocal relationships of exchange. This is absolutely necessary with animals too, and with all living things. Even with a river, we have a relationship that is not simply one of causal action, but of exchange. Abandoning the exclusive vocabulary of causality, especially as we apply it to ourselves, to develop the vocabulary of sociability seems to me to be a good idea.

Romain Boursier

We have compensation or landscape restoration projects, for which we implement an artificial nature, recreated from an initial ecosystem reference. To do so, we address questions of design as much as agronomic engineering, and we place ourselves in a relationship of causality, at least at the start of the project, to initiate the regeneration of the landscape.

A New World

If, in this new ecological era, everything is transformation, how can we not reconsider what we have already produced, and practice this continuous mode of architecture we are calling for by considering possible trajectories? Half-inheritance and half-imaginary, half-goat and half-lion, is the architecture to come not dreamed of in chimeras? A mythological animal gathering the qualities of several creatures under the same identity: does this hybrid depiction not express the capacity for permanent adaptation that our time requires?

Jean-Jacques Rousseau wrote that the land of chimeras is the only one worth living in.[9]

9 Jean-Jacques Rousseau, *Julie, ou la nouvelle Héloïse*, 1761.

Catherine Larrère
Everything that can be called a "landscape," in the broadest sense of the term, is a human/nature co-evolution. There is no scientific reference that says "naturality is this." There are several possible evolutions of landscapes and Patrick Blandin, who is an ecologist and who used to be the director of the Grande galerie de l'évolution, said that where science could not designate nature, it was necessary to desire it, that is, to arbitrate between different human/non-human co-evolutions, and to construct it in a certain way, which is what you call subjectivity, but it is also a political choice.

Romain Boursier
With Albena, we wanted to examine the possibility of using digital tools in landscape projects. At the agency, the modeling and representation of these environments are now a source of creativity in our architectural and urban responses.

Albena Yaneva
We could use all sorts of technologies and styles, as Lyes said. All sorts of tools, either from the first digital revolution, or from the second, like BIM for example, parametric or post-parametric tools, to be able to produce these different cartographies of ecological issues. For me, the main thing is to be able to adapt and rework these technological tools and methods of representation in order to capture the complex ecologies of projects and their dynamic forms. These alternative representations are all the more important nowadays, because if we can visualize new arrangements with nature and new ways for humans and non-humans to cohabit, we can also envisage innovative ways of carrying out architectural projects that will be more adapted to the conditions of the climate emergency.

Alain Bretagnolle
A sort of scripting, since, as we have seen throughout this debate, the question of time has become fundamental.
And talking about scripts, I would like to end on a positive note. Catherine Larrère, you wrote *Le pire n'est pas certain* (The Worst is Not Certain) together with Raphaël Larrère; this is already good news...

Architecture pursues its quest for meaning in a world that seems devoid of it: caring for inhabited environments, considering the project as care, engaging the long term, reconciling natural and societal cycles, and reconnecting the urgency of action to the possibility of new imaginaries. For all of this, transformation is our working hypothesis, founded on the idea that architecture is a temporal art as much as a spatial art, engaging a notion of the project that aims equally to narrate and to build.

This connection between the two action verbs was explored by Ricoeur in an article entitled "*Architecture et Narrativité*," in which he proposed an analogical rapprochement between the connecting (or reconnecting) functions of building and narrating: the first as a configuring operation of space and the second as a configuring option of time, with the parallelism of his demonstration going so far as the inversion of terms—an invitation to consider architecture as an art of narration.[10]

10 Paul Ricoeur, "Architecture et Narrativité," in *Urbanisme*, no. 308, Nov. - Dec. .1998, p. 44-51.

Pre-greening nursery,
University Hospital
Center in Guadeloupe,
Icade / Semsamar,
Architecturestudio,
Babel, l'Agence,
Ingerop.

Les Abymes, France.

Cité des Arts,
Montpellier Méditerranée
Métropole, SA3M,
Architecturestudio,
MDR Architectes.

Montpellier, France, 2021.

Artists are at the forefront on these questions. As José-Manuel Gonçalvès notes in this volume, "Contemporary art is moving from an interpretation of the visible to a formalization of the invisible. Something is changing; artists are in the process of entering a future-oriented, prospective dimension by trying to make visible phenomena that are currently not visible, and by collecting data, especially from scientists. Artists have become hybrids..."[11] If architects must imitate artists on a certain point, it is undoubtedly this one. This bringing together of the sciences and the arts is significant today to avoid the production of sleek, soaring visions, but rather prospects which, although anchored in an occasionally rough reality, reignite the desire to believe, and which carry hope.

11 José-Manuel Gonçalvès, As Explore, "What Set of Actors Can Define the Commons?", November 8, 2022.

Guy Dolmaire Middle School, Departmental Council of Vosges, Architecturestudio.

Mirecourt, France, 2004.

The art of the twentieth century—the art of modernity par excellence, capable of magnifying it while simultaneously delighting in its disturbance—is, of course, cinema. Born with the great western city at the end of the Industrial Revolution, cinema is a powerful vehicle for our imaginations.

In exploring our relationship with technology, cinema opens up new horizons, at times strangely worrying (*Black Mirror*, the anthology series created by Charlie Brooker, 2011-2019) or completely dystopian (*Blade Runner 2049*, Denis Villeneuve, 2017). Or it extrapolates the deterioration of politics and the rise of populism, at times through parody (*Idiocracy*, Mike Judge, 2006) while at other times reality catches up with it (the assault on the capitol by Donald Trump's supporters, 2021). All writing out the great collapse, the sixth mass extinction, the disappearance of biodiversity, the imminent end of the world, the collision of a comet with the Earth. We see nothing coming and are unaware (*Don't Look Up*, Adam McKay, 2022), or at the last moment become aware of the beauty of our Earth home and the fragility of our shelters (*Melancholia*, Lars von Trier, 2011). The living, the invisible, whether virus or alien (*Life*, Daniel Espinosa, 2017): life menaces life, through pandemic imaginaries or political horizons whose harsh reality we have witnessed over the past few years.

Cinematheque and
Multimedia library,
City of Saint-Malo,
Architecturestudio.

Saint-Malo, France, 2015.

Public area of the Saisons
district in La Défense,
Paris La Défense,
Architecturestudio,
Ville et Paysage.

Courbevoie, France, 2021.

Real-fiction: **all these imaginaries start from concerns grounded in reality. Climatic, biological, technological, political, cosmological: overwhelmed by the world we've created, we now live under its threat. These cultural products, although so well made, all participate in a form of complacency, all staging our downfall. However,** *the worst is not certain*, **and the battle of imaginaries remains open. "Catastrophism, this recent construction that affects the western middle classes, is a 'narrative of Everything,' a depoliticized narrative that encourages us to take charge of ourselves privately.**

Tobacco Factory,
Shanghai Tobacco
Group Corp.,
Architecturestudio.

Shanghai, China, 2012.

12 Catherine Larrère and Raphaël Larrère, *Le pire n'est pas certain – Essai sur l'aveuglement catastrophiste*, Éditions Premier Parallèle, 2020. Translated from French: "Le catastrophisme, cette construction récente qui touche les classes moyennes occidentales, c'est un "récit du Tout," un récit dépolitisé qui nous encourage à nous prendre en charge de manière privée. C'est en politisant l'écologie et en adoptant un point de vue local que nous verrons se rouvrir les possibilités d'action, dans leur pluralité."

It is by politicizing ecology and adopting a local point of we will see possibilities for action open up again, in their plurality."[12] The imaginary is a political question, which itself raises a large number of questions: what legitimacy do we have to intervene in cultural contexts? How can we work to make different representations of the world coexist? What shared values can we rely on? How can we understand these expectations in terms of development and maintain a commitment to the ecological?

Jinan Cultural Center, Jinan West Zone Construction Investment Co., Architecturestudio.

Jinan, China, 2020.

Xie Zhiliu & Chen Peiqiu
Art Museum, Shanghai
Pudong Development
Construction Engineering
Management Co. Ltd,
Architecturestudio.

Shanghai, China, 2015.

Western repentance cannot constrain the collective planetary narrative, now in the making: in a different relationship to nature, one more contemplative, more spiritual (*Spring, Summer, Fall, Winter… and Spring***, Kim Ki-duk, 2003). In other ways of living, in a synchrony of human rhythms and the rhythms of nature (***Dans un jardin que l'on croirait éternel***, Tatsushi Omori, 2018). In a more welcoming way, one which finds hope within exile (***Waiting for Happiness***, Abderrahmane Sissako, 2002). In the strangeness of a world which escapes us, which is now being built on the ruins of what we know (***Stalker***, Andrei Tarkovsky, 1979). New possibilities are at work, elsewhere, in the search for another modernity: decarbonized and decolonized, as Lesley Lokko states in her call for Africa as Laboratory of the Future.**

Cinematheque and Multimedia library, City of Saint-Malo, Architecturestudio.

Saint-Malo, France, 2015.

Architecture bears the responsibility of embodying the opening up of these project-based imaginaries: for a new planetary community, and for a new world.

BLOCH

IMAGE CREDITS

Photographs

Architecturestudio: p. 14-15,22-23, 30-31, 43, 44, 50-51, 56-57, 61, 64-65, 82, 84-85, 86, 88, 95, 96-97, 102-103, 106-107, 109, 114-115, 117, 124-125, 128-129, 160-161, 164-165, 180-181, 184-185, 219, 269
Antoine Duhamel: p. 2,18, 34-35, 74-75, 132-133, 136-137, 168-169, 172-173, 208-209, 248-249,252-253, 255, 263, 276-277
Benoit Wehrlé: p. 19
DSY Architectes: p. 26-27
Luc Boegly: p. 70-71, 78-79, 145, 148-149, 275, 285
Marie-Caroline Lucat: p. 90-91, 233, 270-271
Frédéric Baron: p. 144
Georges Fessy: p. 153
Fargeot: p. 176-177
Javier Agustin Rojas: p. 192-193
Martin Stollenwerk: p. 198-199
Marwan Harmouche: 204-205
Arch – Exist Studio: p. 212-213
Gaston Bergeret: p. 219-221
Nicolas Dubuisson: p. 222-223
Changheng Yiming Chao: p. 225, 282-283
Nikos Danilidis: p.257
Coco d'or: p.269
Rania Ghosn, El Hadi Jazairy: 260-261
Christophe Bourgeois: 273
Olivier Marceny: 279, 281
Changheng Yiming Chao: 282-283

Video excerpts

Jonathas de Andrade: p. 13
Joanie Lemercier: p. 227

Drawings

Alexandra Arènes: p.258-259
Rania Ghosn, El Hadi Jazairy: 260-261
Serge Bloch: p. 287

Fragments and Compasses

All of the Fragments and Compasses were created by Architecturestudio and Undo-Redo

Marc-Antoine Durand is an architect, editor, and founder of As Found Editions. He is a senior lecturer at ENSA Clermont-Ferrand and a researcher with UMR Ressources, ENSA-Clermont-Ferrand and CERILAC, Université Paris Cité.

The partners are co-authors of the architectural projects carried out by the firm during the period in which they are or were partners.

Partners:
Martin Robain (since 1973), Rodo Tisnado (since 1976), Jean-François Bonne (since 1979), Alain Bretagnolle (since 1989), René-Henri Arnaud (since 1989), Laurent-Marc Fischer (since 1993), Marc Lehmann (since 1998), Roueïda Ayache (since 2001), Gaspard Joly (since 2009), Marie-Caroline Piot (since 2009), Mariano Efrón (since 2009), Romain Boursier (since 2018) and Widson Monteiro (since 2018).
Former partners:
Jean-François Galmiche (from 1974 to 1989) and Amar Sabeh el Leil (from 2009 to 2018)